Never has any book dealt so realistic
thoroughly with Eskimo life as Peter Freuch...
BOOK OF THE ESKIMOS . . .

The great explorer tells in detail of Eskimo life
throughout the year, in numerous stories drawn
from his own experience. In one of the most unusual essays ever written about Eskimo life, he
speaks frankly of the social structure and the
sexual habits of the Eskimo people, describing
things that are at first shocking to European or
American visitors . . . "fascinating, easy and
pleasurable reading. The Eskimo emerges as a
very odd, impressive customer indeed."

—Book-of-the-Month Club News

Peter Freuchen's

BOOK OF
THE ESKIMOS

edited and with a preface by
DAGMAR FREUCHEN

A Fawcett Premier Book

Published by Ballantine Books

Copyright © 1961 by Peter Freuchen Estate
"The Partner" copyright 1951 by Peter Freuchen
"Dead Man's Cache" copyright © 1957 by
Fawcett Publications, Inc.
"The Day I Harpooned Myself" copyright © 1957 by
the American Weekly.

Photo Credits:
National Film Board of Canada: P. 129 (top); p. 130 (bottom) Gar Lunney; p. 134 (top & bottom); p. 135 (top) Gar Lunney; p. 135 (bottom)
Royal Danish Ministry of Foreign Affairs, Copenhagen: P. 131 (top), Vagn Hansen (bottom)
Richard Harrington: P. 130 (top)
Dagmar Freuchen: P. 129 (bottom); p. 132 (top); p. 136 (top & bottom)

ISBN 0-449-30038-2

This edition published by arrangement with The World Publishing Company

Printed in Canada

First Fawcett Premier Edition: April 1973
First Ballantine Books Edition: December 1983
Second Printing: April 1986

CONTENTS

PREFACE   vii

I. ESKIMO LIFE AND WAYS   9

  1. Eskimo Environment and Origins   9

  2. The Eskimo Way of Life   25

  3. Trading with the Eskimos   48

  4. Love and Marriage   55
       FAMILY STRUCTURE AND MORALS
       AN ESKIMO WEDDING
       ESKIMO COURTSHIP

  5. Eating and Visiting   95

  6. Polar Justice: Crime and Punishment
       Among the Eskimos   114

  7. Eskimos as Servants   137

  8. The Eskimo Mind   140
       LIFE AND DEATH

Contents

MATTER AND SPIRIT

THE ESKIMO IDEA OF THE WORLD

ESKIMO MUSIC AND POETRY

II. ADVENTURES WITH THE ESKIMOS   211

  1. Lootevek: Casanova of the Ice Floes   211

  2. Arctic Nightmare   223

  3. An Eskimo Takes a Bride   230

  4. Dead Man's Cache   238

  5. The Partner   251

  6. The Day I Harpooned Myself   263

  7. Marriage, the Harbor of Safety   267

  8. Hunger   285

  9. The Polar Bear   292

III. THE ESKIMOS: PAST AND PRESENT   301

ILLUSTRATIONS ON PAGES 129-136

PREFACE

PETER FREUCHEN knew the Eskimos better than any white man in the world, his intimate knowledge of their ways being rivaled only by that of Knud Rasmussen, his friend and colleague, who was part Eskimo. Off and on for more than two generations Peter lived and hunted with the Eskimos; he ate and sang and traveled with them. He had for ten years been married to a beautiful Eskimo girl named Navarana, by whom he had two children and to whom his devotion was unbounded. Navarana told Peter many things about her people; she helped him to learn those lessons which books cannot teach and to acquire that wisdom which it would have taken the average human being many lifetimes of experience to match. It was, I believe, due principally to Navarana that Peter had his amazing insight into Eskimo psychology and behavior and it was perhaps because of her that he devoted so much of his time to making Eskimo life less difficult.

Peter Freuchen's first visit to the land of the Eskimos was in 1906, when he went on the Danish Expedition to Greenland. From then on he was a regular (and welcome) guest of the people of the North: in 1910 along with Knud Rasmussen he founded a trading station which he named Thule; in 1912 he went on the First Thule Expedition, made maps of the land around the Peary Canal, and became administrator and manager of Thule—a post he held until 1919. During all these years, Peter traveled constantly, hunting and trapping, living by the meat and wearing the skins of whatever animals he caught, always accompanied by Eskimos with whom he lived as an equal.

Peter participated in the Fifth Thule Expedition which lasted from September 1921 to September 1924. It was on this expedition that he lost his left foot, and it was during the consequent hospitalization, fearing that he could travel no more, that he took up his great interest in reading and writing, especially on the life and adventure among the Eskimos. After his leg healed and he was able to travel to Arctic Russia in 1928 and to West Greenland in 1929-30, Peter retained his interest in writing; he kept a daily record of his experiences and made notes about the people he met. Many of these on-the-spot reports, which he later expanded and rewrote, are included in this book, which is a summation of his knowledge and adventure with the Eskimo people.

In 1932 and 1933, Peter was in Alaska, working on the film *Eskimo*, based on his novel, in which he was an actor but for which he was also one of the directors. From 1933 to the time of his death in Alaska, 1957, he made numerous trips to the Far North. He went through the Hudson Bay Area, traveled in Arctic Siberia, Lapland, and of course Greenland. Whenever he had a chance to go North, everything else was put aside. Between trips he wrote and also created interest for commercial fishing, exchange of reindeer and musk ox, and other improvements of the life of the Greenlanders. He used his imagination, energy, and courage to help the people he loved.

I wish to acknowledge with thanks the assistance of Thomas Coffey and Ove C. Kristensen in the preparation of this manuscript.

DAGMAR FREUCHEN
November 29, 1960

ESKIMO LIFE AND WAYS

1 Eskimo Environment and Origins

THE ESKIMOS have for centuries been the object of much interest and admiration from all peoples of the civilized world, and the reason for this is obvious: Alone of all primitive people, they live permanently in the inhospitable Arctic zone, and have there established a way of life and an economic culture independent of many things millions consider necessary for survival. To put it briefly, the Eskimos possess an extraordinary hardiness which enables them to live where nobody else can.

It is true that there are other people living in the Arctic, as for instance the Samoyeds and Chukchi of northern Siberia, but these are seasonal dwellers who live on the Arctic tundras and coasts in summer, but retire to the forests of the temperate zone in winter. Only the Eskimos confine themselves to the Arctic the year round, and they alone have adapted themselves completely to it.

It might be useful to make it clear what the Arctic is. Perhaps you have been told that it is that part of the globe which is north of 66½° north latitude, and is the realm of the midnight sun. At best, this delineation is only a very rough one. Consider, for example, that it would divide such a typically arctic region as the Greenland icecap in two, and that it would include northern Norway, which is, generally speaking, temperate because of the passage of the Gulf Stream.

The demarcation generally accepted now, therefore, is a July mean temperature of 50° F. This division works out well, because it classifies as Arctic a number of regions that are similar in climate, plant life, and animal life: Greenland and the North American archipelago, the Hudson Bay coasts and the Barren Grounds, the northern coasts of Canada, the northern and western parts of Alaska, the northern coast of Russia, with the islands that are a part of it, and the island group of Spitzbergen.

Climatically, the Arctic is characterized by two features: short cool summers and a small amount of precipitation. The winters vary in rigor and darkness from the low-Arctic to the high-Arctic regions, but although the sun is in the sky through all or most of the summer, it does not give much heat because of its low position. There is less than two months between the last spring and the first fall frosts, and the mean temperature is above the freezing point for only three or four months. Cold air has a lower saturation point for water vapors than warm air; therefore the small amount of precipitation consists mainly of snowfall. This is also the reason why large areas of the northern Arctic are quite bare of snow in winter, so much more so as the violent arctic gales often sweep the landscape clean of what snow may have fallen and deposit it in drifts behind the rocks or the pack ice.

There are three main types of landscape in the North American Arctic: the permanent glaciations called icecaps, of which the Greenland icecap is by far the most extensive— there are several smaller ones on Baffin and Ellesmere islands; then we have the rocky coasts and plains of Greenland, the North American archipelago, and Alaska; and thirdly, the vast rolling plains around Hudson Bay and the region northwest of it, the Barren Grounds.

There are no trees in the Arctic, for the simple reason that the limitation of the Arctic zone, as we have defined it, coincides in general with the northern tree limit. In other respects there is remarkably rich plant life in the low-Arctic zone. The precipitation here can be as much as twenty inches annually, but this still would not be sufficient to sustain plant life if it were not for another arctic phenomenon, the permafrost. This is the thick layer of permanently frozen ground which we meet a few feet down, even at the height of summer. This frozen layer prevents the water from the ice and snow which melt in spring from sinking deep down, and causes it to remain in the upper layer of soil, creating extensive stretches of clay and bogs. Here we get the type of vegetation known as *tundra*, typified in the Barren Grounds. On the low, rolling hills and flat plains, cut through by lakes and small streams, we find low heath, mosses, and grasses, and, in the more sheltered places, even low shrubs like willow and dwarf pine. Where the soil is thin or too exposed to the arctic gale, the plants are low and so scattered that the bare underground becomes dominant. This type of vegetation, often called rock-desert, is the most common in the northern Arctic. Finally, as we come to the rocky ground and coasts of northern Greenland and the islands west of it, lichens become the only plant form that can exist.

The animal life of the Arctic, on the other hand, is abundant, and it is characterized by sea mammals: seal, walrus, and whales that live on the fish, clams, and krill in the waters. Other special species are the polar bear, the arctic fox, the snow hare, the caribou, and the musk ox. It is upon these animals that the Eskimo has based his material culture; he feeds on their meat, he makes his clothes, his bed, his boats, and his summer tent from their skins, and most of his utensils from their bones and teeth. And let us not forget the millions of sea birds and waterfowl that in summer inhabit the cliffs and islands along the arctic coasts.

But no description of the Arctic is complete without the seascape. The Arctic Ocean is in winter completely frozen over, and the ice reaches a thickness of three feet or more along the coasts. This ice forms the smoothest road for dog-sled driving, and without it the extensive Eskimo migrations would not have taken place. In summer, the ice breaks up all along the polar shores. The ice drift follows the south-going ocean currents, particularly the East Greenland Current through the Denmark Strait and the Canadian Current through Baffin Bay and Davis Strait. To the drifting ice floes are added the thousands of icebergs that are continually being produced by the glaciers in the fjords of Greenland.

Conditions all over the Arctic are pretty much the same, but the scenery varies considerably, and while it is a rugged and severe world, it has a majesty and haunting beauty all its own. To think of it as "the white desert" can only be correct in reference to the icecap, that is the only completely lifeless desert in the world. Personally, I have always thought that as a tourist country the Arctic is greatly neglected, and I can think of no place more beautiful than a Greenland fjord in summer. The sun remains low in the sky, coloring it red and yellow, while the black and bottomless abyss of the still water reflects the glowing colors, while the floating icebergs break the rays into blue, green, and blinding white.

Although the Eskimos live in a world where even the smallest deviation from the usual—as for instance, a change in the trek of the seals—can spell catastrophe, a world where danger and death are daily companions, they think it is a beautiful world. They pity greatly those people who live far south, where there is no ice to drive a dogsled on, and where it is too hot for comfort.

The superior techniques of the white man have greatly improved the living conditions of the Eskimos in recent times, but basically they have changed nothing in their culture, which is so admirably suited to the severe conditions of the Arctic. Almost everybody who has visited the Arctic has felt himself obliged to write a book, or at least an article, about The Extraordinary Eskimos, and many have done so without knowing them very well. You may therefore well ask what are my qualifications for writing about the Arctic and especially about the Eskimos.

My first trip to Greenland was in 1906, when I went there as a stoker on board the *Hans Egede,* a little steamer which transported a team (of which I was also a part) whose task it was to prepare for the "Danmark" Expedition to north-eastern Greenland. On this trip I fell in love with the country and its people forever. I participated in the "Danmark" Expedition 1906-08 as a regular member, and when I returned to Denmark I got to know the very famous explorer Knud Rasmussen, who was then forming a plan to establish a trading station at Smith Sound, among the Polar Eskimos.

At that time Smith Sound was unclaimed territory. The rest of Greenland had since 1721 been colonized and civilized by us Danes, but for some reason or other, probably because of the rough traveling conditions around Melville Bay, connection with the Polar Eskimos had not been kept up. Their existence was known, but only vague and mysterious tales circulated about them among the Christian Eskimos.

The first record we have of the Polar Eskimos is from the English explorer Sir John Ross, who tells about a brief meeting with them in 1818. Admiral Peary used them on most of his expeditions, taking advantage of their superior traveling technique, and training them for his fantastic journey to the North Pole; four of them went there with him in 1909. But the first Danish contact was the so-called Literary Expedition in 1903, which got its name because its purpose was to look into the material and intellectual culture of the Greenlanders. Participating in it were Mylius-Erichsen, who later headed the "Danmark" Expedition, the physician Alfred Bertelsen, the painter Harald Moltke, and the young Knud Rasmussen. The latter, in particular, spoke of the Polar Eskimos with love and enthusiasm, and now he was talking of going to live among them. He suggested to me that I go with him, and that we establish ourselves as traders. I was all for it!

But it didn't seem possible to arouse much interest for Knud's plan in Denmark. Following the attainment of the North Pole in 1909, Peary indicated that he would no longer visit the Polar Eskimos. It could therefore be anticipated that they very soon would lack the many wonderful implements of the civilized world to which Peary had introduced them. Further, the Norwegian explorer Otto Sverdrup was working on a plan exactly similar to Knud's. This last circumstance, in particular, caused a few men of vision to give Knud their support, and, although lacking the blessing of the government, we got off to a good start in 1910. In the same year we arrived in North Star Bay and established our station. We called it Thule!

For eleven years following this, I lived among the Polar Eskimos, trading with them but also living like them, and I married an Eskimo girl. I am the last one to have seen these people in their virgin state, and that (mainly) is what I want to write about.

The Polar Eskimos are but a small tribe, less than 300 in number, but they are generally considered to be the noblest strain of the Eskimo race. At any rate, I came to love them as my dear friends, and it is to them that I dedicate this book. Since, as we say in Denmark, every child whom one loves has many names, you may variously find them called Polar Eskimos, Smith Sound Eskimos, Thule Eskimos, or North Pole Eskimos. Only 900 miles from the North Pole, they live north of everybody else in the world, under the most rugged conditions that any human beings can tolerate.

You will also find in this book occasional references to the Hudson Bay Eskimos, whom I visited as a member of the

Fifth Thule Expedition 1921-24, the Danish expedition to Arctic North America led by Knud Rasmussen.

One of the purposes of the Fifth Thule Expedition was to throw some light upon the riddle of the origin of the Eskimo race, which had been puzzling scientists for years (and actually still is). There are several conflicting facts to consider.

First, we must wonder at the complete uniformity of Eskimo culture, all modern influences disregarded. Although the Eskimos are spread over a huge area and relatively few in number, their instruments and hunting techniques as well as other cultural elements have—in spite of local adaptations—maintained distinct resemblances. It can therefore be concluded that the Eskimos developed their unique traits in one certain locality and through the centuries undertook extensive migrations, facilitated by the dogsled. This original locality was probably not a coastal area, for many Eskimo implements appear to have been developed for coastal ice hunting from implements used inland at rivers and lakes. Also, many of the ancient tales of the Eskimos show traditions that must stem from an inland culture.

When we try to relate the Eskimos to other races, we meet difficulties all along the line. Nothing in their economic or intellectual culture points to other peoples of the world. Their language resembles none other. Like many Indian languages it is polysynthetic—that is, words or word roots are chained together in composite words forming meanings that in European-type languages would be expressed in whole sentences. But the scientists cannot classify it as belonging to the Indian language group, though a vague kinship to the Ural-Altaic group has been seen. The Ural-Altaic languages comprise such widely different tongues as, for instance, Finnish, Hungarian, Turkish, Samoyed, Kalmuck, and Mongolian. The most probable explanation seems to be that the Ural-Altaic languages, the Indian languages, and Eskimo have developed from a common ancient Asiatic root.

Racially, the Eskimos differ from the Indians by having much more Mongolian features, such as high, broad cheekbones, small noses, and often slanting eyes, and their babies are born with the blue Mongolian spot at the base of the spine. However, they are taller than the Mongolians, and they are long-skulled where the Mongolians are short-skulled, a point too important to be overlooked. As far as can be divined, their nearest relatives are the palaeo-Asiatic people of northeastern Siberia. The palaeo-Asiatics comprise several small groups, such as the Yukaghir, the Chukchi, and the Koryaks, and are actually the remainders of an ancient people, small dark men of a type approaching the Mongolian. These people followed the retreating ice north after the last ice age and occupied the forests and tundras of northern Siberia, but were later almost completely wiped out by another immigration from the south, that of the Samoyeds and the Tungus-Manchurians.

Then, in 1917, a bit of the veil that covered the Eskimos' mysterious past was lifted quite by chance at no other place than our Thule settlement. Captain Comer of the Crocker Land Expedition, which was then ice-bound, began out of forced idleness, to dig in our kitchen midden. It was slow work digging in the frozen earth, but when we saw what he found we appropriated one half of the midden and started digging ourselves. We also appropriated some of his glory, for the place went down in history as Comer's Midden, while the old Eskimo culture that here was unearthed for the first time was named the Thule Culture.

One of the purposes of the Fifth Thule Expedition was to determine the extent of the Thule Culture. We excavated all of the old house ruins we found, which were many, and our eminent archaeologist, Therkel Mathiassen, concluded that the Thule Culture had extended all along the coastline of the Canadian Arctic.

But another and maybe even more important clue was found when the expedition visited the Caribou Eskimos, who inhabit the tundra between Back River and Chesterfield Inlet. Theirs is the most primitive Eskimo culture in existence, and they were also the poorest people I had ever seen. They didn't own a fourth of the hunting tools that we knew from the Eskimos of West Greenland. They did not have winter houses, but lived in snow houses when their caribou skin tents couldn't be used. They hunted caribou in summer and fished salmon in winter, and thus had no blubber for heat and light. Their houses were sparsely lit by a lump of caribou tallow with a wick of heather in it, and even with many people present the temperature was usually around zero.

Their women were robust, for their life and work were so difficult as to mark them completely. They did their cooking by heather and twigs. This was not so bad in summer, when the ground was free of snow and they could collect their fuel in big bundles, carry it down to the tents, and make festive cooking fires. But in winter it was worse; then the women had to go out and scrape aside the snow to get to the heather, and since they did not have many skins and had to save their mittens, they pulled the heather loose with their bare hands. Imagine what that meant at a temperature of forty below! Their hands were completely malformed, black, hard to the feel as if made of wood, and full of frost scars. Besides, they let their nails grow very long, so that the general impression was that of sinister bird claws. When they came home in winter with their fuel, they couldn't burn it under the open sky, for that would use it up too quickly. Cooking wasn't possible in the snow house either as the snow would melt, and, also, the smoke would bother the master of the house. So adjoining the house they would build a small, low hut with a hole in the roof, and in there the woman would lie down to do the cooking. She had to blow on the fire continually to keep it going, ashes would fly around her face, hair, and shoulders, and her eyes were always red and watering, so that the tears made deep grooves of bare skin down over the otherwise dirt-covered face. You can easily understand that such a woman looked old and decrepit before she was thirty.

The caribou hunt took place twice a year. First in the spring, when the herds migrated north; the caribou were lean, but the Eskimos were hungry and gladly ate the tough meat. Then in the fall the herds would return south to the forests, fat from the grazing on the tundras. In between, the Caribou Eskimos lived on salmon, a poor diet in the cold climate, and they were often starving. But it didn't occur to them to follow the caribou herds or to make deposits for the bad seasons.

It became apparent that their primitive culture had originated in the interior. Not only did none of their implements show signs of their ever having stayed by the sea, but their religion was a typical inland religion, very different from that of the coast dwellers in that there was almost no observance of taboo. Their relatively few taboo rules and simple birth and death customs made it clear that they lived under conditions that were traditionally indigenous and natural to them, and that as long as they could obtain sufficient food, they always felt secure in their surroundings.

The reasoning behind this conclusion is that those Eskimos who came down to the sea to live came upon something that was quite unknown and strange to them, and in their primitive fear and insecurity it gave rise to intricate precautions in the form of taboo rules and more complicated religious ideas.

The late Professor Steensby of Copenhagen had already put forth his widely publicized theory that the Eskimos had originally been an inland people who had come out to the sea from the great lakes in northern Canada, and there adapted their lake and river culture to the requirements of the sea. It would seem that the Caribou Eskimos were living proof of his theory, since theirs seemed to be a remnant of the original Eskimo culture, from the time when the transformation to a coast culture had not yet taken place. It would also seem that the kind of tundra landscape they lived in was the Eskimo's original habitat. Their old tales were—in substance and form—much the same as those we already knew from Greenland and had met in all the Eskimo tribes we visited, thus again demonstrating the puzzling uniformity of all Eskimo cultures.

But all this did not explain the presence of the Thule Culture, nor did it explain the presence of an even older culture which previously had been excavated at Coronation Gulf and in South Baffin Land, and which had been called the Cape Dorset Culture.

Some years later, remains of a later phase of the Thule Culture were found in northeastern Greenland, but it became quite obvious that—nonetheless—the Thule Culture was akin to that of the Alaskan Eskimos! The next step in this exciting detective mystery would, then, be excavations in Alaska.

In the years 1939-50, American and Danish scientists excavated along the coasts of Alaska, and they came up with some pretty gratifying results. They found a layer corresponding to an early phase of the Thule Culture; they found layers corresponding to the Cape Dorset Culture; and they found traces of a stone-age culture that became known as the Cape Denbigh Flint Complex.

To look even further into the past, let us look upon the other forms of life in the Arctic, the plants and the animals. They show a difference from those of the rest of the world by being distributed in both the western and the eastern hemispheres. While America and Europe as well as Asia show great differences in the native flora and fauna of their temperate and tropical zone, the Arctic zone is characterized by the uniformity of species throughout. Most species of animals and plants are distributed around the Pole, very few being confined to either the New World or the Old World. To explain this we must go back to the ice age, which actually was a series of glacial periods during which the northern parts of the European-Asian and American continents were covered by huge icecaps. In between were interglacial periods during which the ice retreated and the climate became approximately like it is now. The last glacial period ended about 25,000 years ago, and we may very well be in an interglacial period.

During the last glacial period, the ice covered northern Europe and most of Siberia, and the biggest icecap was that of Greenland and the North American continent, reaching as far south as the fortieth parallel. However, except for some smaller icecaps, eastern Siberia was ice-free, and so was the greatest part of Alaska. Since the sea level there was much lower than it is now, as so much water was tied up in the icecaps, the two continents were landfast at that point, and in geology the country thus formed is called Beringia. Also, the continental shelf of northeastern Siberia is low and stretches hundreds of miles out into the Arctic Ocean. No doubt this shelf was also dry land and connected with Beringia. In this and other glacial refuges plants and animals survived and developed special traits which enabled them, with the retreating ice, to move in and occupy all of their natural habitat, the Arctic.

With all these facts in mind, I should like to put forth a theory of the Eskimos' origin and development which may seem daring at some points, but which can be defended biologically and archaeologically.

No traces of man from before the last glacial period have been found in Beringia. Yet this would seem ideal as the home country of the Eskimo culture. Particularly the northern plains of the dry continental shelf would provide the kind of tundra landscape that seems to be the Eskimos' ancient habitat, and there were probably great herds of reindeer there. It would also provide the degree of isolation in which the Eskimos—then, as later, the object of the most merciless selection of nature—could develop their peculiar racial, cultural, and linguistic traits. Maybe some development to a coastal culture already took place, as the Arctic Ocean advanced after the ice age. The Eskimos have, in their old tales, traditions of a flood. In all primitive peoples, such traditions have signified the sudden or gradual inundation of

formerly habitable country. The flood the Eskimos tell about
has never been placed anywhere; could it be in northern
Beringia? For my part, I cannot help imagining that the traces
of the original Eskimo culture lie hidden north of northeastern Siberia, under the ice-filled waters of the Arctic
Ocean!

Be that as it may, it has been fairly well established that
the Eskimos, probably under pressure from migrations from
the south, left Asia and crossed the Bering Strait to the
American continent about 6,000 years ago. A branch of them
spread to the Aleutian Islands, off the southwest coast of
Alaska, and established their own special culture that is still,
in language and traditions, closely related to that of the
Eskimos. An Eskimo culture developed on the Alaskan shores
of the Bering Sea, and the *kayak*—that important hunting
aid—was in full use there.

But it is my contention that the bulk of the Eskimos migrated inland, through the tundras of northern Alaska and
northern Canada right over to Hudson Bay. Since the migrations of the caribou herds are roughly north-south, these
early Eskimos may even have entered the forest belt. But
here they clashed with another population wave, that of the
Indians.

The Indians had already before the last ice age arrived
in America from Asia in several groups and migrations, and
they had the continent pretty well populated. With the retreating ice—or rather, with the subsequent advance of the
forests—they moved north into Canada and Alaska. It may
well have been under pressure from them that the Eskimos moved right out to the Arctic coasts. At any rate, we
have—both from historic and prehistoric times—stories and
sagas of clashes between the Eskimos and Indians, mas-
sacres that even the most blood-curdling fantasies cannot
match. Even as late as this, our twentieth century, the cry of
"Indians!" in an isolated southern Greenland settlement
could throw the inhabitants into a state of senseless panic,
and this was true even though the word had lost its meaning
to them hundreds of years before!

The Eskimos could not match the Indians in cruelty and
warfare and had to retreat. It may also be that they simply
followed the migrations of the caribou out to the coast.
They occupied the coasts between Coronation Gulf and
Boothia Peninsula, and their implements underwent adaptation to ice hunting. We are now on surer ground, since this

is the period of the Cape Dorset Culture. The Eskimos spread east to Baffin Island and west right to Alaska. But the broad belt of boggy tundra west of Hudson Bay kept the group known as the Caribou Eskimos back in the interior, and preserved it as a remnant of the original inland culture.

In the region around Point Barrow, Alaska, under the influence of ever richer whale and walrus herds, a new Eskimo culture evolved, based upon the hunting of aquatic animals from *umiak* and *kayak*, and it passed through a period of unequaled prosperity. This new, vigorous, and wealthy culture was the Thule Culture. It spread to the coasts of the Bering Sea and even crossed the Bering Strait to reoccupy a corner of the ancestral home, Siberia. And it spread, through several waves of migration, eastward through the Northwest Passage to Hudson Bay and Labrador, north to Baffin Island, and right over to Greenland. One wave went along the east coast of Greenland and settled northeastern Greenland, but due to worsening climatic conditions that population died out, maybe as early as the year 1000 A.D. Several waves passed through Thule (we counted three layers in our kitchen midden); and the western and southeastern coasts of Greenland, with the rich sealing, became one of the true homes of the Eskimo race. The last migration wave probably overran the dying-out Norse settlers in the fifteenth century.

But in the Hudson Bay area, the Thule Culture was later wiped out by a new migration wave from the interior, probably as recently as the fifteenth century. The tribes we meet, for instance, on the central north shore of Canada, the Iglooliks around Fury and Hecla straits, the Netchiliks of Boothia Peninsula, and the Copper Eskimos at Coronation Gulf, are descendants of these late immigrants. They have more taboos and more complicated religious systems than any other Eskimos, all of which indicates that they have been the last to reach the strange habitat of the coast and adapt to it. The Netchiliks have, in their traditions, many tales about a strange people called the Tunrit who occupied the country before them, but who moved away without protest when they came. They tell about the Tunrits' great skill at hunting, and no doubt they were the people of the Thule Culture. What actually happened to them? Well, there are some indications that they had degenerated and succumbed, others that they all moved to Greenland. One little pocket of Thule Culture survived on Southampton Island in the strange tribe of the Sagdlermiut, who in many respects seem to have resembled the Polar Eskimos. But they were all wiped out by an epidemic in 1903.

At present, the Eskimos are divided into three groups: the Eastern Eskimos, which are the eastern Greenlanders, the western Greenlanders, and the Polar Eskimos, and whose culture descends from late phases of the Thule Culture; the Central Eskimos, whose culture is a recent adaptation of the original inland culture (with the exception of the Caribou Eskimos); and the Western Eskimos, which consist of the Mackenzie Eskimos, the Alaskan tribes, and the Yuit of Siberia, and whose culture is a development of an early phase of the Thule Culture.

Of course, this would not be apparent in places like southern Greenland where the Eskimos—during the last decades —have been emancipated into a fully modern civilization. The Central Eskimos seem to be the weakest group. The census figures for Eskimos look approximately as follows: Greenland, 25,000; Canada, 10,000; Alaska, 16,000; and the Yuit 1,500.

Not all of the Eskimo migrations took place in prehistoric times. At Thule, I got a first-hand account of the last migration into Greenland from my wife's grandfather, old Mequsaq. I should like to tell about it, not only because it is one of the great sagas of the Arctic, but also because it demonstrates how cultural elements were dispersed throughout the Eskimo world.

Mequsaq's original home was at Admiralty Inlet in the northern part of Baffin Island. He was only a little boy when his tribe was hit by misfortune. The weather was continually bad, the game animals stayed away, and starvation threatened. The wise man of the tribe was the great Kritlaq, the greatest shaman in man's memory, said Mequsaq. He understood all things, and he could ask stones in running brooks and interpret the answer. Urged by him, and under his leadership, the tribe broke up and started the long trek north over Devon and Ellesmere islands to Greenland. They stopped at several places, and the trip took several winters, but Kritlaq urged them on. His power was so great, it was said, that when he drove ahead of the other sleds in the night, fire and flames could be seen shooting out from his head!

Several expeditions that were in the area at the same time have reported meeting this strange little group, and they fix the time of their crossing to Greenland as 1864.

Mequsaq told me that, when they had arrived, his father

thought it best to find out if they had traveled far enough. So he went bear hunting and drove as far as snow and ice would permit. He went all the way to Thom Island in Melville Bay. And there he discovered that he had absolutely no desire to continue his travels!

But the Smith Sound area was well inhabited by the Polar Eskimos, and it wasn't easy for the new group to fit in. After a few years in the new country some of them, among them Mequsaq's family, decided to return to the homeland. On the way they had terrible snowfall with bad driving, and since they as travelers had no winter depots, and the hunting was bad, starvation began to ravage them. They ate most of their dogs, but they had to keep some so that they could eventually continue their journey. There were two men in the company, Minik and Mattak by name, who were the strongest and always took bigger parts of the game than they were entitled to, because they were very hungry and didn't know how to comply with their people's customs and be content with what was theirs.

They became more and more savage. And one day, when Mequsaq's father was hunting with the other men, they entered the house, intending to kill them all. Mequsaq's older brother defended himself well, but the two boys had to see their mother and their sister stabbed to death and carted off to be eaten! They tried to get Mequsaq also, and they cut one eye out of him, a knife landed deep in his neck, another in his back, and for the rest of his life he had deep scars from the fight. But he saved his life.

When the father returned and heard this, he decided to set out after Minik and Mattak to revenge his wife and daughter. But his dogs were too weak from hunger, and he didn't have much strength himself, so he gave up this resolve. The rest of the party now moved together into one large igloo to defend themselves better against the two cannibals.

One night, some time later, they woke up as they heard sleds arrive outside the igloo. It was Minik and Mattak again. But when they saw that the men were home and ready for defense, they didn't try anything. They hung around for a while, and nobody dared leave the house.

It turned out that the two cannibals had seen tracks in the snow showing that some had died from hunger and been buried in the scree, where there were loose stones to build graves from. It was seen that the two men went there and returned with two corpses which they put on their sleds and drove away with, to eat them. After that time Minik and Mattak were never heard from again.

But even when the light returned and hunting became better again, it was still feared that the two men would return. Asayuk and his sister Itusarssuk were children then, and they were always put behind the skins covering the walls of the igloo when the men went out hunting. There were no women to stay at home with them, since Minik and Mattak had killed those who had survived the hunger. Asayuk often told me how he sat together with his sister behind the drapery so as to be out of sight in case wicked men should enter.

But when they had been sitting there for a long time, they felt their hunger very keenly, so they crawled out and ventured outside the house. He remembered clearly how they looked around them for the cannibals. When they saw the sleds far out on the ice, they became afraid and ran back in to hide behind the skins.

When their father, Krumangapik, came nearer, he saw that the snow block that had closed the igloo had been thrown aside. He feared that his children had been abducted and killed. He ran inside quickly and saw that they were still there. Then they all laughed a lot at his fear, and that was the first laugh they had had in a long, long time. He had come home with game, and the hunting stayed good thereafter, so that they regained their strength and kept their dogs alive.

But since they didn't have any women, they didn't feel any desire to travel for several winters in order to get home, and they knew that there were better chances of getting women in Greenland. So they crossed again from Ellesmereland to Etah. And they stayed there ever since.

There was, however, some strife before a regular family life could be established in the new country. A circumstance that helped them was that the Polar Eskimos did not have any kayaks or any bows and arrows. By one of those strange mishaps of the many wanderings between regions of different nature, they had lost the use of these things. Thus they could not hunt in the summer when there was no ice, and their winter depots were few and small and usually used up too early.

Therefore, when the darkness was at its deepest these people went into the houses, lay down and covered themselves with skins, and moved as little as possible. They had no blubber for their lamps, they had nothing! And they didn't go outside and never ate before the sun came up over their middens, when they could see to go out hunting. By that time they were usually so weak that they could barely reach those seal blowholes that were nearest to the settlement. Only after they had eaten for some days did they regain strength to hunt as usual. Their dogs were usually dead except for a few strong ones which had perhaps sustained themselves by eating the others.

Mequsaq's father and his group taught these people the use of the kayak for hunting seals and walrus, and the use of the bow and arrow for hunting caribou in the mountains. For this they were held in respect, and when we came to Smith Sound, the Baffin Islanders were thoroughly integrated, and the Polar Eskimos were a wealthy people who always had plenty of skins and lots of good things to eat in their houses.

Knud and I had to try to adjust to this rugged world. You might like to know exactly what our new surroundings looked like. We built our station on the rocky south shore of North Star Bay, also known as Thule Fjord. In this fjord are two islands, of which one, Saunders Island, was the biggest bird cliff in Greenland. The fjord was surrounded by mountains, behind which the icecaps could be seen. Three glaciers went down to the fjord and filled it with icebergs, which provide the Eskimo supply of fresh water. We didn't have much real snowfall, yet we often had spectacular snowstorms, when the wind was such that it swept myriad ice crystals off the top of the icecap and carried them out over the coast.

Average temperature at Thule during the winter was ten below zero, that in the summer just above the freezing point. The ice broke up very late in spring, and the drifting ice and the icebergs filled the waters all through the short summer. Melville Bay, while it formed a beautiful icy road to southern Greenland in winter, was notorious among navigators as the worst waters in the Arctic in summer. Only for a few weeks in July and August could ships get through to us, and we had to rely on one ship a year to supply us with all the things we needed.

For three months of the winter, from November to mid-February, we didn't see the sun. On the other hand, it didn't leave the sky for the three and a half months from May to mid-August, and we had brilliant, though cool, summers.

This severe and beautiful country became my home; with all my heart and soul I came to love it and its people.

2 The Eskimo Way of Life

EVERYTHING about the Polar Eskimos, the way they look, the way they live, and even the way they think and feel, is largely determined by the extreme arctic conditions under which they live. In their isolated existence north of everywhere they love to receive visitors, and when they come running toward you to welcome you, all excited, they may, especially because of their heavy fur clothes, seem thickset and somewhat ferocious. The way to alleviate this impression is to smile. Deceit they have never known; they take a smile for what it is and return it. They smile often and willingly, and you soon learn to know them as warm and friendly, with a great capacity for humor and compassion.

But Eskimos are strong. There can be no sissies among the people whose neighbor is the North Pole, and since, as they themselves say, "there is strength in beauty," they are also handsome, free, and graceful.

The first impression one gets of the women is that they are far from primitive. They wear their hair in a low bun on the back of the head, kept in place with a bit of string or ribbon. It is long, straight, and blue-black, loose strands framing a broad oval face whose eyes seem to brim with savage, unashamed passion. Yet their manners are modest and docile. When they are seen wrapped in several thousand dollars' worth of furs, with their strong white teeth gleaming in a perpetual smile that spreads to the black eyes, one cannot wonder that white men have been taken with them. They seem to have more natural grace, more zest for life than their white sisters. When one sees them inside their houses, one notices their small and well-shaped hands and feet. They have broad cheeks and small noses, but otherwise the Mongolian features are not very dominant in the Polar Eskimos.

The men usually have pretty well defined features, sometimes with classic aquiline noses. Not until they are well up in their twenties do they grow a little beard on the upper lip and on the chin, lending them what would be a certain sardonic elegance if it weren't for their always blubber-smeared faces and hands. They wear their black hair long and falling loosely to the shoulders, somewhat greasy and unkempt, but perhaps held a little in control by a narrow band around the head. Even so, it falls down in their faces all the time, forcing them to make many oblique movements that—together with their broad smiles—give them a certain coquettish grace. This becomes so much more surprising when you realize with what ferocious heroism they procure the daily sustenance for themselves and their families.

Both men and women wear boots of sealskin, called *kamiks*. They are roomy, and inside there are stockings made of hare skins. For further protection of the feet, always the most exposed part of the body, they put a layer of dried grass in between the two pairs of soles, and this is changed every day. The men's kamiks reach the kneecap, where they meet a pair of shining white bearskin trousers. These are worn below the waist, somewhat loosely around the hips. A coat of fox fur covers the rest of the man—this has a hood which can be turned up to protect the head completely. The mittens are of seal or caribou skin.

The Eskimos have discovered that for maximum protection against the cold the hair of the fur must be outside. Under the coat they wear birdskin shirts with the feathers inside. These are the only tight-fitting garments. Otherwise, the skin clothes are loose and do not overlap too much, so as to allow for ventilation. For it is important that they be kept as dry as possible. If they should get too wet from perspiration and then be taken off, it could be difficult or even impossible to put them on again, as they would be frozen stiff.

In summer, the fox fur coat is replaced by a seal fur coat which is less warm. And in particularly clement weather, the birdskin shirt is often worn alone. When new it has a handsome dark yellow color.

The coat has a snip both in front and behind, and the hood and the sleeves are brimmed with foxtails. Sometimes the men will wear two foxtails sewn together around each leg, just above the kamik, to take the bite off the cold air coming in.

The women's costume is essentially the same as the men's, but their kamiks are much longer. They reach the crotch, and instead of trousers they wear short panties made of foxskin. The kamiks are brimmed on top with the mane hairs of the male bear, the longer the more elegant. The coat hoods are made of sealskin, pointed, and edged with foxtails.

The children, darling little creatures with shining eyes, vastly spoiled by their parents, are dressed like the grownups according to their sex. Only the babies, carried in their mothers' *amauts,* differ from this pattern. With the Polar Eskimos, such an *amaut* is really an expansion of the back of the mother's coat, made so that the baby sits in comfort in the nude against the mother's nude back. While there is a hood to protect the baby, the mother has a loose hood for her own use. This mode is necessary since it might sometimes be necessary to feed the baby under rough weather conditions, and the mother can then just shift it over to her breast under the protection of the coat. It is true that a healthy, normal baby will do all kinds of things on the mother's back! But that has to be tolerated.

The women are cleaner than the men. They wash themselves a little, or rub themselves down with a little blubber oil, after each menstruation. As for the men, they might go for years without being washed. However, the hygiene is not in an altogether bad state because both men and women take most of their clothes off, getting their bodies "aerated," when they are inside the house.

The familiar igloo is used by the Polar Eskimos only as a temporary shelter during travels. Most of the winter they live in permanent winter houses made of stones and peat. Permanent, that is, for the winter, for each spring they are left by the inhabitants and automatically become public property the next fall.

You enter the winter house through an entrance tunnel, usually about fifteen feet long so as to provide both ventilation and protection against the outside cold. Since the house usually faces the sea, it is on a hill which the horizontal tunnel cuts into. The floor of the tunnel is laid with flat stones, the walls are piled-up stones, and the ceiling is made of flat stones covered with peat or turf. It is low, so that you have to crawl in on your hands and knees.

In the tunnel, you will find a strange little instrument, a little saber of wood or bone, called a *tilugtut.* When snow is falling or drifting outside, thousands of snow crystals will be lodged in the long hair of your skin clothes. If you enter the warm house like that, they will melt and make your clothes wet and heavy. Moreover, if you soon have to go out again, they will freeze. The tilugtut is used to beat the clothes free of snow while still in the entrance tunnel. During this procedure, it is a good idea to call out a few remarks, like: "Somebody comes visiting, as it happens!" so that the people inside are prepared to see you. It is true that an Eskimo home is open to visitors at almost any time of day or night, but there are strained relationships everywhere in the world, and it is neither wise—nor polite—to show up in the house without a word of warning!

The entrance tunnel ends up just inside the front wall of the house itself, and you find yourself a couple of feet below the level of the floor, which you then step onto. Now you are in a room, rarely more than fifteen feet in diameter and roughly circular, inasmuch as the wide front wall, the converging side walls, and the narrower back wall of the house are curved evenly into each other. It is about nine feet high from floor to ceiling, but the roof slants toward the back wall. Besides, the whole back half of the room is filled from wall to wall by a big platform about three feet high. Since the house is sunk a little into the earth to give it extra protection against the gales, the platform usually represents the level of the ground outside. It is laid with flat stones which are extended along the front edge so as to create an overhang, under which there is storage space. On the sides, they extend into two side platforms that rest on stone supports, but also have storage space under them. What is left of the floor, which is also laid with flat stones, is then only a space about seven feet square in the front center part of the house. It serves well when game or frozen meat has to be brought in for the family meals.

The walls of the house are double, two layers of stones with peat or earth filled in between them. The roof is made of flat stones, deftly built up and overlapping each other, at last reaching so far toward the center that a main stone slab can rest on them, their outer ends being weighed down with boulders for stability. The size of a house largely depends upon how many large flat stone slabs can be found for their purpose. Only when an extra large house is wanted will the Eskimos solve the problem by building pillars up from the platform to support the ceiling.

Lumber in sizes sufficient to support a roof was rare before the white man came to Thule. Sometimes the Eskimos could barter a few little pieces of wood from the whalers, precious objects that they guarded with their lives. Also, they would find a little driftwood on their shores, and some of them believed that it came from forests that covered the bottom of the ocean like those in the white man's country. Actually, the driftwood was supplied by the rivers of Siberia and had drifted across the Polar Basin. After several years in salt water, it had chipped and was hard and difficult to work with. But its presence caused the Eskimos never completely to forget the use of wood.

The platform in the house is the family's sleeping bunk. Here they sleep in a neat row with their feet toward the back wall. Against the back wall are usually piled extra clothes and skins so that it isn't too cold. The bunk is covered with a thick layer of dried grass, upon which skins of musk ox and caribou are spread. The family and its eventual guests sleep under blankets made of fox, hare, caribou, and eider duck skins. The natural colors of these animals' feathers and fur are used to make beautiful patterns.

Only when it is overcrowded are the side bunks used for sleeping, but they are less desirable because they are colder. Otherwise, the blubber lamps are placed on the side bunks. One of them may be used to place a piece of meat or game on for everybody to nibble on. Then there is a bucket or sealskin basin for ice to thaw in for drinking water. Whenever possible, the lady of the house gets this ice from one of the icebergs floating in the fjord by the beach. That water tastes fresh and sweet. A dipper is placed in the basin or bucket for everybody to use when drinking, and this dipper is usually passed around after each meal.

On the other side bunk, there would then be knives, trays, and other household gear. The storage space under the bunks is used for skins and other property. On the walls may be pegs of caribou ribs or antler for hanging things on. Under the ceiling is suspended a framework of wood or bones. As it is for drying clothes on, it is directly above one of the blubber lamps. It is very important especially for the kamiks and stockings. Every evening, when the master of the house comes home from the day's hunting, his wife takes his kamiks and stockings and hangs them up to dry overnight. In the morning she chews them carefully till they are pliable and soft enough for his feet, and she puts new dried grass in between the soles.

For this purpose, the women go every fall up to the rocks to cut grass off, dry it in the sun, and carry it home. The best harvest is naturally around the bird cliffs, and they have to get a whole year's supply for their families before winter.

Both men and women are usually undressed around the house. The wife is only in her scant foxskin panties, and she sits placidly on the main bunk most of the time. Her cooking pots are suspended from the ceiling over the blubber lamp; everything is within her easy reach, and no bustling around is necessary. Since she has to cut and sew the skin garments of the entire family, that is what busies her most. Like a Turkish tailor, she sits with her legs stretched out at right angles to the body, her favorite position, with her work between her toes. Her most important tool is the *ulo,* a curved knife with a handle in the middle of the blade. From intuition, she cuts her skins in the proper pieces and sews them together, rarely measuring anything. The furs of the blue and the white fox are woven together in intricate patterns, and her work puts the finest Paris furrier to shame. With small, hardly visible stitches she weaves her narwhal sinew thread in and out until the skin pieces look as if they had grown together.

No wonder the needle is one of the most important Eskimo tools. It can be fatal, during a trip, if a torn garment cannot be repaired to protect against the cold, or new garments cannot be sewn. It is perfectly truthful to say that the lack of needles has caused the death of many travelers in the Arctic. For this reason, the woman's ability to sew well is one of her chief attractions.

The husband also undresses in the house. He may keep his bearskin trousers on, or he may be in the nude. When his clothes have dried, he ties them together in a bundle with a thong and hangs them up under the ceiling by a hook. That is in order to get as few lice in them as possible.

The house has one window, which is in the front wall above the entrance. The windowpane is made out of the intestines of the big bearded seal, which are split and dried and sewn together, then framed with sealskin, and the whole thing is put in the wall opening and fastened to the sides. One cannot see through such a window, but it lets quite a good light through. At one side there is a little peephole to look out of. More important, the ventilation of the house is provided through another and larger opening in the upper corner of the windowpane. Fresh air comes in through the entrance tunnel and is often regulated by a skin covering the entrance hole. This skin, when weighed down with a couple of stones, will also keep the dogs out of the house when the family is asleep. The dogs are rarely allowed in the house, anyway, but in very rough weather they may be resting in the entrance tunnel.

The flow of air out through the hole in the windowpane is regulated by a whisk of hay stuck in it. It is easy to see when the air is getting close because the flame in the blubber lamp starts to burn low. And although no draft is ever felt, the house is always well ventilated.

Although the blood and blubber from the killed game smeared over floor and side bunks often give the new observer the impression of an animal cave, he will soon realize that the stone house is ingeniously suited to the arctic conditions. And it is well heated and lighted by the blubber lamps.

The Eskimo lamp is cut out of soapstone. It has a deep depression in the middle, at one side of which a whisk of long-burning moss is placed. Lumps of blubber are put in the lamp, and as the moss burns, the blubber melts and is sucked up in the moss to be consumed. By placing the lamp on three stones or on a tripod, and slanting it at the right angle, one can regulate the flow of blubber to the side where the moss-wick is. A stick serves to open or close the wick, making it narrow or wide according to whether a large or a small flame is wanted. This demands great practice, and only Eskimo women know this art to perfection. The lamp is kept burning at all times; only when the house goes to sleep the flame is made very narrow, and the lamp is filled up with fresh blubber. If it is properly regulated it burns easily through the period of sleep.

There are two types of lamps. One is oval, with a slanting bottom to help the regular flow of the blubber; the other is kind of shell-shaped, with a row of little knobs along the long curved side. This latter is a prototype of the Thule Culture, and is the one used by the Polar Eskimos.

This is rather significant, for there are few household possessions that play as big a part in Eskimo domestic life as the lamp. The wife has to tend the lamp, and it belongs under her jurisdiction. The more lamps she can take care of the cleverer she is, and many lamps are a sign of wealth and prestige. Since there rarely is any permanent place called home, the lamps become the symbol of the home.

In a Polar Eskimo house, though, there were rarely more than two lamps, one on each side bunk. It is the younger woman who runs the household and has all the power. The widowed mother-in-law is a dethroned ruler. She loses her say over the lamps when her son brings home a wife, although the young bride may have a kind disposition and leave her one lamp to take care of. In these situations there are no false sentiments. There was once an Eskimo girl who married a white man and was going with him to his country. Her happiness made her feel so generous that she told her husband she would let his mother have one lamp to take care of so the old lady wouldn't feel neglected. But poor little Aqradaq soon learned differently, for in the home of her husband there were no lamps to tend. At first alone, later with her baby and an Eskimo nursemaid, she remained in an upstairs room and was not permitted to come down when there was company. She was like a prisoner, and she cried and pleaded with her husband to send her back, or she would die. It was not the isolation she minded, but the humiliation of seeing her mother-in-law run the household.

A constant concern of the Eskimo household is the lice, even though Eskimos get rather used to them. The wife delouses the husband, particularly his long hair, when the plague becomes too bad. And the husband, I have seen, often delouses the children and eats their lice with great relish, only once in a while handing one to the tot so that he also could have a little pleasure from them.

In their cold climate, cleanliness (the little they could have of it) was not the answer. Lice don't die from a little exposure to water. I have made scientific experiments along this line. Once I soaked a T-shirt filled with lice in water overnight. When I dried it and put it on without picking it clean, the little animals were right there.

And once I took some specimens of these unpopular creatures and put them in a test tube. I put it out in the cold of winter for four days, at a temperature of forty below or more. But when I took it inside the warm house again, and poured them out in my hand, it wasn't long before they started wiggling again.

The house is not the scene of all social life in wintertime. There are usually five or six houses in a settlement, and at a central point the men have built the meat rack. That is a high scaffold of stones on which all the hunters lay their catch so that it is out of reach of the dogs. Around it there are one or several cooking places, that is, fireplaces built up of a couple of stones and sheltered with walls of snow. When the weather permits, the whole settlement congregate around a lot of boiling meat at a cooking place and have their evening meal together. Men, women, and children sit and stand around with their portions of steaming meat and eat while they gossip. The whole ceremony is a good expression of the fact that the fight to obtain sufficient food is so difficult, so important in these barren regions, that every meal is a festive occasion.

For the Eskimos' placid living in the winter house is only a temporary thing. Most of their time is spent hunting or traveling around to get various materials needed for the household. It is not out of any desire for nomadism that the Eskimos are on the go all the time. It is simply that the goods of life are so thinly spread over their vast hunting grounds that they must constantly travel to get them. Take the Eskimos of the Thule district, for instance, who were scattered along a long coast and few in numbers. At only three places in the district could they get soapstone for their lamps and pots. Before Peary came, all their knives were provided from the famous meteorite stones on Salve Island in the northern part of Melville Bay (the stones are now in the American Museum of Natural History). But before they could go there to chisel parts of them off and beat them into shape with their crude tools, they had to go way up north to Humboldt's Glacier, there to find a certain kind of agate that was suited to use on the soft ironstone.

Seals were essential for kayak skins, boots, and summer coats, and when they had procured these, it might suddenly be necessary to go to another place to get bearskins for men's trousers. Foxes were to be found around the bird cliffs, so it was necessary to spend some time there. And so on. It may easily be seen that the Eskimos had to develop superior traveling methods, which in turn enabled them to perform their long-distance migrations.

The dogsled is the principal means of transportation in the Arctic, and until modern times, the only means used for long-distance traveling. The firm sea ice is the best road for dogsleds, so these are seldom used when the ice has broken up in summer. Around Thule that was only one month out of the year.

The type of dogsled used in Greenland has two runners about seven feet long and shod with steel. It is more than four feet wide and has about ten thwarts sitting closely together. On the back are attached two stanchions with a crossbeam on top. They serve to support the load, and the driver can help push the sled by means of them. The dogs are hitched to the sled in fan shape. Each dog has a little harness to which is attached a single trace of sealskin line. All the dogs' traces are the same length and meet in a little ring which again is attached to the sled by means of two strong lines. The ends of the runners are upturned. Pulled by about ten dogs, such a sled can transport 800 pounds or more under good conditions.

The sleds used by the Polar Eskimos are almost similar, the differences being that the stanchions are only about three feet high, and the sled itself is longer and narrower. In the old days, when wood was scarce, such a sled would often be made out of whalebone and caribou antlers lashed together with sinew; this was a formidable task.

A Polar Eskimo's dog team is his pride and glory. He tends to have no less than eight and preferably twelve good dogs, and it is his pleasure in life to see them well-fed, and to hear himself praised and envied on account of them. In all matters, the sign of manhood is the ownership of dogs, so much more as he trains them to help him hunt bears, the big animals that provide him with skins for his trousers.

This is the reason why dogs in the Thule district are tied by the houses, while those in southern Greenland and Canada are allowed to roam around, freely foraging for themselves. The Polar Eskimo's dogs are so trained to hate bear that a bear happening by could frighten them into running away from the settlement and thus losing their way, perhaps never returning to their owners. They are therefore tied with sealskin lines, and already as puppies they have their teeth dulled with a file so that they cannot chew their lines or traces to pieces.

For this reason it is always a problem to have suitable dog feed. They cannot chew, and the walrus hide—which is what they are most often fed—must be cut into pieces for them to swallow. If it is frozen, it must be thawed. On the other hand, the meat stays a long time in their stomachs when it has been swallowed like that, and during travel the dogs should not be fed more than every second day. Even so, you don't get their best performance out of them on the day they have been fed. It is on the day that their stomachs are empty that they are the fastest and most lively.

Knud Rasmussen and I were well supplied with powerful dogs at all times because Knud's uncle, Carl Fleischer, the colony manager at Tassiussak, was one of the finest dog breeders in Greenland. Even if he had had to give Knud his last dog, he would not for the honor of the family tolerate his nephew's use of an inferior team.

Every year that I lived at Thule, the mail journey was an important annual event. I had to leave Thule on about January 15 so as to make connection with those mail sleds that transported letters and packages down south to Holsteinsborg, where the steamer from Denmark arrived on April 20.

Often I made several trips a year down across Melville Bay, and I know its mountains and its ice so well that no place there is strange to me, and I could find my way there even in the middle of the dark months. For navigation can be a problem in the High Arctic. At Thule our compasses pointed southwest, toward the North Magnetic Pole, and the misdirection was constantly varying. In the dark months, therefore, trips were usually made with the beginning moon. Another direction finder was the so-called *sastrugi*, snow crystals on the ice which the wind has arranged in stripes pointing in its direction. Since the southwest is by far the dominant wind in all of western Greenland, it was no problem finding one's direction when sastrugi were present. Only on new ice, and with the moon hiding, did we have to rely completely upon our knowledge of landmarks silhouetted against the sky.

Melville Bay is something special. No other place in the Arctic has been the scene of so much adventure. It was the road of migration when the Eskimos came from the north and took over Greenland, and it was the background for the whalers' heroism in the years when whale oil was one of the necessities of civilization, when sailing ships were dominant, and large ships' crews every year made their way through the notorious pack ice of the Bay. Here we crossed during the dark months every year.

There was adventure in the journey every time, and spirits were high. The first night we always spent in a cave on Saunders Island—a cave about which the Eskimos who accompanied me could tell many mysterious stories of ghosts and spirits.

The next day we reached the settlement of Cape York. It is placed on a rocky precipice so that the houses look glued between the boulders. We were usually the first guests of the winter at the place, so they were happy to see us and fed both us and our dogs to capacity.

After Cape York, the secret of the trip was to pull out to the new ice away from the coast. There wasn't as much snow, so traveling was lighter, provided the ice had not packed itself together. But sometimes the ice could be like a mighty ocean stiffened in a surge of fury, and we had to turn left and right to find the best passage. In the darkness we often ran straight into mountains of ice and broke up the sleds. No trip over that stretch was commonplace.

If there was snow, we would usually see bear tracks in it, for every fall the bears migrated in great number across the ice and up the promontory at this place. The dogs were trained to smell if they were old or fresh and promising, and if it didn't carry us too far off course, we let them run in the tracks so that they could have the pleasure of looking at the pawmarks of their archenemy.

It takes some training to go bear hunting in the dark. When the dogs smell bear, they are taken with fury, they jump forward as if the sled had no weight, and the one who falls off can't catch up with them again. Nobody can worry about him! The only thing to do is to follow one's sled and hope that it gets stuck in some pack ice. If you stay on the sled, you must sit in the darkness and mind the balance and lean now to the left, now to the right, and hope that the sled doesn't turn over.

Then you cut loose your best dog, the leader of the team; he disappears in a wink. If then, from the darkness out ahead, you hear a howl as he is hit by a paw, you know that there is a bear, and you let the rest of the team go. They dart up to the bear to surround it, they jump wildly around it under its constant attacks. The bear is adroit like a cat, it tries to beat the dogs back and flee, but they are all over it. It is difficult to get in to shoot, and in the darkness it is necessary to walk all the way up to the bear.

When you see the bear like this, in its awesome height and wrath, you understand why the Eskimo with his spears considers the bear his most distinguished quarry and talks about "the great lonely roamer" with the greatest respect. It is out of this same respect that many of those hunters who had guns nevertheless preferred to attack the great animal with their spears, particularly if they were two or three together.

"A bear is so constructed that it does not like to have spears in it," say the Eskimos. As if to prove what they say, the bear—as they run right up to the beast with their incredible courage and hurl their puny weapons at it—takes the spears that have lodged deeply in its flesh and breaks them as if they were matchsticks.

When the bear finally is felled, the dogs calm down with a strange suddenness. They lie down on the ice and watch without excitement as their fallen enemy is being skinned. According to Eskimo custom, all the hunters present are to get parts in the quarry, in this case both of meat and skin. There are three pairs of trousers in a bearskin. If there are more than three hunters present, the ones who threw their spears last will usually be generous enough to leave their parts of the skin to the others. The hunter who fixed his spear first in the bear gets the upper part. That is the finest part, for it includes the forelegs with the long mane hairs that are so much desired to border women's kamiks with. The headskin doesn't really count, for it is only good for a seat on the sled or to put under a wetting baby in the amaut. So the hunter measures with his whip handle from the neck down, and marks the length of his own thighs on the skin and cuts off at that mark. The next hunter does likewise with the next piece, and the third one gets the rest.

Since the white men like to have a whole bearskin with head and claws on it, a rule was made in the Thule district that if the hunter who had "first harpoon" needed the skin to sell in the shop, he had only to say: "I skin with claws." Then he had to give his mates parts in the meat only, not in the skin. Often it is the intention of a young man to get himself income easily and quickly, just by saying these four little words. But they are difficult to pronounce. For they show that he isn't able to catch foxes enough to trade with; in addition, they make his friends trouserless. Often a remark is heard about "the good sense in keeping the skin whole!" and "This is a nice skin. Here is a man who uses his good luck when it comes along!" Such sarcasms do not fail to hit home. But then the young man breaks out in a Homeric laughter: "Naw, now I must laugh. At last, there is something amusing to tell others! Game mates think that the bear was to be skinned with snout and claws so as to rob them of the much desired trouser skins. Of course, it was a joke. The skin belongs to everybody!" With that, he feels relieved and can—since he shot the bear—go up to the next two in line and measure the length of their thighs with his whip handle to transfer it to the bearskin. There is much satisfaction in this gesture.

Bear meat tastes good when you don't get it too often. But with the new ice in September, lots of bears always came to Thule. They went ashore at Pitufik, where the American airbase is now. Bears are wise, they know their geography. They crossed the glacier and came directly down behind Cape York to Melville Bay. This way is shorter, and they passed onto one of the richest seal places in the district.

But some of them didn't get so far. They lay down to sleep by the edge of the glacier. They thought it peaceful there, and they let themselves be snowed down. Not all bears hibernate, but if they are fat enough they like to do it. From the warmth of their breath a cave formed over them, and they slept until the light returned. Then they came out, miserably lean, and for some days they had to practice walking on the ice, for they had been sucking their paws, which thus became sore.

Almost daily we saw bears go ashore over there, and we killed so many that we got bored with the taste of their meat, which is best raw and frozen, anyway. Now our pot was hung up on a tripod formed of three harpoons, and we continued boiling meat till nobody could get another bite down. And the dogs got their well-deserved part.

Our fire was usually made on blubber and lit with moss, which we all brought along. These campfires lent the trips across Melville Bay a certain romantic mood. Knud and I always lived like Eskimos and traveled like Eskimos. We didn't carry a tent with us, but in good weather we would just simply sleep in the shelter of some pack ice. And I will always remember the festive hours when the flames from the blubber fire welled up. I used to go away from the others for a little while and take in the scenery. The huge blubber fire against the background of the contour of the mighty mountains, the little skin-clad figures darting back and forth, unloading sleds, cutting up dog feed, and doing all the hundred things that are necessary in a camp on the ice.

When the meat in the pot was done, the fire attendant called out, and we all crowded around the pot with our knives in hand. We had to take our mittens off to eat, of course, so it was nice to be near the heat, and it was always amusing to see the savage faces, framed by the fur hoods and with the long black hair sticking out, in the shifting glare from the fire. During the long winter darkness, we rarely saw each other's features sharply, but here by the cooking fire we "discovered people again," said the Eskimos. Joy, joy!

When the meat was eaten, the pot was passed around, and we drank as much of the soup as we could. Soup from bear meat is fat, it tastes strong and spicy as it goes down. Of course, a pot that has been over a blubber fire is very sooty, so we were not exactly handsome to look at when the meal was over.

When nobody wanted more soup, the owner of the pot always had a dog that needed something extra for the road, so the dog was invited to come up and lick the pot clean.

If the fury of the gale was over Melville Bay, we had to build ourselves an igloo to camp in until it had abated. To build an igloo, the Thule Eskimos use a snow knife, which is really more like a broad-bladed saw.

A typical igloo is about twelve feet in diameter and nine feet high, and inside it has—just like the house—a platform about three feet high, serving as sleeping place. If a family is out traveling, building the igloo is the man's job. A woman could do it, as she may sometimes have to in order to save her life, but she would never admit to it; it is decidedly a man's job. Carefully, but with the speed of years of practice, he cuts out the large wedge-shaped blocks. The base circle consists of about fifteen large blocks. As the walls get higher, and the rings narrower, he cuts the blocks smaller, and he has to step inside to put them up, while somebody may help him by handing the blocks to him from the outside. The last circle has five blocks in it, and he closes the top hole with a block in which he bores a hole for warm air to escape. A well-constructed igloo will never collapse, only sag in the middle, but the rising heat from the people and the blubber lamp would eventually melt it completely if it were not for the little airhole in the top which—incidentally—is regulated with a whisk of hay just like the airhole in the house.

When the igloo is completed, the man cuts a low arch for an entrance hole, and he crawls outside and builds an entrance tunnel which not only serves to keep the direct impact of the cold away from the igloo when somebody enters or leaves, but which also becomes storage space for hunting gear and other things which they do not want to leave on their sled.

In the meantime, the wife and the children have been tightening the cracks between the snow blocks with snow, and they throw snow over the whole construction. As soon as the igloo is finished, the wife takes her skins and cooking gear and goes inside to arrange the bunk and make the igloo livable.

The construction of an igloo takes perhaps an hour for an experienced hand, and it is usually used only overnight, but sometimes it is lived in for several days while a storm exhausts its fury. It is because of the ingenious invention of the igloo that arctic travelers can take the gale in their stride, and actually even welcome this change in the routine of daily travel.

The dogs take care of themselves. They huddle together at a place where there is a little shelter from the wind, and they curl up with their snouts under their bushy tails. They fight and yammer a little while they all try to get the place in the middle where it is warmest, but finally they quiet down, and they let themselves get covered completely by the drifting snow. In this snow cover they can keep themselves alive and warm for many days if necessary.

If it is anticipated that an igloo will have to be used for a longer period, it can be secured in the following manner: The man lights a fire inside it. He closes the hole in the ceiling, leaves the igloo and walls up the entrance. As the heat builds up inside, the walls melt, and the water from them is absorbed by the porous snow. Then the igloo is opened again, the fire is put out, and the full cold of the outside is let in. The watery walls freeze to almost solid ice that can withstand any gale. But so as to keep them cold from the inside and also protect the inhabitants against moisture and seepage, the woman lines it with a drapery of skins inside. Usually, this is simply the skin for the summer tent that now is hung up inside the igloo by means of lines going through small holes in walls and ceiling.

When they leave the igloo to continue their voyage, the last thing the travelers do is to relieve themselves, using it as a comfort station.

This is due to one peculiarity about the Eskimo dogs: they love human excrement more than anything else in this world. Out in the open, distressing situations can therefore arise. The process has to be done quickly, because of the cold, but the dogs crowding around can make it even more difficult. If there are other people in the party, somebody will take position in front of the suffering one and keep the dogs at bay with a whip.

But while the igloo is available, everybody takes advan-

tage of it. Afterward, of course, the always hungry dogs
are let in so that they can do away with the garbage and
other things they can find.

This was an added factor in the problem of hygiene at
our Thule station. Water closets were out of the question
because of the low temperatures and the lack of running
water. I had built a three-walled shelter where a certain
amount of privacy and protection could be obtained. But
loose-running puppies and single dogs came rushing up in a
horde when they saw somebody "with bowed head," as the
expression went, come walking toward this shelter, and they
flocked around ready to jump in. Only one could get the
warm mouthful, of course, but to obtain this honor they
would willingly let themselves be bitten bloody, and the violent fight wouldn't subside until a long time after.

I hired a special boy to accompany guests out to the difficult spot. Qupagnuk (whose name means "the snow starling") was not very old, but from the time he could walk
he had handled a dog whip, and his ability at hitting home
was phenomenal. Proudly, he took position in front of the
shelter and defended the occupant's peace.

This Qupagnuk I had taken into our house because he led
a miserable existence. His real name was Ungarpaluk ("the
little harpoon"). But because his father had died, and his
widowed mother did piecework about the various households
to earn her keep, there was no real home, and the boy was reduced to foraging for himself. Somebody would throw a pair
of old kamiks to him, or they would let him have other
dilapidated garments. He was so full of lice that nobody
liked to have him sleeping in their house, and he usually
slept in the tunnel of an abandoned house. He was happy,
though. He played with the other children, and he looked
well fed. But he was always hungry, so when the hunters
were feeding their dogs he came running to get his share of
the walrus hide or meat. He jumped in among the voracious,
battling dogs, who often bit him in the face and on the
hands, and he saved himself a bite or two. This got him the
name of "Snow Starling," because the Eskimos said that just
like that little bird he had to pick up a little to eat where it
was found. And he responded willingly to the name of
Qupagnuk. When I first saw him at Cape York, I pitied him,
and I announced that I thought it was shoddy of the great
hunters there that they couldn't bring home enough food to
give a poor orphan suitable clothes and nourishment. I

referred to their own children, whom they watched over and stuffed with all the delicacies the house had to offer.

They listened to me a little—patiently, as they always did. But then one of them said: "Pita, you speak both wisely and at the same time like the newborn man you are in this country! An orphan who has a hard time should never be pitied, for he is merely being hardened to a better life. Look, and you will see that the greatest chief hunters living here have all been orphans. Myself, I can remember how Qisunguaq was left behind by starving foster parents and still made out by seeking out the winter depots of the foxes and at the same time training himself more in hunger than people thought possible. Today, it is impossible for Qisunguaq to feel cold. Look at Angutidluarssuak, who always manages to cross the treks of the game animals, and who endures all hardships and can live without sleep more than anybody else. His childhood was spent in constant starvation, and for several winters his only food was stolen from the hunters' meat graves. Look at little Iggianguaq here. Here see a man who may be slight to look at, but who outdoes everybody in bear hunting because he never gets tired of long-time sled driving."

I thus understood that the Eskimos had their own method of caring for orphans, and perhaps not such an inhuman one. But I nevertheless took Ungarpaluk with me to the station.

To return to the igloos, around Hudson Bay it was a lot faster to build them than in Greenland. People dug down in the snow at the same time as they built up, and their snow knives, broad-bladed curved knives, formerly made of bone or antler but now sold by the trading stations, were a lot more efficient in cutting the snow rather than sawing through it. It must be said that there is often much more snow around those regions than you ever find in Greenland, and in order to build his igloo the Hudson Bay Eskimo must first find out if the snow is deep enough. For this purpose he has a special snow guage, a thin stick of bone or tusk, about three feet long, which he holds gingerly with two fingers and sticks down into the snow. The feel tells him how deep the snow is and of what consistency, and he is able to start his igloo at the most desirable spot without wasting any more time. In half an hour he puts up a sizable one.

As a whole, since so many of the Canadian Eskimos do not use permanent winter houses, they are more ingenious at snow building than the Greenlanders. Among the Musk Ox People I once saw an igloo that was built specially for drum dances, and which could house more than sixty people with room to spare in the center for the performance. The other igloos were grouped around it and had corridors leading into it, so that the whole complex was like a sheltered village.

When the Hudson Bay Eskimos got in trouble, it was usually because of lack of game and not because of failure of transportation, for their sleds and their sled driving have many advantages over those of the Polar Eskimos. Even when they have wood, they do not have to be concerned about making the sleds light, for most of their land is flat and barren. Since they usually stick to land when out in a sled, they do not have to worry about rough ice. The land is almost entirely covered with snow. They can, therefore, make their sleds much larger, and a Hudson Bay sled of the type that I used during the Fifth Thule Expedition, though it is only two and a half feet wide, is up to eighteen feet long and furnished with a lot of thwarts sitting rather far apart. The dogs, usually ten or twelve of them, are hitched to the sled in a double row, not in a fan shape formation as in Greenland. There are no stanchions on the sled, but I put some on mine because I was used to them.

Since there is so much soft snow, the Hudson Bay Eskimo does not use steel shoes for his sled; he covers the runners with a thick layer of mud. This mud he procures in the summertime and stores for the winter, when it is to be used. When he prepares his sled, he brings several balls of mud into the house to be thawed. Then he puts it on the sled runners in layers several inches thick. When it is frozen stiff, he planes it down with a knife until it is even and smooth. Finally, a thin layer of ice is applied to the mud; for this he obtains a pot of lukewarm water and brushes it on with a foxtail or piece of skin.

The sled runs on this thin ice crust, and very smoothly at that. During a day's journey it might get worn off; then the driver will very often use his own urine to renew it, since it has just the right temperature. Moreover, it gives a tougher ice. But it is a matter of great concern not to get the ice crust chipped. The driver has a thong which is attached to the fore end of the sled. If he sees a stone sticking up through the snow, he hurries to throw the sled out to the side by pulling in the thong. If the ice crust gets chipped anyway, it has to be repaired immediately, since it can reduce his speed considerably. This is quickly done with a piece of meat which is chewed free of all fat and then applied to the crack in the runner.

I had no real trouble finding my way in the foreign country, for by that time I was well versed in the Eskimo language, and I could always get rather exact topographic descriptions from the Eskimos who had taken the same route. They have a very practical custom of always giving descriptive names to landmarks. *Pingo* everywhere means a round-topped mountain; *Kuksuaq* is the big river; *Tassersuaq* is the big lake, etc.

The sled being the man's property and pride, it has a certain significance as a symbol. One of the first days I was in Canada I met a party of Eskimos whose dogs were in bad condition. The women were running by the sleds instead of sitting on them. My Greenland Eskimos and I invited them to sit up on our sleds. They smiled hesitatingly, then they asked for permission from their husbands. This was granted, and happily they mounted our conveyances and settled down. This with the exception of a young wife whom I invited to sit on my sled. She turned her hood down and pointed to her head. I didn't understand her meaning, and urged her to climb up so that we could continue our trip.

Only later did I learn that they had all understood that we had taken these women on our sleds because we wanted them for company the following night. But this woman had her hair hanging down loose, which was a sign that she was having her menstrual period. So it was in order not to cheat me that the honest girl had shown what state she was in. When I invited her anyway, they all laughed a lot, for they thought I was saying that it didn't bother me in the least.

Old woman who have lost their sexual attraction are exempted here, of course, and everywhere among the Eskimos you will find these unattached old females whose only pleasure is to travel from place to place, meet their relatives, and gossip. If they get a yen to go where you are going, they just settle down on your sled with their little bundles. To chase such a woman away would be a dog owner's eternal shame! For she will surely say with a toothless grin: "Perhaps your dogs cannot pull my weight!" And she will spread the story wherever she goes.

There is one place in the Eskimo world where dogsleds are not known at all. That is in the southern tip of Greenland, where the sea doesn't freeze over at all. Here, the *umiak* is used for transportation. The umiak is a large, deep boat made of one or two layers of sealskin tightened over a framework of wood or whalebone. It is rowed with regular oars, and the Danes call it the "women's boat," because it is rowed only by women.

The umiak has always been thought by outsiders to be a regular feature of the Eskimo world, yet it is not really common except in the two extremes of Eskimo country, namely Alaska, where it is used for whaling, and South Greenland.

The performance of these large skin boats is a delight. They float like giant birds on the waves and take no water except for a little spray from the waves. Even this could add up considerably if it were not for the escort of the kayaks. On a trip, the umiak is surrounded by kayaks, like a battleship surrounded by destroyers, and they take the impact of the waves.

On my first umiak trip I sat in the stern of the boat watching the kayakmen. But at length I couldn't sit idle while the women were working, so I insisted upon taking an oar, much to the amusement of both the men and the girls. A couple of hours of the pace set by the girls left me exhausted, and I had to hand the oar back to the embarrassed young woman who had been trying to coach me.

The stamina of those girls was astonishing. When we reached our destination they had been rowing for thirteen hours, yet they attended the common merrymaking in the evening and danced for five hours.

The Greenland *kayak* is also a skin boat, about fifteen feet long, very slender, and round on the bottom. The kayakman wears a watertight garment of sealskin, and the manhole is covered with skin in which there is a wooden ring that closes tightly around the hunter's waist. The hunter's hood and sleeves are tight-fitting also, and neither man nor boat takes a drop of water.

During a storm the kayakman must be able at will to turn his craft bottom side up and then make it turn up again. For if he sits upright and lets a breaker hit him, his spine may be broken. No, he throws his boat over and takes it at the bottom. Many kayakmen who are well practiced in this sport prefer to hunt the seal in stormy weather with big waves, because they can get much nearer to the seal under cover of the waves.

The kayak is principally a hunting tool and the most

important one in Greenland. The hunter has his harpoon lying on the deck of the kayak. The Eskimo harpoon is a six-foot-long shaft with a detachable point of walrus ivory. Through the point goes a line. When a seal is harpooned, the shaft falls off and floats around to be picked up later. The point stays in the seal which—if it is still alive—dives to the bottom of the fjord, and drags the line with it. The other end is attached to a sealskin filled with air that works like a drift anchor and also tells the hunter where the seal is. Sooner or later it has to come up again, and then he can kill it with one of his pikes.

This form of sealing was used all over Greenland both summer and most of the winter (except among the Polar Eskimos), and it was the basis of the old Greenland culture. But it was a very dangerous form of hunting, what with the rough and capricious weather around the cliffs and reefs of the fjords, and it was considered a natural death for a man to be lost while out in his kayak. Every evening, the women went up on the hills around the settlement and gazed out over the sea, each one waiting for her husband. That picture of the worried wives and mothers standing up there waiting evening after evening will for me always be the symbol of old Greenland.

But the danger was not lurking in stormy weather alone. The Greenland fjords are peculiar for the spells of completely quiet weather, when there is not enough wind to blow out a match and the water is like a sheet of glass. The kayak hunter must sit in his boat without stirring a finger so as not to scare the shy seals away. Actually, he can only move his eyes, as even the slightest move otherwise might mean game lost. The sun, low in the sky, sends a glare into his eyes, and the landscape around moves into the realm of the unreal. The reflex from the mirror-like water hypnotizes him, he seems to be unable to move, and all of a sudden it is as if he were floating in a bottomless void, sinking, sinking, and sinking. . . . Horror-stricken, he tries to stir, to cry out, but he cannot, he is completely paralyzed, he just falls and falls.

This trance may last until perhaps a slight ripple of wind on the surface of the water brings reality back to him. It is the notorious kayak illness, a nervous sickness, but none the less real. It has claimed quite a toll of otherwise able-bodied hunters who were not capable of pursuing the only profession they knew of, because—every time they would go out in a kayak—they would be stricken with panic. It has meant poverty and ruin for many a Greenland family.

The Polar Eskimos cannot use their kayaks for more than a couple of months out of the year, so with them sealing on the ice is much more important. This is also almost the only form of hunting they can continue during the dark months, since the moon gives them sufficient light to go out on the ice and watch the blowholes.

For at this time, Smith Sound is completely covered with thick ice, and the hunters take advantage of the seals' need to come to their blowholes to breathe. The hunter takes up his position by such a breathing hole and waits patiently. It is cold, of course, but he doesn't dare to move his foot the slightest bit. If he does, the snow and icy crystals on the ice might crack and betray his presence. The seals are sensitive and suspicious animals. If there is no snow on the ice, as is the case when it is new, the hunter puts bearskin soles under his kamiks so that the hard soles won't sound against the ice. The slightest sound is clearly heard by the seal in the water, it flees immediately, and the long wait starts all over again.

Every seal uses many blowholes, and each blowhole is used by many seals. How they find them in the dark is a riddle that no naturalist has been able to answer to my satisfaction. The blowhole is quite small at the surface of the ice, and it expands dome-shaped down to the water, for since the ice is often three feet thick, the seal must be able to get its entire body into the opening and yet only show its snout to the outside world. When the hunter hears the seal come up in the hole, he must take care to wield a powerful thrust with his harpoon just as the seal is under the little opening in the surface of the ice. He cannot see the seal, yet he must hit it directly in the head, and often he kills it with the first thrust. Seals are quite nervous and faint easily from just a light blow on the head. But it might happen, if it is a big seal, that the hunter has to fight with it for quite some time to hold it there. Once the seal is dead, he chops a wider hole in the ice to get it up through it.

Apart from the seals caught at the blowholes, the Polar Eskimo family lives mostly on the provisions collected the previous summer during the months that the darkness lasts. This is therefore also the time to go visiting, both to the neighbors and on longer trips, so as to taste each other's good things.

But the hunter's wife has one important task to perform, that of setting and tending the fox traps. For the fur of the arctic fox, which has been poor all summer, is beautiful again now with the beginning of the dark period. While her husband is at the blowholes, the wife borrows the dogsled and goes out to set and tend her traps.

These are permanent constructions built of stone. The flat stones are used to form a kind of cage which is hidden under peat and snow. The bait is at the bottom of the cage, and the fox can enter at its front. When the fox takes the bait, he releases a string which has been holding the stone which closes the cage, and there he sits. Of course, these traps become more effective as the winter goes along and the foxes become hungrier and hungrier. Sometimes, also, snares are used, and when we arrived at Thule we introduced steel traps since we were interested in getting as many skins as possible traded in. Until that time, fox trapping was considered the woman's work, the reasoning being that they didn't fight or run away, the cowardly animals, and therefore they were not worthy of a man's attention. Now, with our arrival, the possession of many foxes meant wealth in the white man's goods, and soon the men began to realize what a cunning animal the fox really was, well worth busying oneself with.

But the women still trapped for their own use and that of their families. And the care of the furs was their responsibility, at any rate. They chewed each skin carefully for hours until there wasn't a speck of fat left on it, then they tanned it in hot water and dried it. That was all that was necessary in the clean germless air. And the foxes from the Thule district have always been considered among the finest in the world.

3 Trading with the Eskimos

As THE ESKIMO CAME into closer contact with the civilized world, their opportunities for trading with white men became more frequent. But trading was a completely foreign idea to Eskimos and they had to learn it from the bottom. European and American people think that anybody can trade; if there is only something to pay with and something to sell, trading seems easy enough! But it was not so with the Eskimos.

Living in the world's most inhospitable country, happy to be able to wrench from it the bare necessities of life, they had never developed any trade. There were of course exchanges, but these were always in the form of gifts. For the Eskimos always feel an obligation, whenever they receive gifts; they want to give *qooyanasat*, i.e., "something to say thank-you with." But this is quite different from payment. The exchange of one thing for another of similar value never occurred to Eskimos.

When Knud Rasmussen and I established our trading post at Thule, the land of the Polar Eskimos was not as yet under Danish rule, and the people there had been trading almost solely with Scottish whalers, the *upernatleet*, as they called them, meaning "those who arrive in spring." The whalers never permitted them to choose what they wanted, and gave to them only sparingly from such stores as they happened not to need for themselves. After all, they didn't want to spoil the Eskimos by teaching them the monetary value of things!

Then, a few years before we came, the great American explorer Robert Peary had come to the place and, as the whole tribe just consisted of some two hundred people, he became a provider of American goods for all of them, giving them guns, tools, and other goods in return for their services on his many expeditions. He did not care much for fur; neither did the natives have much time for trapping when he was using them on his expeditions.

As for Knud and me, we arrived with the backing of a small private capital, and we didn't have many goods. But Knud explained to the Eskimos that if we got a lot of fox skins, we could exchange them in Denmark for more goods that would arrive the next year. The natives could supply quite a number of fox skins, most of them blue foxes, for we usually got only a couple of white ones in about a hundred blue skins. To start in trading with an entirely new tribe is always an experience, and, as our stock was limited, the natives felt sorry for us when we were departing with our goods. They always came as my guests and stayed in my house, and the regular trading was done in the following way:

Each man trades just once, or maybe twice, a year. The first time is when the ice has formed and the fall foxes have been caught in sufficient numbers to make a good showing. A man always brings his wife and all his children, as this is a great event for the year. It is dark during the four months from October 19 to February 24, and when the sledge comes out of the darkness all the inhabitants of the village gather around and lots of ceremonies are gone through to show how glad the visitors are to be there and for the inhabitants to tell them how welcome they are. They come into my house, after the dogs are looked after and everything taken care of, and get something to eat. My boiled meat is followed by tea with sugar, and it is a big feast for everybody. All the villagers come in too, listening, talking, and telling.

We discuss the weather, the hunting in the summer, the dogs, the scandals of different places, and other events. The only matter we don't talk about is foxes. Next day the same thing—eating, dancing, talking—and the next day and the next, until I for my part think that the hospitality has come to an end. Then I just casually ask the man whether he has caught any foxes this year.

"Me, foxes?" he answers. "Nothing doing. One is a poor hunter as far as that goes, but especially for foxes."

"Well," I say, "I'm sorry, because I'd like to have a few foxes just to send home to the white people's country when the ship arrives next summer, and I ought to have a few absolutely first-class ones; and I know that in that case I will have to see you to get the very best grade."

"Oh!" the man yells out. The big, nice white man has made a mistake. "Oh, you don't know how unable I am to catch foxes. And what about it? Even if I had a few skins in my possession, what do you think my awful lazy and dirty wife would do with them? She can't tan skins. In fact she can't do anything."

The wife sits listening, but doesn't protest.

"Well," I remark, "I saw a couple of bags out on the load which is now on the meat racks, and I thought they contained fox skins."

"Well," the man says, "maybe there's just a couple of fox skins in the bags, but we just use them to wipe the grease off our hands and other dirty things; and anyway, they are full of oil and far below such skins as your eyes should be bothered with looking at."

"Good!" I say. "But just the same I might like to have some of them. What about looking at them tomorrow?"

We arrange that, and the man keeps on for half an hour complaining that tomorrow will be his day of shame and dishonor. "Oh, why did I bring those lousy skins with me! Oh, why couldn't I get a real able wife to work like you, and you" (he points to every woman present). "Now I know that I have seen this place for the last time, because after the laugh that will be made over me tomorrow I will never show up again, even if I am tough enough to survive it, which I doubt."

Next day comes, and after breakfast I again have to encourage the customer to show his merchandise. Groaning and lamenting, he goes for his bags, the wife following him. Now comes the big moment of the year. They bring in a couple of sacks, each containing some fifty blue fox skins, and they have beforehand assured themselves that the whole village is present to witness their triumph. As if they were being dragged to the gallows, they open the sacks and pour the contents out. Now it is my turn. I look at the skins amazed, surprised and beaten.

"Well," I say, "as usual, those are the best skins in the year. I knew they would come from you; and they certainly did. Here is something I will have to mourn about for years, because I am unable to get those foxes."

The man raises his head, interested. "What did you say? Are they too poor for you to accept?"

"Oh, no; not at all. Just the opposite. You will have to take every one of your skins back with you because I have nothing to pay with. The trading goods that came out this year were especially bad. We haven't got enough of them and they certainly aren't of a kind that can pay for such skins as yours."

"Pay!" yells the man at the top of his voice. "You don't think that I would show myself low enough to take any pay for those poor skins? I will feel myself happy if you'll accept them. Oh! Pay! My ears must be thick or my mind is turned crazy, because the sound I got in my head made it seem as though it was your intention to pay something for those terrible skins."

This takes some time, but finally I put in a question. "I am unable to pay for the skins but anxious to show my gratitude through my poor gifts. What could you be thinking of wanting in case I should be presumptuous enough to compare my unworthy goods to your valuable furs?"

He starts in, talking to himself, trying to remember but it is impossible for him. "What do I want! What do I want! Oh, I am a man without wishes. I don't know if I want anything."

It is then up to me. "Don't you want a gun?"

"A gun! A gun! Oh, a gun had been in my mind and in my dreams for a long, long time; but I, the man you listen to now, am a terrible hunter. Why should I have a gun?"

"Well, I will give you a gun. You need a knife, too, and you need some tools. And what more?"

Now that the big time is here he doesn't know what he wants. But I have the skins, so I invite the man, his wife, and his children to go into the store and look the things over. They get the key and go down to the store. They go in, closing the door carefully behind them, and spend the best day in the year going through everything. There isn't one gun that isn't taken down and looked over; no kettle but what is unpacked and examined, but packed again and put in its place. All the knives are tested, every pipe sucked at. The scissors are looked over, the needles taken out, and the dry goods, hardware, everything is gone through—soap and what else. They spend the whole day in that store.

Meantime, I get a chance to look these skins over and figure out my prices, and finally, in the evening when the couple come back, the man has his wishes. He never tells what he wants, but he relates of what fine knives he saw, both those with the white handles and those with the brown, and the small ones with the point. He goes on: "And then I looked at the files. My, what beautiful files! Just what I needed last summer when I gave up my routine laziness and happened to work a little. And I saw out there that you have axes. I guess the big hunters—of course not me, but the real big hunters—they have plenty of use for such axes for chopping up the frozen meat in the wintertime." And he keeps on as if he were sent out to advertise the store to the public. He is interrupted by a sort of yelling or crying from the background. It is his wife, carefully instructed by him, who now breaks in complaining what a bold and fresh husband she has, keeping on asking like a beggar even when it has been proved to everybody that he has nothing to pay with. This, of course, only serves to cause me to protest that his skins are marvelous, unmatched so far, etc.

When the man has been talking for some time, I turn to the wife. "What about you? Aren't you going to trade? Don't you want something?"

She blushes and looks for a place to hide. "Me? Certainly not! What should I want? Am I one who deserves anything? Oh, no; I have no wants, no wishes at all. Haven't I been a guest in your splendid house? Haven't I spoiled the fur he brought? Don't talk to me. Why does a big, strong man direct his words to a poor woman and make me ashamed?"

"But wasn't there something you would like?"

"I would like to have—oh, I happen to be without wishes; only those people who are worth something should have something."

"Well, but I just want you to take something with you."

And after several more excuses, she tells what she might like to have. A few needles, just to possess them, because she can't sew, and it is only because other women have such things and know how to use them. And she wanted some scissors, and she wanted thread. Maybe for the children some undershirts would be good, and some for herself; also combs. And "I would like to have a mirror, even though I, of course, will never look at myself in it. But sometimes real women lower themselves to visit me. And a kettle and some cups; maybe a pot. But because I am so bad I will not ask for a sewing box, but I looked at one out there which was good, so I will have something to think about. Of course I don't want it. And then I saw——"

But here her husband interrupts. "Wait a moment! I have to go outside and beat my fresh and shameless wife. Oh, I am a poor man at everything, and here you see I can't even educate my wife. Where is my whip? What can I have to lash her with?"

The wife keeps on asking, and finally I have to stop her from asking for more. Meanwhile I have figured out how much they can have for each skin and write it down on a piece of paper, sending them out to my clerk, who now is in the store ready to deliver the goods. It pays better and saves me lots of talk and time when I'm not there. They look at the piece of paper I give them as a nun looks at the Holy Bible. Now the clerk has his troubles out there while they are making their choice between the different cups, the different kettles, the guns, and what not.

And now comes the end of the trading, where they show their smartness and prove what fine business people they are.

The man will come running in. "Oh, I'm so sorry; when I told you what my needs were I forgot to ask for tobacco. I'd like to have some tobacco."

"All right." I allow him the tobacco.

A few minutes after he will be back with his purchases.

"Well," he will say, "I saw a knife out there I would like to have instead of this one, though it will ruin my sleep to part with this one, too."

I let him have the knife.

The wife will be there. "There was also some red cloth. My, I would rather have that than some of the things I got, but I'll begin to cry when I have to give them away again."

Then the man comes again. "When I am going out on long bear hunts my thoughts will go back to this hatchet, and I'll be thinking of having had it in my possession, because I'll have to give it back and procure a saw I saw out there. I have the whole time been thinking of a saw, but my tongue refused to pronounce the word."

I let him have the saw. And they keep on. The only way to stop them is to have lunch ready. Big helpings of meat; whaleskin in mighty plates, piles of frozen bear meat, bags of duck eggs frozen hard as stones, but delicious to bite into like apples—all given to make them use their mouths for everything but asking for more. And the deal is closed.

Next day the departure takes place. The dogs are harnessed up and attached to the sledge. The man and wife are loading and lashing their stuff on the sledge. But sure enough, he comes in at the last moment: "Oh, I forgot matches! Why didn't I mention a saw file! If I had only asked for a little more goods! Enough for a harpoon shaft!"

The smartest man is the man who remembers most. He gets a reputation amongst his countrymen. Of course the perfectly straight-minded man doesn't know about this and doesn't allow for it, but the seasoned trader keeps back four or five fox skins to make up for the forgettings and additional wishes.

When everything is loaded on and the woman and children placed on top of the sledge, the man gives a signal to the dogs to rise up and be alert. Then I come out with a package in my hand, giving the wife some tea and sugar, or whatever else I know she would like. Of course these things have been allowed for, too.

The whip cracks and away they go. They soon disappear in the darkness, coming again late in the spring before the ice breaks and they have to go to the places where there is open water and the summer keeps them from communication with the outside world.

4 Love and Marriage

Family Structure and Morals

LIFE IS SO HARD for the Eskimos, and the different chores they must perform are so specialized, that each man must always have one woman to take care of his skins, his clothes, and his food. Through necessity as well as an ancient custom, which in many cases amounts to a taboo, all work is rigorously divided between man and woman. Even so, both of them have plenty to do.

The man has the more heroic tasks of fighting the polar bear, harpooning the fierce walrus, or outsmarting the tricky seal. Sometimes he must endure the long wait at the seal's blowhole for many hours during the cold nights. In the springtime, when the sun is in the sky day and night, the man must seek out every opportunity to catch game. Not only must daily needs be taken care of, but meat caches must be built and filled for the coming winter. So when the weather permits, he hunts continually, sleeping and resting as little as possible, wandering around in the open with the dog team.

The woman with her children and her needlework stays at home. She has to scrape the animal skins and prepare them while they are still fresh. She sews the clothes of the entire family, cooks, and keeps the house warm. Also, meat must be laid out on the sunbaked rods and dried for traveling provisions. The man cannot sit there looking out for the birds that come and want their share of it: this is the woman's work. And the woman is expected to do this and many other things at the same time as she is chewing the skins or sewing garments.

If a man loses his wife, he is immediately destitute. He can no longer claim a household of his own, and has to move into the home of a married couple to have his clothes dried and mended, his boots softened by a woman's chewing the soles, and his stockings turned inside out every night, and to be supplied with fresh dried grass in the morning. In return for taking care of his needs in such a case, his hosts claim all his catch.

On the other hand, a woman who loses her husband, and who is not taken to wife by another hunter, is reduced to the state of a beggar. She must live on the mercy of other people, only now and then trapping a fox or fishing some trout. She has never learned hunting since, Eskimos believe, "the great animals would be offended and go away from our shores if they were hunted by women." And if the woman happens to lose her husband during travel in desolate places, she frequently starves to death along with all her children.

Thus man and woman stick together as a close unit, and the woman's work is considered just as essential as the man's. This of course is not official; the man is reputed the stronger one, and his physical prowess makes him feel far superior. To regard a woman as having anything to say would make a man ridiculous, and he never lowers himself to mention his wife when he is out hunting with his fellows. For if by chance or mistake he mentions her name, everybody will laugh and shout at him: "My, my, here's a fellow who is longing for his wife! Why don't you quit and go home to her instead of exposing yourself to the cold and the difficulties out here!"

But in reality women have great power, as in our society. If you want a man to do something, to go traveling with you or to do some job, your surest bet is to get his wife interested. You can be sure that the man will come along if the wife wants it, although officially she has nothing at all to say. An old friend of mine, Odark, once admitted to me: "People travel according to women's wishes, never according to their commands!"

The fact remains that man and woman are indispensable to each other; they form a basic economic unit. Consequently, marriage between Eskimos is usually a matter of mutual interest and sheer necessity rather than of love in the sense in which we use the term. On the other hand, married people are generally very devoted to each other and as a rule remain faithful to each other throughout life. But Eskimo love for—or rather devotion to—each other has very little to do with sex. It is considered rather ludicrous if a man can find pleasure in only one woman; as for the woman, it is considered a great honor if she is desired by many men and can give them pleasure. For this reason, Eskimos have never understood why white people put so much significance on their so-called *wife-trading*.

The Eskimos' rather free sexual mores are based on the necessities of their way of life as well as on their point of view concerning marriage. Consider first the impossibility of washing clothes in the low temperatures of the north, along with the fact that Eskimos rarely have a second set of clothes. As a result of this situation, people are used to going naked inside their houses while their clothes are being cleaned. This is not only to get away for a time from the warm skin clothing and to get fresh air for their bodies; it also allows them to pick out the lice from the garments that are bundled together and hung up by a string from the ceiling. An old adage has it that "we would rather be a little chilly and be the only ones in our clothes."

From their childhood, therefore, Eskimos are used to seeing men and women in the nude, and absolutely no shame is connected with the human body and its needs. This is not to say that wherever Eskimos get together there is promiscuity. On the contrary, if several families should happen to occupy the same house, there is strict order in sleeping arrangements. All lie in a row facing in the same direction. An older daughter will usually be closest to the wall. Then comes a younger daughter or two, then the mother. Next to her sleeps her husband, and beside him the boys. Then follow the boys of the next family, their father, their mother, then their sisters, etc.

More important in understanding the Eskimos' sexual ethic is their point of view that sexual desire is entirely natural and normal, something like the desire for food and sleep. White people, seeing that Eskimo sexual morality is quite different from their own, have tried to change it, or to take advantage of it, at the same time calling the Eskimos "heathen pigs." But there is this much to say for the Eskimos: they stick to their unwritten laws very strictly, and any digression from the rules will be reported and retold and commented upon—and very often punished.

When an Eskimo goes on a hunting trip, it is essential

to his success that he take a woman along with him. When I drove with Eskimos from Thule across to Ellesmereland to hunt musk oxen, in my earlier days, women were absolutely essential as traveling partners. For musk oxen are hunted early in the spring when it is still cold; and it was very practical, when we came to the place where we intended to camp during the hunt, to build an igloo and install women to make it habitable, if not comfortable. When we returned from the hunt to get food and rest, they would have ice chopped and melted for fresh water, and the igloo was warmed by their blubber lamps. Further, they had dry stockings, mended mittens, and other clothes completely ready. And if we were lucky enough to bring in the raw skins, they stretched them on a frame, scraped them, and dried them. In this manner, we were able to bring thirty or forty large musk-ox skins home on our sleds after each trip.

If, however, we had been alone, we would have had to stop hunting early at night to return to the igloo to light our fires, melt ice for water, and boil meat. We would have had to bring spare boots and mittens from home, as there would be no time for drying them. The musk-ox hides could not be scraped or thawed out; they would have had to be brought home raw and frozen, and we could have carried only ten or so in our sleds, as they weigh so much more in that condition.

Now perhaps a man intends to go musk-ox hunting, but his wife is unable to go along. She might be advanced in pregnancy or have a very small baby, or she might be sick. In such a case, the problem is solved by leaving her with a neighbor, who graciously consents to let his wife go along on the hunting trip. Another case might be that a woman wants to visit some relatives far away, and for some reason or other her husband has other plans. It might then be arranged that she go with some other man who is headed that way—provided that this other man will leave his wife behind to do the housework.

Thus one may often see men with other women than their wives. This does not necessarily mean a divorce or lack of harmony between husband and wife. People look very liberally at such arrangements. As a matter of fact, it would be difficult to find a more tactful people than the Eskimos. If anyone sees a man and a woman traveling on the same sled, it does not concern him the slightest bit whether they are married for good or just for a short time. When it started, or how long it might last, does not matter to him. Nobody asks questions—that is considered rudeness in the extreme—and everyone treats it as the most natural thing in the world. Wherever the couple happens to visit, the woman is given the same status as if she were the hunter's real wife.

I myself, during one of my first visits to Thule, had occasion to appreciate this Eskimoic tact. I was expecting my Danish girl friend, Michella, to join me. But the ship that summer brought no Michella, only one of those clumsy letters it is as embarrassing to write as to receive. She was not coming, and I hardly found life worth living any more. But then, some weeks later, I was active again, trying to forget as I made plans for a trip up north to hunt walrus. An Eskimo, Tatianguaq, came and wanted a word with me.

"It appears that you are without woman's companionship," he said. "My poor wife wishes to see her family up north. It is not impossible that one would benefit a little bit from her company. It is supposed that she knows the best way to travel; she can help set up camp and dry clothes. Also, a man's pleasure at night is increased by the presence of a sensuous woman in his sleeping skins!"

In this modest way, Tatianguaq let me know that he knew my problem and wanted to help. There was of course another side to the coin: he had for some time been having a little difficulty with Ivalu, his beautiful wife. She had been on board Peary's ship and there learned to like the white men's form of courtship. A temporary separation might set matters straight. As for me, I was more than ever—due to my keen disappointment—feeling akin to these kind and carefree people, and I was ready to adopt their way of life. So Ivalu and I started north.

But not without the comedy that was expected in such cases. I had my sled packed and loaded on the appointed morning. The appointment was with the husband, and Ivalu had not shown her face at our house while the negotiations were taking place. When I started out and turned down past the Eskimo houses to get my companion, not a soul was in sight. Ivalu wasn't up yet. I called her; nobody answered. "Ivalu, Ivalu! What is the matter? Come out, we are going on a trip visiting!"

"Somebody sleeps, why go on a trip? Don't speak to a poor woman!"

I entered the house and saw immediately that a new fox-skin fur coat had been sewn, and new kamiks were laid out. Ivalu was on the bed, about to lie down for more sleep. Tatianguaq sat by the wall and looked at me with an embarrassed grin.

"Women have women's minds," he said.

I wasn't sure whether this meant that our agreement was canceled and that a retreat was difficult to perform. Besides, I really needed someone who knew the way across the glacier. So I insisted that she was to come—now! An old woman was lying farther in on the bed reminiscing about the days when men had fought for her and desired her company on sled trips. She got quite carried away, and Ivalu seemed determined to stay in bed.

"Hurry up, my dogs are waiting!"

"Let me wait. A woman is without knowledge of your dogs' decision."

"The decision is that we are going north to the settlement."

"You are witless! Listen to a man speak without meaning! No journey has been decided for me."

"Nonsense, you are going with me. Hurry to get dressed!"

Several visitors had entered the house now, mostly women who followed the developments with ill-concealed interest. Ivalu enjoyed her triumph and tried to prolong it as much as possible. "Take another woman. I have no desire for journeys in the cold, and others are better than I to help a man!"

The situation was embarrassing, and I turned to Tatianguaq saying that I didn't like to force his wife, and hadn't we better give up the whole thing?

Ivalu became attentive immediately. It began to look like a victory she didn't want. Here she had been advertised as the one who had conquered this strange white man whose whole desire had been for one woman who never came. She had been looking forward to entering settlements in triumph as my companion. But on the other hand, with so many spectators, she couldn't very well give in as if she were destitute for men's attentions.

"I don't want to go with you. Also, it is not supposed that you would want me along. (Pause.) Of course, you could trust that I will run between the stanchions of your sled to lighten it, and I will take care of your clothes if you force me against my will!"

But Tatianguaq was getting impatient. It was early in the morning, and he had to go sealing.

"Let my kamiks be supplied with grass under the stockings; since my wretched wife seems to be leaving my house for a while, it is expected that Ilaituk will take care of things!"

It had been Ivalu's hope that I would use violence to get her on my sled, so that she could attract the whole village with her screams. But I just went out, saying that she had to make haste. The last I heard as I crawled out was her opinion that I was without my wits and that I would never get her down to my sled. I cleared the dogs' traces, got other things ready, and pretty soon Ivalu appeared, dressed in her new traveling finery.

"Come and sit on the sled, we have to leave!"

"I am not coming down to your sled. What do you want with me? Others can serve you better!"

"I said that you were to hurry!"

"Some words were spoken into the air!" she called back.

She was beautiful and enticing to behold. Some people had crowded up to watch, but nobody wanted to appear to be listening. It was mostly women who had gone outside to pee—a business that can be prolonged interminably—and everything could be seen and heard. Finally I ran after Ivalu; she tried to evade me, but without any great haste.

"Is your traveling gear ready?" I asked.

"What traveling gear? I don't know what you are talking about. Why are you saying this to me?"

"Because you are going with me on a trip."

"Take somebody else who might possibly want to go. Not I! Go away from me. My husband will shoot you, he is already making his gun ready."

Then I caught hold of her and lifted her up. She kicked a little and cried out that the lot of women was an unhappy one. And if only she had a husband who dared to defend her, for this was very distasteful! We reached the sled, and the dogs saw me carrying something; it was half dark, and it was natural for them to suppose that it was something to eat. So they crowded around us, and I had to put Ivalu down to bring them to order. Now, of course, I was afraid that she would run away while she had the chance and make a show of us once more. But not at all!

"Oh, you fool at training dogs," she said. And then she took the whip and swung it with a talent I myself didn't possess. She scolded and shamed the dogs, and then she gave them the starting signal. I pushed on the stanchions to get the heavy load going, and the dogs rushed off at full speed, gay and yapping with anticipation. I could hardly keep up with them. But Ivalu jumped up on the sled and made herself comfortable. I saw her wave to her husband and to the other women. She was now sure that the event would be related to everyone in the tribe and that her role as an honorable and reticent woman had been carried out to the extreme.

We drove across the Wolstenholme Fjord and into Granville Bay. When the excitement at the departure had dissipated, I asked her if she had sleeping skins with her. "No," she said, "but I suppose you have. It is to be hoped that we are not going to sleep on the sled until we reach the houses of people again?"

What do you say to your lady on a sled trip? I tried a lot of things, but it was like water on a goose. First I said that I was happy to have her along. No answer.

"Aren't you happy too to be along on the journey?"

"No, no joy is felt," she said sullenly.

I tried something else. "Do you know the way up across the glacier?"

"It is not desirable to drive across the glacier. There it is always windy and cold."

"Yes, but there is no ice to drive on around Kangarssuk!"

"You are saying senseless things. What you said is known by all. People are not without thoughts."

"Yes, but it was just to talk some words to you."

"Let men speak to men, and be silent when they are with a poor woman," she said. So we were silent for a while. Not for long, for I have always been a talker, and I wanted—like any man—to feel that I was master of the situation.

"Are you afraid of me?" I asked.

"Certainly not. What should I be afraid of? Hold your speech when nothing sensible is being said!"

This was a conversation to cool the passions, particularly since it was twenty-five below with a cold gale blowing from the north. But the journey became smoother; the dogs adopted the trot that is natural to them—that is, too fast for man to walk, and too slow for him to run. I jumped off the sled and practiced the two paces walk and one pace run that is required. But the girl sat and shivered in dignity. Every time I asked if she was cold, I got the same answer: "Be silent, somebody is thinking."

I was hoping that the thoughts were about me and our imminent adventure, and I asked several times to find out.

At first she didn't answer, but later her mood became somewhat warmer.

"Somebody is thinking of meat," she said suddenly, as if wanting to be friendly. Perhaps also to make me stop and prepare a meal. But it was too early for that, and I wanted to get to Granville Bay without stopping. When we had been driving along for some hours, she again said she was beginning to feel a little desire for food. She had not eaten that morning. Why? Because she had been nervous anticipating what was to happen.

Only then did I feel a little pride. I had been very much in her thoughts. Silently we went on, and I decided to reveal more of my personal affairs to her and make her understand—what she was to understand I didn't know. Nothing came of it, for when I had been lecturing for a while without getting the usual conjectures about my stupidity and lack of rational thought, I turned to her and discovered that she had fallen asleep sitting on the sled.

I had been thinking that I could find a soul to relieve my desperation. I was even intending to nobly bring her back to her husband untouched by me and completely like a sister who had been with her brother on a trip visiting people. I had been thinking of her as one trembling bundle of nerves, horror-stricken at what was in store for her.

And then she was sleeping quietly and without apparent feelings of any kind. An Eskimo woman can lean on the stanchions and sleep calmly. She follows the movements of the sled with her body, and when she has had the sleep she needs she wakes up, as quietly as she fell asleep.

But let us draw the veil of discretion over the rest of what transpired between Ivalu and me, and say only that it was a satisfying journey for both parties. When we returned to Thule after an absence of almost three weeks, she jumped off my sled while we were still driving up the frozen beach. Without a word or a smile of goodbye to me and our now ending love affair, she ran up toward her house, laughing and shouting to everybody as if she had left them only an hour ago, and nothing at all of importance had happened.

Besides exchanges of wives for practical reasons, the Eskimos practice a more casual exchange—sometimes just for the fun of it, sometimes as a means of persuading nature. In the first instance, it might happen when men are out hunting—Eskimos hunt together, as a rule—that they decide to visit each other's wives the following night. They consider it a marvelous joke, and they keep their plan secret from their wives until it is time to go to bed. Then each husband goes outside and enters the other's house.

The women are always supposed to accept the one who comes. I have heard of a case where a woman refused to give herself to the visitor. In the morning, when the men came out, the "betrayed" man complained to the husband and said to him: "Now you have enjoyed my wife, but I was not allowed to come near yours." The husband felt that the honor of his house had been spotted, and to make up for it he beat his wife thoroughly in public. It only made her more stubborn, and the same occurrence took place the next night. More complaints ensued, and more beatings, until finally the man with the presumably low sex appeal felt that it was below his dignity to give a woman and her behavior such great importance. So he told the husband that he could have her, that she had no attraction whatever.

As a means of persuading nature to greater generosity, wife trading was—in earlier days—often ordered by the *angakok*, the local conjurer. When the hunting had been bad, and starvation followed, the absence of game was thought to be caused by certain evil spirits, and it was up to the wise man to find out why they were offended and to try to appease them. Often he ordered a common exchange of wives. This indicates, of course, that sex plays a role in the Eskimo supernatural world—a thing which they themselves would not readily admit.

The *angakok* would then designate which wife was to belong to which man, and if—in the course of some days—still no game had been caught, he would try another combination, and wait a few more days for success. If thus all the men in the village had visited all the women, and it had not improved the hunting luck, the *angakok* had to find some other means of persuading the great woman who lies at the bottom of the sea and who sends out the animals to be taken for food.

There was also the rather popular game of "doused lights." The rules were simple. Many people gathered in a house, all of them completely nude. Then the lights were extinguished, and darkness reigned. Nobody was allowed to say anything, and all changed places continually. At a certain signal, each man grabbed the nearest woman. After a while, the lights were put on again, and now innumerable jokes could be made over the theme: "I knew all the time who you were because———"

Several old stories deal with this popular amusement. It should be said that—crude as it may seem to us—it often served a very practical purpose. Let us, for instance, say that bad weather conditions are keeping a flock of Eskimos confined to a house or an igloo. The bleakness and utter loneliness of the Arctic when it shows its bad side can get on the nerves of even those people who know it and love it the most. Eskimos could go out of their minds, because bad weather always means uncertain fates. Then suddenly someone douses the light, and everybody runs around in the dark and ends up with a partner. Later the lamp is lit again, the whole party is joking and in high spirits. A psychological explosion—with possible bloodshed—has been averted.

Other old stories tell of occasions when animals played a role in the exchange of wives. Hudson Bay Eskimos told me the following tale about "wife trading and the whale."

Once upon a time, the men at a settlement decided to swap wives, but one of them—who always had odd ideas—proposed that they should not do it the usual way with the men going to the women. This time the women were to leave their tents and go to the men they were told to visit.

When the women were kicked out from their tents, they stood there feeling very embarrassed, as they were shy to go visiting each other's husbands by themselves. Now, it must be told that at that certain place the whales used to come very close to land. A big harpoon was attached with a strong line of walrus hide to a rock on the shore; thus there was no waste of time when a whale came near. While the women were standing there, telling each other that this was a most awkward situation, a whale came running in spouting right under the cliff. One of the women shouted in great excitement: "If women must act like men in one way, let them do it in another way, too!"

And with that she ran down and grabbed the harpoon and hurled it, and it fastened in the whale's blubber. The huge whale got very offended at being harpooned by a woman, and he ran at full speed away from the coast, broke the walrus line, and disappeared out to sea.

For many, many years after that no whale came close to the coast again—until a great *angakok* conjured up the soul of the big whale and promised that no woman should ever be present at a whale hunt. At that same time, it was promised that women should never again be forced to visit other men—the men should always come to them.

The Eskimos around Hudson Bay offered me this story as an explanation of why they always locked their women up in tents when they went whaling. There was a strict taboo against women even looking at a whale hunt.

At Hudson Bay, I once traveled with a married couple, Aguano and Qinorunna; they were en route to Pond Inlet to meet another couple, with whom they had a strange arrangement. The two couples met every spring and traded partners. Aguano had had Qinorunna for a whole year, and now he was going to give her to his friend and receive the other wife in exchange. This had been going on for several years, everybody was very satisfied with it, and I could get no other explanation than that "it was because of a certain idea."

I found out that the two men had been friends from childhood, and it must be said that none of the women had any children. Here we come to an important factor in the family life. Quite a few women are sterile (it has erroneously been supposed that it is because of the early start of the sexual life), and as all Eskimos love children, and also need them to give support in their old age, it is considered a great misfortune for a woman to be without children. I have known cases where men have divorced sterile women and remarried in order to have children. In some instances this has brought forth tokens of real love in the sense that we know it in the Western world.

I remember a man, Samik, whose wife did not bear him any children. After a while, he chased her away and married a young girl with whom he subsequently had three children. The first wife was inconsolable. Time and again she returned to Samik's house, only to be kicked out, beaten, and mishandled. She kept coming back, and for a long time she refused to have anything to do with any other man.

A couple of years later, though, she married a young hunter, and now positions were reversed. For she lived very happily with the young hunter who—although she was much older than he—appreciated her because of her great abilities in tanning skins, sewing clothes, and keeping house. And now Samik turned to her with his old affection—and she refused him flatly. He tried to surprise her when she was once looking into her fox traps. He entered her house when he knew the husband was out hunting, but she would not have him. She told me that she had once been so much in love with Samik that the fact that he had preferred someone else to her had hurt her too much; she could never be happy with him again.

Visiting a wife behind her husband's back just isn't done. It should be clearly understood that, in each case of wife trading or wife borrowing, it is strictly an arrangement made between the men. The wives have little or nothing to say in the matter. The man who dares to visit a woman without her husband's express consent not only delivers a mortal insult to the husband, he also becomes an eyesore to his tribesmen, being guilty of a serious breach of all good rules. His behavior is related with the utmost contempt and, in many cases, it calls for decisive action by the husband. In order to save his honor, he might drag his wife out and beat her in public—whether the affair be her fault or not. He might seek out her paramour and take his revenge upon him. Among some Canadian Eskimos, fist fights take care of the matter, but in other tribes—as the Polar Eskimos—blood revenge was quite common, and everybody would consider such a killing justified when there was no other way of saving the husband's honor.

But, conversely, it could also be a dangerous insult to a man to refuse to partake of his wife's embraces when he had clearly indicated that it was permitted. It was like saying that what the house had to offer was not good enough. Eskimos have no such thing as servants, but the man is master in his house, he makes decisions for everybody; everything that is brought in by those living in his house belongs to him, because his wife does the sewing and cooking for them.

From this stems the fact that it is regarded as unfaithfulness in the extreme if a man catches his wife doing some sewing for another man without his permission, or rather, his order. He will immediately tear the clothing from her, cut it to pieces, and beat the wife terribly outside the house, and the story will be told not only to the neighbors, but it will run up and down the coast as a sensational scandal worthy of many comments and explanations.

Sometimes you will find a hunter so mighty and strong that he can afford to keep two wives. He will claim to have so many skins to prepare and such a great supply of game that it would be too much work for one woman, but this might of course in some cases be only a subterfuge. He might have fallen in love with a young girl while his elderly spouse, even if she no longer attracts him physically, still is a good housekeeper, and it pays to keep them both.

It is rather funny to visit a man with two wives. When you come into his house, one of them will do all the talking, welcome you, and tell you to give your outer clothes to the other one, who will mend them and dry them and otherwise be of service. You can then be sure that the husband is sleeping at her side of the house. For each of the two has her special side of the house and her own lamp to take care of.

Next time you come, you may find that the other woman is the ruler of the house and orders her co-wife to please the guest. Then she is being preferred, at least for the time being. They always know exactly where they stand, for when the husband returns from the hunt they will spot his sled from afar, and they will both run out to meet him with dry mittens, a choice morsel of food or some other thing that can show their affection. He then takes great delight in just dropping the gift offered by one of them while he accepts and enjoys what the other one brings, takes her up on his sled, and lets her co-wife walk to the house.

Because of the general scarcity of women among the Eskimos, polyandry is quite common. In such cases, people live in a triangle so that a woman enjoys two husbands. Nothing can be more delightful for a woman, for then she sleeps in the middle of the igloo while the two husbands have their places by the cold snow walls. She never has to carry ice or water into the house. As soon as she expresses desire for something to drink, her two beaus will start a race to be the first to bring it to her. They have to mend their own stockings and mittens, and they are in every way competing for her affection and sympathy.

When they are out hunting, they have to think of their wife. While we free men with just one wife always eat the tongues and the hearts of the caribou right away, the two co-husbands will always tuck the best parts of the game away to bring home to their wife. They thus maintain a permanent rivalry, so to speak, being all the while the very best of friends.

The scarcity of women among the Eskimos has one very definite reason: girl babies are considered less desirable than boy babies and are often strangled at birth and left out to die from exposure. This would seem like extreme cruelty to us, and in modern times it hardly takes place any more. But in former days it was often a matter of pure necessity. Consider a country where you have no insurance for old age and no way of gathering a fortune of any kind, where life is difficult, and the only way you can protect yourself against sure starvation when you are too old and weak to hunt is to have sons who will take you into their houses and let you live out your time in contentment. It is an old Eskimo saying that "a son is a better provider than a son-in-law." As soon as a daughter was married, her skills were lost to her parents. She would go with her husband's parents and owe them all her loyalty and support.

An Eskimo woman never weans her baby until the child is three or four years old, often later. There is then a lapse of at least three years between pregnancies. It follows that, in order to get a son, a couple would often have to let a newborn girl die, always right after birth before "they would get too fond of the child," so that the woman could become pregnant again sooner. It was, in fact, often out of courtesy to a friend or neighbor with a son that Eskimos let a little girl live; she would later make a wife for the boy. The couple were then regarded as married from the time of the girl's birth, and almost always respected the plan of their parents, marrying when they came of age to do so.

Since the Eskimos take such a natural attitude toward sex, it would seem that sexual perversities are rare among them. From the time of the wars with the Indians, they have strange tales about unnatural practices which they claim are rather common among the Indians, though they say it is unusual to find such things among themselves. It is true that I have no recollection of hearing of them among the Polar Eskimos. But among the Hudson Bay Eskimos, I heard about some pretty startling things. Here are a few samples.

One case of homosexuality was mentioned, that of a certain Panimuaq, who was said to have had relations with his adopted son. But it was said that he hanged himself out of shame.

Relations with dogs were apparently not uncommon, and no shame seemed to be attached to it. The same was the case where dead caribou and seal were involved, although it must be said that men who resorted to this procedure were thought to be rather ridiculous.

I know of the cases of two wealthy hunters, with two wives each, who had frequent relations with dogs. And there were even special taboo rules to observe during such a romance. The intercourse had to take place when the dog was in heat, out of respect for its natural instincts. About a man who was mentioned as an ardent devotee of this means of obtaining sexual satisfaction, it was said that he once hurt his collarbone because he tried intercourse with she-dogs out of season. An evil spirit struck him with sickness to punish him for seeking love with a dog at the wrong time.

Copulation with dogs must always take place out in the open. The only place where cover might be sought was where two ice floes in the pack ice stood up against each other, so as to form a small shelter.

Then there is the age-old tale of another woman, who had relations with her dog and bore young which were dogs with human hands and hairless bodies. She had been confined in the open air in the shelter of some rocks, but her fellow-villagers had been ashamed of her and had pushed stones down over her and crushed her and her brood. The Eskimos believed firmly in the truth of this account.

Sometimes, sexual abnormalities were believed to give magical powers, as in the case of the man who was believed to be a great shaman because he had relations with his mother.

Incest was frowned upon, but in all cases of sexual deviations it was the rule that they were not to be concealed, that they had to be confessed openly. Only when the doer kept it a secret to himself was he believed to be possessed by an evil spirit (our equivalent of being sinful). As long as he talked openly about it to other people, it was considered to be a matter of no great consequence!

The Eskimos have nowhere mixed with the Indians nor with the primitive races that neighbor them in Siberia. Yet they do not seem to mind interracial marriages. Many Greenlanders have Danish blood in them. Admiral Peary had two sons with Alakrasina, and Matthew Henson had a son with Ivalu, and these three young men grew up to become the best and most intelligent hunters of the tribe. In recent years, intelligence testing has been carried out in Greenland, and it shows that the mixture between Eskimos and white people is fortuitous, since those with mixed blood tested fully as intelligent—on the average—as white people, and are physically probably superior.

An Eskimo Wedding

An Eskimo wedding does not always mean that the young

couple will establish a household of their own or that they
are able to support themselves. The newlyweds almost always join the household of either the boy's or the girl's
parents, most often the boy's. This is necessary, first, because
the young bride still has to learn the more difficult domestic
chores, such as how to cut out the various skin parts for
clothing and how to sew them together. The young man on
his part must continue to learn from the older man about
hunting, trapping, and the like. In the second place, it
might be several years before the two have collected enough
tools, cooking pots, skins, and bedding to build a home for
themselves.

In the meantime, then, newlyweds stay with their family
or other people. Whatever game is caught, whatever is earned
by the young man belongs to the owner of the house.
Separation from the parents' house is effected gradually, just
like independence from the parents themselves: the young
couple will go on hunting trips alone, live in an igloo or a
tent by themselves, and stay away for longer and longer
periods at a time.

The groom's very first task is to dress up his bride, for it
cannot be too much emphasized that a wife makes the reputation of a house by her looks and her apparent comfort.
Among the Polar Eskimos, fathers always let their young
girls go around in miserable old rags. In southern Greenland, it is just the opposite: young beauties are dressed in
gorgeous colors, are given bead embroideries and what not.
They shine, they entice the male population in every possible way. But later, when the church has given its blessing,
and the holy rite keeps the two parties nailed down in
matrimonial bliss, wives gradually become sloppy. After an
absence of a few years you may see young women who used
to charm you out of wit and senses looking slovenly and
indolent.

In northern Greenland around Thule, still another practice prevails.

There, a father—no matter how wealthy he is—will not
waste good skins on a marriageable daughter; it is up to
the groom to dress her up, and you may be sure that he
wastes no time in doing so. For she is his publicity, and it
is a man's pleasure to see his wife neat and content.

At the Thule settlement near my trading station, I began
to notice a little girl who was wretched to look at, dirty,
and with clothes made partly of dogskin, partly of worn-out

hand-me-downs. Her mother, Kasaluk, had had two children with her first husband. The one, a little boy, she had to kill during a hunger period, but the girl, little Mequ, had "found life sweeter than death" even under those circumstances, so the mother allowed her to fend for herself. She survived and later had gone to live with her grandparents up north. Then Kasaluk was married to Uvdluriak, the great hunter at the settlement, and Mequ had been brought down to take care of her younger half-brothers and half-sisters.

The little Mequ had only rarely visited our house. But once—while she was there—I gave her some bread, which was a great delicacy to her. She was happier than any Eskimo girl before! And a few days later, she came with a pair of mittens she had sewn for me. She just laid them down in front of me and said: "To express thanks for the bread!" Then she was gone again, as quietly as she had come! She was shy and not used to speaking to important men without being asked!

During that period I had become more and more Eskimoic. Once Ivalu had come to visit me and stayed overnight, and I can't even maintain that she was the only woman I had pleasure from when my travels took me around in the district, or when I—while fox trapping—camped in igloos or caves with members of the fair sex.

One day, when I passed by the tents with Knud, Mequ was sitting outside with her little brother.

"How sweet she is, really," said Knud. "If I were ever to marry up here, she would be the only one along the whole coast, from the south and right up to here, that I could imagine would be intelligent enough, and clever enough, and beautiful enough!"

I didn't ponder the matter; but for the first time the thought of marriage occurred to me. Knud was right. This business of borrowing another man's wife was not exactly what we ought to promote in the district, and therefore we shouldn't participate in it, either. It never came into Knud's mind to reproach me about the conduct of my private life, but his remark hit home with me. This little girl, just reaching the marriageable age, seemed really so pure and fine to me—in spite of her dirty dogskin pants and the torn kamiks. Her smile and good cheer covered it all. Also, it was known that her stepfather could furnish her with magnificent skins if he wanted to. But this just wasn't done. Because of the hunger period some years before, during which many girls had been killed, there was a lack of women among the Polar Eskimos and several young men had already been to see Uvdluriak.

One day we heard that Samik, a feared and often wrathful man, had raped Mequ while his wife happened to be visiting us. It caused quite a bit of excitement, but nothing could be done. The missionaries remained silent when their own little flock wasn't concerned—but it happened to be one of them, a man named Seckman, who brought me the bad news. He asked if we shouldn't do something. We then went to see Uvdluriak, but he didn't think that any harm had been done. He had no intention of starting a feud with his neighbor. Shouldn't people rather laugh at such a witless hunter like Samik, who preferred an immature girl to his own excellent wife?

Later that winter, I was staying alone in our house with a servant woman, Arnanguaq, who took care of the lamps. Everybody else was away on trips. Arnanguaq was married to our handyman, Minik, who happened to take the position that "he did not want to make appointments for exchange of women" with anybody. But even if Arnanguaq did not fear any attack from my side, she invited Mequ down to the house for the night, so that she wouldn't be alone with me.

We undressed and went to bed. Our lamps were burning low, the wicks had been made small so that the blubber could last until morning. Suddenly, in that romantic half-dark, I was possessed by a power stronger than myself. I threw my skin covers aside, reached over and grabbed the young girl, and swung her over to me on my bunk. She didn't say a word, and neither did Arnanguaq.

Thus I was married and, to the extent possible for an explorer, settled down. Mequ was so small and fine of build. Her hands were soft, as if she had been manicuring them all her life. But the night of our marriage she had had to do a lot of dirty work, and her entire body was filthy, her clothes too miserable for description. My remembrance of the night is somewhat misty, but in the morning I told her that I didn't intend to let her go home, that I wished to keep her with me.

Her reaction was a little less lyrical than I had expected: "Then somebody else must bring my mother the needle that I borrowed from her!"

She pulled a needle out of her hairtop, where she had kept it tucked away. Possibly it was only a message; Arnanguaq went with the needle. In the meantime, we went to the big house to have breakfast. Emilie Rosbach, the missionary's wife, had the food ready. Naturally, she was much too well-bred to say anything. I put Mequ down at the table by my side, and there she sat, for she didn't dare to move. She got a fine cup, she got bread and tea. There was sugar to put in the tea, but as she didn't seem to think that it was proper for her to take any of it, I put two teaspoonsful in her cup. In those days a clearer announcement of marriage couldn't be made in Thule.

I was aware that I had to guard Mequ for some time. Since I had not abducted her properly, as any decent groom would, it would be a while before people realized that it was a permanent arrangement. So she went with me wherever I went, except that I couldn't take her with me out to my caches to fetch supplies; her clothes just weren't good enough for even short sled trips. Pants of dogskin, the greatest shame to a man! But it didn't take long to make up for that, for we had plenty of foxskins. I didn't have any sealskins for kamiks, however, so she had to go to her mother to get them. She went with rich gifts: the little children got canned milk, the mother became the proud owner of a beautiful pair of scissors and a royal supply of thread. Mequ was now completely rehabilitated after her former miserable state—which was by no means due to Uvdluriak's stinginess, only to custom. Besides, her husband now had the joy of seeing his little wife grow more well-dressed and civilized from day to day.

She had of course a lot to learn. I remember clearly one thing which became the cause of much amusement. It happened on the second day she was living with me; we lived in the little house, where it was cold, and in the morning—when we had entered the big house to eat and warm ourselves—I told her that she had to be washed.

She looked at me in great astonishment: "What are you saying? Don't you remember that I washed yesterday?" When I then said that in the future there was to be washing and bathing every day, she almost feared that she had been seized by a madman. But later she became one of the great agitators for personal hygiene in Thule.

There was no great excitement until Knud returned home. Rasmussen wasn't a man to let a wedding just pass by. He sent word north and south, east and west, that with the next full moon the wedding would be celebrated in the grandest manner. This was a little against people's taste, though. They found it immodest and a little bit tactless to blazon abroad that two young people now had agreed to stick together. What concern was it to others?

But the feast had to be great. I was myself ordered to deliver everything I could, especially eggs from my caches. So I made my first sled trip with Mequ, and we stayed away for a few days. Only then did I discover what I had been missing. On a sled, a Thule woman is as good as a man. She arranges the dogs, she swings the whip expertly, and she helps to pack and secure the load. Her cheer lights up the darkness! We were staggering around in the Polar night to find my depots, but we had a wonderful time. For Mequ it was the introduction to an entirely new life in which she, for the time being, remained a bit lost, but was very happy.

Once my axe slipped down from the sled, and it was impossible to find it again. When I expressed my annoyance at the loss, Mequ asked if it meant a lot to me. I said that it was bad luck for a man to lose his axe. "Will it be the right thing to show understanding of the loss by crying a little?" she asked. But then I said that she shouldn't worry, for at home I could get another one from our stock.

"It is unknown to live under conditions where belongings are so numerous that they decrease in value," said Mequ.

She was learning, and before long she was running our house with great administrative ability. She became the first lady of Thule, even deposing such authorities as our housekeeper from southern Greenland, Vivi, and Emilie Rosbach, and her own mother, Kasaluk.

Our wedding feast was a great success. Knud had announced that he wanted to see who could bring the most and the best, and the celebrations finally amounted to several days' sumptuous eating. It wasn't quite easy, at first, for Mequ to be hostess to older women who had known her since she was born. She had been fatherless, and even if she lived with the old Mequsaq, she wasn't as well protected as were the children of great hunters. Now she was the one who had the right to call out that boiled meat was ready, and to say that she hoped the guests would eat well to get her pots empty, so that she could fill them up again. Vivi and Emilie, two mature women, had to step into the background, and there were some frictions.

During that first year of our marriage, we actually had it best when we drove away and took it upon ourselves to visit people all over the district, taking part in the hunt, or bringing them supplies so that they could make more out of the fox trapping.

Mequ's intelligence and authority became more and more apparent, and she called upon them almost as if using magic. The Eskimos commonly have several names, of which one is the calling name. Often the calling name is changed in order to mark a great event or turning point in the person's life. At Christmas, shortly after our wedding, Mequ decided to use one of her other names; she was now to be spoken of as Navarana—"in order that some greater ability, hitherto concealed, might appear in her."

From then on she was called Navarana. After Christmas, we drove south to Cape York to see people there. There had just been a violent gale from the southwest which had broken up the ice around Parker Snow Bay so we had to go behind the Cape and up across the glacier there. It was a hard turn, and I didn't think the dogs were able to drag the sled. Navarana walked quietly between the stanchions while I yelled and shouted and beat the dogs—with little result. She must have thought strange things, seeing my impotence. Then I got the idea to walk in front of the dogs, enticing them to follow me; I gave the whip to Navarana and proceeded out front. But then I saw something new. Navarana let a tempest break loose. She started to use the long whip as it had never been used before, letting every single dog feel the smart on its back, and her encouragements rained down over them in one fury. At first, they didn't quite understand that a new partner had joined the firm.

"Oh, you strange dogs who are not ashamed to be lazy, you whom a mere woman must remind of your duty. Run forward quickly if you want to avoid the lash. Hurry up, dogs! Hurry up, dogs!"

The dogs howled and began immediately to fight, the stronger ones falling upon the weaker. But that only resulted in more pain and more smarting cracks over them. There was nothing else to do but to move along; it turned out that they could very well pull the sled when they wanted to. Up they came, past me, walking there to entice them. Navarana didn't stop because she passed her husband. She was moving now, and she wanted to move faster. I tried to run after the sled but couldn't catch up. She carried on so that I almost became afraid of the devil that had been hiding behind her quiet demeanor.

Only when she had reached the ridge of the glacier did she let the dogs stop and wait for me. I struggled up at last, and there she stood by the stanchions, smiling. She had already cleared the traces, and now she handed me the whip.

"It is difficult to mount the steep side of the glacier. It so happened that a woman forgot how hard it is to move when the hands are not at the stanchions!"

I asked if she wouldn't rather continue the driving, since she did it so much better than I.

"Can a poor woman get dogs to obey? A man's dogs know only his command words!"

Down from the ridge was easy, but it became more and more precipitous. She then taught me to put the dogs behind the sled, while we sat down on it and hit with the whip out back; thus the dogs worked like brakes. It was the first time I saw this method and I was to use it a lot later on.

Down on the ice we ran into another snowstorm and had to give up. The snow was too loose to build an igloo from, and we couldn't reach the cave at Agpat, since the ice was all broken up. Navarana again had the solution to our problems. She told me to turn the sled over so that it made a shelter. Behind it, out of boxes and other baggage and our skins, we made a cave and crawled into it. We were laughing very hard because we, who had a big and wonderful house at home, and who intended to go see friends in warm shacks at Cape York, now had to let ourselves be snowed under. We were talking about how wet and cold our clothes would be in the morning because we had slept in them, about how hungry we were, and about how we couldn't boil meat. These things showed how completely witless people are and worthy of ridicule.

We then fell asleep in our strange lair while the storm raged around us. The next day it was the same thing, we couldn't see three feet ahead of us for drifting snow. Wet and cold, we stayed right where we were, and I don't know how long we remained so. Suddenly the storm quieted down. We could see the moon, and we got up in a hurry. The cold went to our bones, but we had plenty of work digging the baggage out of the snow, getting the dogs ready and getting everything cleaned of ice and snow. All the while the moon was shining down on us, and I asked Navarana if she could see the mountains by their shadows, for the moon was in its third quarter.

"The mountains?" she asked. "What mountains?"

"The mountains in the moon."

"But isn't it a man, then?"

I started to explain that the moon was a cold globe, and that irregularities in its crust could be seen clearly, and that even the single mountains had been given names by people on earth.

This was completely new to Navarana. She told the old tale about the sun and the moon being brother and sister pursuing each other, but never able to meet. I explained how unreasonable this was, and defended my ideas, which were founded on scientific observations.

Navarana looked very serious: "Yes, I have been thinking that the woman who is taken by a white man must assume his beliefs. Is that what the minister is talking about on Sunday?"

I said no, it had nothing to do with religion.

"Yes, but my grandfather has told me about the creation of the world, about the sun and the moon, and about the earth's creation. It sounds unreasonable, I know, but we people think only weakly, we see only close by. Outside our thoughts there is only mist. But now I will take up your beliefs, and it now happens that a woman forgets the man in the moon!"

In this manner we discussed things during our trips. I was by no means smarter than she was, it was only in certain fields that I could make up for the knowledge she gave me.

We arrived at Cape York, and Navarana was now a lady of high rank. We moved in with Krolugtinguaq, chief hunter of the settlement, and one festive meal after the other was arranged in our honor. In the meantime, Navarana was playing with the other young people and having the time of her life. We couldn't stay long, though, and we would now try to force the ice around the Cape even if it was still unsafe for our return trip. We found several times that between the ice floes there was thin ice that couldn't hold. The storms and the strong currents cut the ice up from beneath.

"Are you afraid?" I asked one day, when we were driving over ice where the dogs got their paws wet every minute.

"Is a woman afraid when she is traveling with her husband?" she said. "Women leave the care and the worry to the man when they are on his sled."

Such words made me proud and strong.

When we arrived home, I was informed that the strong gale had broken the ice around Dalrymple Rock. Now that it was about to settle again, there was a chance of a good catch of walrus, because these animals could get closer to Saunders Island, where there are mussels and where they like to stay. Consequently, I left Navarana at the settlement and joined the hunters on the ice. It was a healthy life, but somewhat dull in the evenings when we were running around playing to keep ourselves warm. One day, a fresh young man had a bright idea.

"Somebody got the desire for eggs," he shouted. "There are eggs on this island. Let us go get eggs!"

The others seconded his motion, and the whole crowd scurried up to get—my eggs. It so happened that I was the only one who had collected and cached enough of them, and I had sneakily counted on them for myself and my guests. As a man of honor, I could of course do nothing but join the chorus and express my satisfaction that my wretched eggs were allowed to be included in the meal. They came down with bags filled with the stone-hard frozen eggs. Some were gnawed on the spot, like apples, others were put in the pot until it was filled up with eggs. Nobody gave it a thought that these eggs belonged to me. Had I owned the eider ducks? Had I done anything but hide the birds' eggs? Nobody in this country knew how to be content with an egg or two. Here the fun was to see how many could be downed. And every man had ten fingers and ten toes, that was enough to count on. We filled the pot several times.

When I returned home, I could really begin to appreciate my little woman. She had taken wonderful advantage of her visits. What she had paid with, I don't know, but now she had fine kamiks of white sealskin with a beautiful border of bear mane.

I told her of my experience with the eggs. She said immediately that she would take care of that, since I seemed to be so fond of eggs. I told her that she was not to ruin my good name and reputation as a hunter by passing my complaint on to the others. She turned her big black eyes toward me and looked at me as if I had wanted to avert a misfortune or heavy insult to both of us: "Do you really think that I could do that to you?" she said seriously.

She went down to her mother and said that she felt sorry that it would not be possible to treat guests to eggs this year, since the hunters had used them out on the ice and didn't leave any to take home to the women.

The next day, Kasaluk told her husband that she strongly

feared that the walrus hunt would be of short duration this year. In her dreams, she said, she had seen that the ice was strewn with eggshells, and in the same vision she understood that this insulted the walrus so that they would decide to go elsewhere. The hunters talked the matter over. They agreed of course that a mere woman's dreams should have no influence. But for the sake of all eventualities it was decided that it was better not to eat any more eggs as long as the walrus hunt lasted. As a result, plenty of eggs were stored up in my quarters.

Such a clever and precious person was Navarana. She gave me some of the happiest years of my life, until the Spanish flu took her away in 1921. And she bore me two children, a boy who was named after his great-grandfather, Mequsaq, and a girl, Pipaluk, who is now a well-known writer.

Eskimo women used to talk about giving birth as being "inconvenient." This is not to say that it was any fun, but they had a remarkably short period of confinement. The women used to sit on their knees while giving birth. If the woman was in a tent or a house when her time came, she would most often dig a hole in the ground and place a box on either side of it to support her arms, and then let the baby drop down into the hole. If she was in an igloo, the baby had to be content with the cold snow for its first resting place. If the birth seemed to take long, the husband would very often place himself behind his wife, thrust his arms around her, and help press the baby out.

Among the Hudson Bay Eskimos, things were a little more difficult. In that community, childbirth was surrounded by a number of taboos that virtually isolated the poor woman. Nobody, for instance, was allowed to touch her. So if the husband had to help her, he would place a strip of skins around her just above the fetus, tie it with a loop at her back, and pull it tight. The baby was immediately wiped clean with a piece of skin and placed in the *amaut* where it would spend its first year. The skin piece was guarded as a precious amulet to ward off evil.

At Thule, in one case, I gave some skins to a woman to prepare in the morning. She brought them back in the afternoon deploring that it had taken so long, but she had had a baby in the meantime!

Another time we were traversing a glacier while traveling in the company of an Eskimo couple. While up there, the husband came and told us that his wife was going to give birth. I told her that this was very inconvenient, since there was no snow from which to build an igloo. Couldn't she wait? She said she might, and in two hours we managed to get down from the glacier, and we all helped build the igloo while everybody joked about the event.

As soon as the igloo was finished she went inside with her husband, and we waited about an hour. Then the man came out and told us that he had a son. But the mother was a bit tired, and they had decided not to go any farther that day. We went across the bay, and the next morning, when we woke up, there were the happy parents with their newborn child waiting for us.

Navarana was true to form regarding these things. One day, while I was sleeping she came to tell me that Itukusuk had caught a narwhale. Did I want to go down there and eat *mattak?* I said that I was sleepy, I had just returned from the hunt, but I would come later. It was during the summer, daylight lasted through twenty-four hours, and every man had his own sleeping period in that part of the world. Later I woke up again when she came back home. I asked if the mattak feast was over already, but she said that she had an upset stomach, and so she had come home to sleep. She went into our other room, and I resumed my sleep. After a while, Arnanguaq came to report that Navarana was in labor.

I became very excited and called Knud, who was sleeping in the loft. He had himself taken an Eskimo wife. His wife had borne him two girls; he had experience in those matters, and I wanted to ask him what to do.

He said that, as far as he knew, coffee had always played a role in the proceedings. It was during the first world war, we had not received supplies (especially coffee) for a long time, so I said that this was quite impossible. Knud then revealed that he had preserved some coffee beans tied up in a piece of cloth for the occasion. Consequently, we resolved to go to the brook for water.

Before we could leave the house, though, we heard a loud yell: "Anguterssuaq! A big boy!" It was Arnanguaq, acting as midwife. Somewhat dazed, I went with Knud for the water, and when we returned, we went inside to see Navarana. She said that it was more tiresome than she had imagined to bear boys and so she wanted to be left alone. It was only three in the morning, she still had time to get a nice sleep.

Knud was sleepy too, and the coffee was forgotten. I was

too happy to sleep. I went outside and sat down on a rock and started laying all kinds of plans for my boy. I resolved to stay in Thule the rest of my days, to teach him hunting, economy, and industry, and to be to him everything that a father could be. He was to avoid all the stumbling blocks I had run into myself. In short, I sat there daydreaming about my newborn boy that I hadn't even seen. And I stayed there until Navarana came out herself and told me to come in and see him. She got out of bed at the usual hour and tidied up the house.

In the evening, Knud threw his coffee party. The entire Thule population was there, of course, and he opened the dance with Navarana. She didn't stop dancing till very late. Our firstborn had arrived in style.

When our boy was five days old, Navarana put him in her *amaut* and mounted the Thule Rock with him to show him his future hunting grounds where he was to perform great deeds and bring much game to the house—and whatever else an Eskimo mother wishes for her child.

An Eskimo mother doesn't wean her baby until her next pregnancy sets in, however long that might be. If she does not become pregnant again, she often nurses her lastborn for many years. It is considered a sign of a woman's youth and agility that she still has a child to nurse and milk to give, and only when she has finished her usefulness to her children is she really old. I thus saw several times, both among the Hudson Bay and the Polar Eskimos, and even in southern Greenland, mothers giving the breast to fourteen-year-old boys who were already sporting in kayaks and taking part in the hunt.

Otherwise, the mother doesn't interfere much with the children once they can walk and run around. Under her watchful eye, they are allowed to play freely around the tents or houses and even with the dogs. Instinctively, they show no fear of the dogs, and it is amusing to see how these otherwise so ferocious beasts are completely complacent when it comes to children. They will gladly tear a bear or a fox to pieces, but when a little tot starts pulling their tails, poking their eyes, or riding on their backs, they suffer it in quiet dignity.

Our children didn't get any education, as such, at Thule. Once, on a summer day, I was busy in the shop, and Mequsaq and Pipaluk were playing outside with their little friends. Their game was to crawl up on a big slanting rock and slide down its smooth side. Up and down they went in one wild tumble.

Then I heard their grandmother, Kasaluk, come out and shout to them: "Oh no, dear children, don't do that! Think of your poor father who has to drive long stretches in the cold and dark to get skins for your pants. Now you are wearing off the fur. It is unreasonable, you must not do it!"

Then she went back inside, and the children resumed their sliding down the rock, a wonderful game in any latitude!

After a while, the same amiable woman came out again: "But dear children, now you are still sliding down the rough stone. Please remember that your father has to provide all the foxskins and bearskins that you are wearing out. There won't be any seats left in your pants. You must stop that immediately and show that you are sensible and economical children!"

Whereupon she went into the house again, and the children continued their fascinating game. A third time Kasaluk came out: "Oh, dear children, now I must admonish you to stop this game. Think of your poor father! He had to drive around in the cold of winter, fighting the bear and looking to his fox traps, so as to get new skins to replace those you have worn to pieces on the rock. Children, please think!"

It was finally dawning on me that the children were disobedient and also extravagant with their pant skins. I found that the moment had come to show up in parental dignity and demand that the respect and the economy be maintained in full. So I went out there.

"What is going on here?" I asked sternly. "How remarkable!" I tried to speak my finest Eskimoic so as not to make myself ridiculous just by using wrong words. This was a serious affair!

The grandmother concurred, very pleased. "Yes, truly remarkable," she tuned in. "Very remarkable! How one must rejoice in this sad sight!"

Her words seemed confusing to me, and I asked for an explanation.

"Yes, it is very clear that no pants can stand for this sliding down that rock. Those children ruin a lot of things. That can only please us older ones!"

I didn't think so at all, but the woman was my mother-in-law, the incarnation of an international authority who understands all things and who must command respect. So I said petulantly, "No, I don't think it is so wonderful. I have to drive around in the cold and the dark, hunting the bear and looking to fox traps, and now they are wearing the fur off their pants by sliding down this stone!"

"Yes, but you see, nobody can help thinking by seeing this foolishness. Children ruin things without giving it a thought; they have no cares. But every day of their lives they become wiser and wiser. Soon the time will come when they never will do that sort of thing. They will remember their unnecessary wear on their pants and regret it. Everyone must rejoice by recalling that we start out as thoughtless children, but with every day the good sense increases in us. At last we become old and sage. Just imagine if it were the other way round, so that we were born clever and economical, and our wisdom decreased with time. Then misfortune would dwell with people! Therefore, it is joyful to watch children's careless play!"

There was the Eskimo educational system in a nutshell. They had invented progressive education long before the Americans! In their defense, it must be said that their stern and barren country had of itself forced its stern rules upon them; their ethics were so strict, their ways of disapproval so definite and so pitiless, that the youngsters quite automatically grew into upright members of society.

And they loved their children. A man would lose his honor if he hit a child. The father of a flock rarely had a leisure hour with his family in which he didn't take out his knife and carve out of bone or wood dolls for the girls and animal figures for the boys. One thing that Eskimos developed to perfection was the bull-roarer. These artfully carved thin blades of bone or wood, sometimes ornamented, had little cuts along the edges at regular intervals. They were attached to a string, and when the child swung them in the air, they would give a delightful humming sound. Sometimes the bull-roarer would have two holes in the middle; a thread was passed through them, and by pulling with both hands the string would get more and more twisted, and the bull-roarer would go like a propeller and make almost as loud a sound.

Other games popular with the children were various versions of "house," "hide and seek," "tag," "hopscotch," just as in other civilizations all over the globe. As already mentioned, the children played freely with the dogs, and both boys and girls were expert trainers and drivers even before they became of age to use a sled.

The girls were made to help their mothers very early, for it took a long time to teach them the many chores a woman must do. As for the boys, they were always encouraged to play with toy harpoons and other tools, for soon they would have to go out with the men on the hunt, tagging along with their undersized instruments; and by the time a boy was fourteen he was usually expected to have brought his first seal home. This, of course, called for a celebration; everybody from near and far was called in to take part in the young hunter's catch. To an Eskimo boy, this was the introduction to the ranks of the grownups.

Another event that called for a big eating feast was when a tot had worn out its first pair of kamiks. The happy parents would throw as big a party as they could manage, and among the Hudson Bay Eskimos, particularly, the little kamiks were kept as invaluable talismans.

The grownups had their games, too. Among the women, making figures with a string was often used to while away hours that because of the weather or other circumstances couldn't be passed in any other way. A sinew thread about three feet long would be cut off, and the ends tied together. A woman would stretch it out with all her ten fingers, tying it in a certain pattern. It was now up to the next woman in the circle to pick up the string with her fingers in such a manner that it would form a new figure. Thus the most intricate figures would be formed, many of which had names and originated in a long-forgotten past. Learned men have written whole volumes about the intricacy and the symbolism of this strange pastime.

In Greenland, both at Thule and down south, a kind of soccer was sometimes played. The ball was sewn out of walrus skin and stuffed with grass or feathers. The participants were usually divided into two teams, and often there were tournaments between settlements. At other times, the players were divided into couples, each couple against all the others, and it could develop into a real brawl. There were no rules to the game, anything went, and there are records of injuries and even fatal accidents during particularly heated games.

Eskimo Courtship

Eskimo girls marry so very young that a girl will often continue to play with the other children right up to the time of her first pregnancy. A boy, on the other hand, has to hunt well for many seasons before he has accumulated enough property to establish a home, so the husbands of the twelve-year-old brides are frequently grown men, two or three times as old as their wives. Only when a young man is a member of a well-to-do father's household can he afford the luxury of marriage at the age of eighteen or twenty.

Among the Eskimos, sexual life is not directly connected with marriage and the simple biological need for the opposite sex is recognized in both men and women, young and old. Toddlers of both sexes are encouraged to play together with a freedom that would outrage a mother in America, and the game of "playing house" can—among Eskimo children—assume an awfully realistic appearance. The mother of a six-year-old girl once confided in me: "You should see my daughter and that little boy next door. They're as cute as they can be, just like husband and wife. But I wouldn't for anything let them know that I was watching."

Parents never worry when their teen-agers fail to return home at the usual hour. They take it for granted that the young people have found a vacant igloo nearby and are spending some time there, either as a couple or as members of a larger party. In fact, at a larger settlement there will always be a house called the Young People's House where young people can sleep together just for the fun of it, with no obligation outside of that certain night. Nobody takes offense at this practice, for no marriage can be a success, Eskimos believe, without sexual affinity.

But a good hunter has additional considerations when he is choosing a bride. To an Eskimo, a wife is more or less an advertisement. The degree of ease and comfort in which she seems to be living is the measure of his ability as a hunter and provider. Although she has a thousand tasks to perform, she is never required to do any heavy or dirty chores. Her value to him lies in how neat, gentle, and loving she can be; hard work would only weaken her for love-time. Chewing skins and sewing is the woman's job, but flensing the animal is the man's job; cooking the meat for the guests is the woman's task, but taking it down from the meat rack, chopping it up, and bringing it into the house is the man's. The wife's composure and attractiveness tell the guests of the husband's wealth. It follows that a girl who shows industry and talent, and who keeps herself neat, is much desired for a mate.

On the other hand, the busier a hunter keeps his wife sewing, entertaining guests, and bearing children, the prouder she is of him. Coquettishly, she calls him "the terrible one" because he keeps her in such slavery, and it is every girl's dream sometime to be able to shout: "Oh, a poor woman does not have the ability to prepare all the skins that a man can bring home. How I envy those women whose husbands give them only a few skins to prepare!" With such a speech, she can make the other wives green with jealousy.

If such a neat and clever girl should also happen to be fat, then she is really the village belle. An Eskimo cannot give his wife jewelry, new hats, or other things that will demonstrate his wealth, nor can wealth be demonstrated in clothing: all the women's apparel is pretty much alike. It is therefore essential that she appear well fed! As a result, there must always be lots of food—and fattening foods, too—at his house, and his family will enjoy respect and a good reputation. A fat girl is always popular because, as a wife, she will be easier to keep in style, and stoutness is identical with beauty among the Eskimos.

This reminds me of Inuiyak who was one of my Eskimo helpers during the Fifth Thule Expedition and whom, when I was about to return to Denmark, I paid with such gear as I was not going to use any more. He got sled and dogs, axes, knives, and a gun. All of a sudden he became a tycoon among his people, and his first thought was to get a wife. In Repulse Bay he asked for a few days off, and came back with a bride. Being so rich, he had of course no difficulty in getting the fattest one in the place. When Inuiyak came driving up with her on his sled, he made a big to-do out of puffing and panting so that we all could see how hard he had to push. We gave them a real celebration, but the next day we regretted it. We had counted on Inuiyak to take a load on his sled for us on the month-long journey we still had left. But he was no longer the same man!

"My wife is so fat," he bragged. "No dogs can drag this heavy burden. She is too big to run, so others will have to take those boxes!"

This was shouted in a loud voice so everybody could hear it. The intention was to flatter the beauteous lady; being in love has strange effects on people. So Inuiyak wasn't very useful to us any more.

Another standard of beauty among the Eskimos is the nose. Once, when I was a contestant on "The $64,000 Question," quizmaster Hal March asked me why Eskimos rub noses. I said that the custom was of no particular significance, other than olfactory. But now I'd like to modify that statement. Although white people are much too fascinated with this business of rubbing noses, it is a fact that noses *are* important to the Eskimos, and perhaps in a sensual way. A girl must have a petite nose, and if a man really wants to deliver a well-styled compliment, he will tell her—cooingly—that her nose is so little that it completely disappears between her broad flat cheeks.

Fifty years ago, when I first visited Greenland, I stopped overnight at a settlement where there was a girl with an unusually large nose. Her mother took one look at me and almost kissed me. At last, she said, there was someone in the village uglier than her daughter. I say "almost kissed" because Eskimos don't kiss. They bump noses together momentarily in greeting, but there is never any pressing lips together, not even when boy meets girl.

Unlike almost all other primitive people, the Eskimos know nothing of cosmetics, probably because in most places the vegetation is so scant that vegetable dyes were not developed. Still, I came across a couple of cases where women thought of "helping nature," almost causing unhappiness and dire disaster.

One incident took place in the northern part of Greenland's Upernavik district, which at the time was Christianity's outpost. The boy was a prominent figure in local life, son of a Dane who had married an Eskimo; he had learned the trade of carpenter, which put him in the upper class. Because of his strangely indistinct features he was usually called "Snotface." The girl's name was Bala: she was the daughter of a great hunter and known for her domestic ability, but above all she was noted for her enticing chubbiness. Her clothes were well-sewn, and her sealskin pants were of a particularly miraculous fit, clinging tightly to delicious curves. There was mass, and there was fullness of form. "Snotface" started sleeping poorly at night, dreaming about this female horn of plenty. The two had met several times at informal dances at the settlement, and finally "Snotface" proposed. Her answer was yes, and a letter was sent off to the minister to please perform the wedding on his next inspection tour.

I happened to be on the same boat as the minister, and that automatically made me a guest at the celebration. A feast to remember! The groom himself was colorful as a Christmas tree: white anorak, blue pants, fancy kamiks, green scarf, red hair, and strings of beads and colored pictures on the cap—Raphael's angels and other such things. The dinner was delicious and the food plentiful. The bride served us, and the groom presided at the table, expressing his satisfaction both with the meal and with his imminent fate.

We continued our journey the next day; the minister had many chores of baptizing, preaching, marrying, and giving last rites in his vast district. But already at our next stop we were met by a dogsled—an express sled, I might add. The man on it shouted aloud that he was looking for the minister. His entire being was shrouded in the dignity the importance of the occasion gave him. For here was a letter, and it was sealed with lacquer. Solemnly he handed it to the minister, who hastily broke the seal and read. Accidents and death are everyday business so far north, and there was reason to fear the worst. But the tragic message turned out to be that of a soul in torment. "Snotface" wanted an annulment. His bride had been revealed as the daughter of deceit personified. His love had turned into hate. A divorce was demanded. Most Respectfully Yours.

So it was bad work the minister had done, but he defended it bravely. That same evening he wrote an admonishing letter: What God hath wrought one day cannot be sundered by mortals the very next. Time will even out all differences. Remember the holy rite, the vow before the Lord's altar. No, he said, he could not agree to a divorce. With kind greetings in God. Yours Truly.

The next day's travel carried us even farther away from "Snotface" 's woe, but even so, another express messenger with a letter caught up with us in the evening. Daily mail delivery in Greenland! This was very extraordinary indeed!

"Snotface" was giving his explanation in intimate detail this time. He insisted that the marriage was built on a foundation of falsity, and that his life's happiness was forever lost. Bala's deceit had—literally—been unveiled. "Snotface" expressed certainty of the fact that he could have had any girl he wanted. But now he had been betrayed and gypped.

It appeared that Bala had falsely been wearing panties that she had fabricated out of her father's thick knitted sweater, and which, moreover, she laid double! Here she had been promenading borrowed magnificence, her bulging shape had charmed "Snotface" out of his wits and aroused his soul's most beautiful dreams. Now that the vow had already been given before the altar, he had discovered that leanness incarnate and bony angles were hiding under the ostentatious exterior. "Snotface" gave vivid expressions of his hatred of vanity and woman's propensity to fraud.

It cost the minister an extra trip and numerous Bible quotations to maintain the sacred alliance. But, I am happy to say, he finally succeeded.

Farther up north, among my wonderful Thule Eskimos, where choosing and discarding a bride was a much simpler matter, I never thought that vanity could wreak such havoc. But there lived a man, by name Napsanguaq, who had a daughter, Arnanguaq, who was a lovable woman, delightfully plump and clever at sewing. But she was not married, even in a country almost destitute of women. Alas, she did not have enough hair on her head for it to be set up in a top such as women must have to look neat. The hair hung like miserable little wisps around Arnanguaq's pretty face. Whoever would take such a girl as wife and expose his house to ridicule?

Napsanguaq was really worried. The daughter was a wonderful help in the house, but a son-in-law would be better. Napsanguaq needed a hunter to help out, now that he was growing old.

They went musk-ox hunting in Ellesmereland, very far away. A whole year elapsed before they came back, and their return made a sensation. Not only did they have many skins and much news to tell, but Arnanguaq had in the meantime grown hair on her head so magnificent and abundant that the other females almost went mad with envy.

The young men in the tribe responded splendidly to the new challenge, and so violent was the sled traffic to and from Napsanguaq's domain that the track through the snow assumed the looks of an icy highway. The courtiers brought gifts, and the game they caught went to the household as long as they were guests. Things were really looking up, and one fine day it was rumored that a handsome young buck named Aqioq had been preferred. The girl was betrothed, and not much later I heard that the young couple were spending their honeymoon on a lonely little island. I transferred their names to my list of married people, keeping the statistics up to date.

One day we heard the baying of dogs as if a sled party was approaching, but it turned out to be just one traveler, Napsanguaq. He was alone! No family, no festive crowd packed together on one sled, no dashing son-in-law tagging along! One very quiet man drove up, greeting nobody. Something was the matter, but since he hadn't stopped out on the ice, it couldn't be a death. I was mystified, but among the Eskimos discretion is a must. It is rude to ask questions that could embarrass another person.

I did the trading with Napsanguaq, and he informed me that he would be leaving again the next day. This was so unusual that I could allow myself to ask the reason.

"Alas, it so happens that the sight of other people's faces is not desired. These things were badly needed; if not, I would have stayed home."

"But what is wrong? What has happened to make you leave both your happy face and your family behind?"

"The lie has entered our lives. It has been the cause of comments among people that a young woman was different from what was expected and desired!"

I had to *drag* Napsanguaq into the house, we sat down alone in my room, and he confessed all.

Arnanguaq's coiffure had attracted the eyes of men, their senses had been inflamed, and a state of happy excitement had ruled the settlement. Aqioq was the swiftest hunter, his catch would add greatly to the supplies of meat and skins in the house. So he got the girl and carried her away to the little island where their young love could bloom in peace.

But unfortunately there is only one room and space is scarce in an igloo. It is difficult—even impossible—for a lady to guard the secrets of her toilette. It soon turned out that Arnanguaq's tonsorial glory was a swindle, a deceitful masquerade! It was black musk-ox hairs she had combed into her own sparse strands. She had matted them together artfully, but it does happen that hair has to be reset. In order to look passable she couldn't very well let it go for more than eight days or so. The groom discovered the trick, and in that instant his love was gone. For what he saw would inevitably be seen by many others, and then the laughter would resound, derision would fill his house, they would even make taunting songs about it. The scandal was certain, and Aqioq wanted none of it.

He drove the girl back to Napsanguaq, threw her off his sled, and said thanks for the loan, but he had had enough. A woman whose hair reminded him of a man's was not to his taste. Aqioq drove south, and Napsanguaq was left behind with both his daughter and the shame. Arnanguaq herself was even worse off than she had been originally, for, matrimonially speaking, she was now a "reject."

My heart was bleeding for her. Ever since I had set foot on Greenland I had time and again been called upon to straighten out other people's love affairs. I don't know why people showed me this extreme confidence, which many times made me feel like a roving "Lonely Hearts" club. Anyway, I was getting to be an expert in the field, and in this case I went all out. I felt strongly with Arnanguaq in her heart's yearning for nuptial bliss, and she had to be saved for marriage.

When Napsanguaq went home, I went with him. Most of the houses in the settlement were being lived in at the time, so I got the audience that was necessary for the success of my mission. And so I started to give them of my rich experience and worldly wisdom. After the meal at Napsanguaq's house—in which the whole population, as was the custom, took part in honor of me as the guest—I found a convenient moment in the conversation to start my speech.

"I have seen instances of this sort in many countries," I said. "Women wish to be attractive to men, and who are we to blame them for it? Among white women—even among the wives of the best hunters in that faraway land—I have seen those that improved upon their looks."

An elderly woman cut in excitedly: "Yes, but here we are dealing with a woman who wished to be more beautiful than it was nature's intention she should appear to be before people!"

"Yes, that is very true. But I know women in many places who add to nature's intentions and subtract from them almost at will. Women who add a little hair where it is needed, color where it is lacking, and even replace teeth that have fallen out. Nobody censures them; their reputation is the very best!"

My listeners were gaping in utter amazement, but to doubt the reliability of the speaker didn't enter their minds. It had to be so.

"Yes, but if the husband sees it, what then?" asked several.

"He is pleased that his wife will look nice and happy and show that she is comfortable and well-treated in his house!"

This started them thinking, I could see. The publicity value in the case was now beginning to appear to these people north of everybody and everything. And I continued exposing the methods and wiles of civilization to them. A little color makes a woman look well rested, a little hair shows her younger and more attractive, so that her husband is envied by strangers. I talked and talked, and Aqioq listened. He understood that the pride of a man is demanding. In this, as in so many things, the woman is his help and support.

And during the night he sneaked up to Arnanguaq while

her parents discreetly looked away. The marriage was again in effect.

Another time, I had the opportunity to be counsel to Apilak, whose fame is based on the fact that he accompanied Dr. Cook on his ill-fated North Pole journey. Apilak was married, but his heart was big enough for two wives, and so was his wealth. He had, however, fallen in love with a girl who was absolutely impervious to his advances. Apilak—who ordinarily was a loving father to his children and a good provider—was beginning to go off the deep end as the lady turned a deaf ear to all his prayers. He sent out invitations to sumptuous banquets, using all his meat stores. He sang lustily and long to the accompaniment of the drums, but his ladylove remained cold.

One day, Apilak killed one of his best dogs right outside her house. The intention was to show her that his most valued possessions meant nothing to him when he thought of her.

Two days later, he stuck his knife twice into his little daughter's leg so that she screamed with pain. The idea was to show the girl once again that nothing else in the world meant anything to him; he had even forgotten his children.

But nothing happened, so something extraordinary had to be done. One day, when there was a big village gathering, Apilak rolled his sleeve up to his shoulder, took his powder horn, and poured out a streak of powder—from the shoulder to the hand, making a little heap in the palm. He lit the powder, and searing flame ran up and down his arm while his face never moved a muscle. But all that happened was that the women became frightened and ran off.

I arrived at the settlement a couple of days later. I had heard about Apilak's behavior, and now I was told everything about his strange courtship. I had come with the intention of walrus hunting, and I urged all the men to accompany me out on the ice. Most of them did, including Apilak.

When we wanted to rest during the hunt, we built an igloo. At night, while the others were asleep, Apilak and I lay awake. Things were still bothering him, and finally he started talking about his elusive beloved.

I took the occasion to scold him for his cruelty to his little girl. I looked at his arm that was festering. The sores in the hand were constantly breaking anew when Apilak threw his harpoon, but as a man with dignity he made no complaint. While I bandaged his sores, I spoke to him of my personal experiences; I informed him of my opinion of women and the best way to win them. You can't succeed by beating around the bush, the personal element is the great appeal. Go to the girl herself, talk to her, influence her heart, I told him. I talked enthusiastically, and my words sounded convincing—or at least I thought so.

Soon after the ice broke up, the chances of getting any more walrus were gone, and we returned to the settlement, where we spent the time visiting, eating, and talking, as one usually does when the time is inopportune for hunting, just letting the hours slip by as easily as possible.

Suddenly we heard the screams of a woman, the cries of children, and many excited shouts. We rushed out to see what was afoot.

It was Apilak, the great lover, who was busy with the "personal element" I had recommended. But with his own interpretation of it: He had grabbed the girl by her hair-top and was swinging her around in a circle, while she was stumbling and crying and screaming loudly. I ran over to them, but the lover had finished and stood beside the girl, who lay sobbing on the ground. From their talk I could tell that personal matters were being discussed. So the rest of us withdrew. Soon it was announced that Apilak had left the village with his beloved on a sled. A little trip away from other people where, alone, they could exhaust their passion for each other.

The final result was that Apilak had two wives. In the long run, the girl could not resist him. This showed that even among the Polar Eskimos, where women are not supposed to have a mind of their own, it pays to go directly to the heart of the matter.

But let us consider the case of an ordinary young hunter who wants a certain girl as bride. Maybe he has been with her in the Young People's House, or just the sight of her and her good reputation have made up his mind. It would be beneath his dignity to go up to the girl and propose, and it could also be embarrassing if her answer was no. So he starts visiting her house, or rather, her father, and sits and talks with him or eats with the family. The girl can then reveal to him a lot about her like or dislike of him by the way she takes his outer clothes and takes care of them, by the way she serves him food, etc. But she says nothing, and he only talks to her father and her brothers about the hunting and such matters as silly women know nothing about.

He may then start bringing presents for her. He would not give them to her directly, but he just casually "forgets" them when he is leaving. It might be a choice piece of fur, a piece of ribbon or a mirror from the trading post, or the like. If she ignores the gift, or even throws it out of the house, saying something like "Something was forgotten which is too good for a poor woman to use," then her feelings are cool. If she should go to the extreme of cutting the fur or ribbon to pieces in public outside her house, then his case is hopeless. But suppose she accepts his gift and uses it conspicuously: that amounts to a public declaration, and the young man's next step will be to ask her father's consent. Very often the father makes his decision according to his friendship or esteem for the young man's kin. Officially, the girl's mother has nothing to say, but she is actually an active agent in persuading the father one way or another, and just as often as not the marriage has already been "arranged" between the two mothers before the developments have reached this stage.

If the young man gets the approval of the prospective father-in-law, he has permission to take the girl, and that's all. And I mean just that: he takes her.

5 Eating and Visiting

THE ESKIMO'S DEAREST PASTIME is visiting. More often than not, he takes his meals in somebody else's house, his family with him, or else he himself has guests, as many as his provisions can accommodate. Visiting is an important social function and is governed by a great deal of etiquette. A man's reputation is to a large extent dependent upon how often he invites, how well he serves his guests, and the perfection of his manners as a host. Consequently, the best pieces of the game that he catches are reserved for visitors. And when he has had a good catch, he is the happiest man on earth. He stands by the entrance to his house and calls out: "Come visit my house! Come visit me!"

The rest of the four or five families at the settlement—those who have seen him come home with game, and who have more or less been expecting his invitation—come running immediately. As they enter his house, they simply say: "Hereby somebody comes visiting!" The women take off their long kamiks and their outer garments and crawl up on the bunks, the men sit down on the skins that cover the floor, while the children and the youngsters either sit or stand in a flock by the entrance.

Then the man of the house says how happy he is to see his guests, and for a little while everybody just sits around talking about the hunt, the dogs, or the weather. Suddenly the host gets a bright idea.

"Do you happen to want something to eat?" he asks, and the other men then answer him that of course they didn't expect at all to get something to eat, but that if he wants to give them food, then they know that no place in the world will they get such good things as in this particular house!

"Alas no!" says the host. "You are in bad luck. It so happens that I am a bad hunter, and I have nothing to treat you to. But if you will lower yourselves to taste the poor carcass I can offer you, then let me go and fetch it in!"

Then the great hunter goes out to the meat rack and gets his best piece of meat. In order to get it in through the narrow entrance tunnel, he puts a strap around it and hands one end of the strap to the young people just inside. They pull the meat in with loud shouts about how heavy it is, how this great hunter always has big things to offer, etc., all to flatter their host.

The meat is placed in the middle of the circle, and the host takes his axe and begins to chop the frozen mass to pieces. When this is done, he takes a little piece and begins to eat, but says in a highly worried tone of voice:

"Alas, I have to throw it all out again, for it tastes so awfully bad. The dogs have soiled it, all kinds of dirt is on it. I can't offer it to such excellent guests."

Upon this invitation, everybody grabs a piece, each man hands one to his wife on the bunk behind him, and soon there is noisy chewing and smacking of lips only interrupted by loud praises of the incomparable delicacy that is being consumed here. The men say only little, but the women are gabbing continuously, as women everywhere are wont to do. It is beneath the dignity of an Eskimo man to pay any attention to the women, and if the noise from them becomes too loud, he may look about him in astonishment.

"What is this!" he shouts. "Is it getting to be spring? Where am I? It sounds as if the auks on the cliffs are quacking. Are there really birds here, or is it women that are nearby?"

That quiets the ladies down a little, but then everybody laughs, and the gaiety starts up again. The host's wife is busy boiling meat from the newly caught game over her blubber lamp, and when everybody has had enough of the frozen delicacies, they start in on the steaming walrus or seal meat. The polite guests fart and belch to show how well they are digesting the treats of the house. They continue eating until they are too gorged to get another bite down. If a guest gets tired, he will simply go to sleep where he sits and start in on the meal again when he wakes up. If it becomes apparent that the provisions of the house are about to give out, another hunter will stand up and ask to be allowed to show what his house has to offer. Thus the party goes from house to house, and the feast may last for days.

Among the Hudson Bay Eskimos, the women are not allowed to take part in these feasts. It is thought that boiled meat is man's food, too good for women to have, and a man would make himself ridiculous if he ate it in the company of his family. No, he goes outside his house and announces loudly that there is boiled meat. This is an invitation for all the other men in the village to come to a feast. With serious faces, they form a single file and enter the house of their host. They have their big knives in their hands and hold them up in front of themselves like sabres. Inside the house, they take position in a circle without saying a word.

The host begins the proceedings by making a little speech that is always approximately the same: "Alas, I have waited so long before inviting you because I was embarrassed on account of my bad house. I do not know how to build houses as big and handsome as yours. Moreover, I have nothing decent to offer you. The rest of you, you are used to catching young, fresh, and good-tasting animals; I must be content with half-dead carrions that are an insult to the palate. And finally I have only the miserable wife who sits here. She is unfit for any work, and she is particularly impossible at cooking meat, so this meal is going to be a terrible scandal for my house."

Whereupon the men sit down, and the wife starts serving the meat. This is her only function at the meal. She has a kind of fork made from a caribou antler or a walrus rib, with which she lifts a lump of meat from the pot. She then licks it carefully so that soup and blood won't drip too much over her husband's fingers.

The husband takes the meat and puts it in his mouth— or at least, as much as he has room for. He then cuts off the rest and hands it to his neighbor, who cuts off a mouthful and passes it on to the next man in the circle. The lump of meat keeps circling like this until it is eaten up, and the host receives a new lump from his wife. It is desirable to have a little fat with the meat from time to time, so the host cuts off a piece of blubber and sends it around the circle in the same manner. The men rub the various pieces around on their faces so that the blood and smear often cover even the foreheads. If a piece is lost on the floor, the man who picks it up is expected to lick it clean. Water to drink with the food is provided in a basin made of walrus skin or sealskin. The water is from melted snow, but it is far from crystal clear, for it has been melted in the same pots the meat is cooked in. And these pots never get washed, only wiped off with a piece of skin at every new moon. The water is therefore brown like thin coffee, and on its surface caribou hairs, matches, and other little things are afloat. On these occasions my beard was very useful, as I let it sift the water for me. Afterward, when I wiped the beard with my hand and saw the amount of dirt and slime it contained, I was ever so happy that I had avoided using the razor.

As you may easily understand, I much preferred life with the Thule Eskimos. There, the fair sex were allowed to enliven the parties with their charm, the pots were kept fairly clean without any consideration of the position of the moon, there was always freshly melted water, and each man got his individual piece of food untouched by others except, perhaps, the hostess, who handed it to him only to press him to eat more.

I was early acquainted with the magnificent hospitality of the Polar Eskimos. Knud Rasmussen and I even skipped unloading the little ship *Motor* in which we went to Thule together in order to take part in a food orgy which he got started by announcing that he had been longing to taste the good things the place had to offer. We were invited to Uvdluriak's and there for the first time I tasted rotten *mattak*. This dish, which is a great delicacy for the Eskimos, consists of huge flakes of narwhale skin that have been kept in meat caches for several years. In the low temperature they do not become rancid, they just ferment, so that the skin tastes very much like walnuts while the blubber, turned quite green, tastes sharp—almost like roquefort cheese. Next we went to the house of Tornge, who served caribou meat with tallow. Knud let it be known that he would consider it an offense not to visit all the other tents, where people no doubt were expecting us with such specialties as they had in store. At last, we were so gorged that we both lay down on the bunk where we happened to be and fell asleep. We were awakened by a message from the irate captain of *Motor,* who asked us if we had any intentions of further activity in this place.

We were not too eager to have the crew stay over the winter, so we got the unloading organized in a hurry, and *Motor* took off. Then we started building our house. Knud said that we had to procure food supplies for the winter. We had not brought provisions from home except for some canned goods to be kept in reserve. The intention was to "live off the land"—a prospect which I found very exciting, and which Knud was even more crazy about, for he loved the native foods. So the next day he announced that he was tired of building houses and that he was going to secure provisions for the winter. He explained to me that if we became too dependent upon the Eskimos, it could be embarrassing for us, and that good relations would suffer.

In short, I was put to raising our house, assisted by a couple of boys, while Knud—together with all the hunters from the settlement—went out to get walrus. I worked and hammered bravely. The house was some kind of patent house that had been sent with us as an experiment, but it was difficult to build and not really too appropriate. It was warm enough, but fragile, for on the outside it was mortar so soft that if I pitched a stone after a dog, and it hit the wall instead, it stayed imbedded there.

The boys and girls discovered this very soon, and it became a new game at the place to cover the walls with stones. Later on, the exterior was covered with wood, and many years after that it was used as a schoolhouse. I looked at it with pride every time I revisited Thule, reminiscing about the Archimedian constructions I had had to use to raise the chimney.

It took me three weeks to build the house, and when Knud returned, he started a series of house-raising feasts in grand style. Actually it was one single celebration, but it lasted a couple of weeks. At the time, there were eight families in the settlement, and they all seemed capable of eating at every hour of the endless day. As I have mentioned, sleep was permitted during the banquets, but expressions of satiety in the form of air explosions from every possible opening of the body seemed to be good substitutes for sleep. Knud was at the head of them all. He sang and told stories; he cooked and arranged food orgies the like of which had rarely been seen. His ability to drum up edibles was formidable. We didn't have to supply much of them, ourselves. It was Knud's special art—during a meal—to start reminiscing about gigantic feasts of yore. Then his eyes assumed a dreamy look while he softly mumbled something about tail of narwhale, well fermented, rotten eider ducks, or other beautiful treats.

Immediately, somebody or other jumped up and demanded to be allowed to show that also in this place such palate-caressing articles could be prepared. Knud expressed a little doubt—but no more than to make it a challenge. The result was always that the man and a couple of his friends ran off to fetch the delicacies. They might otherwise have been set aside for the visit of a dear relative or some such purpose. Now they went to Knud and his guests, almost the entire settlement. Our house seemed to have inexhaustible riches. How we procured all that was consumed I don't know; that was Knud's department. He just told somebody or other to go out and get some cooking meat. If then the poor fellow went out to obey the glorious command, and it happened that he returned to report that there was no more meat on the rack, Knud turned a little joke in his direction so that everybody present laughed at him. The man couldn't bear this loss of honor; he went out again and came back with all he could carry. There was no point asking where he got it from: meat was considered common property, so it didn't really matter.

We just ate, and I learned what was good. The diet of the Polar Eskimos is actually healthful and varied. When you have meat and meat, and meat again, you learn to distinguish between the different parts of an animal. The breast doesn't taste at all like the muscles of the hindlegs, for instance. And little by little I learned the finesse of Eskimo food preparation. One of the greatest delicacies, narwhale skin, is either served fresh and raw, or it is preserved with dried meat in big skin bags filled with blubber. Seals are used either as boiling meat or put in the meat cache to ferment, whole and unskinned. Then their meat tastes strong and sweet

as sugar, and the liver is particularly desirable, tasting somewhat like preserved cranberries.

A good man to visit was Angutidluarssuk, whom I got to
know when we first went down to Cape York to make ourselves acquainted with the people of that settlement. As always, we paid a visit to every house, including that of the
poorest man in the tribe—a big, strong, and thoroughly lazy
fellow by the name of Kritlak. There was no exterior sign of
his economically poor state, however, since all the houses
looked alike, and since he served us generously with seal
livers that he fetched from the other men's meat racks.
Honor forbade them to protest; it would be like admitting
that a poor seal liver was after all of some importance.

We were then invited to the house of Angutidluarssuk.
He was one of the greatest hunters of the tribe, but oddly
inconspicuous and quite ugly in appearance. He was not at
all unsympathetic, though. His gentle demeanor and his kind
smile made people forgive him his incredible filthiness. His
hair was always caked together in a mass of grease and dirt
because he wiped his fingers in it. His clothes were more
than modest, and he always wore pants from thin-haired bears,
while his son and his foster son and the children of poor
neighbors sported the most elegant pants that could be made.
He walked very badly, with a kind of waddling. One day,
while several of us were standing on the ice near Saunders
Island watching breathing holes, a bear came walking toward
us from the direction of the open water. It quickly saw us
and tried to beat a retreat to the thin new ice, so that—in
order to get it—we would have to cut off its retreat by running
around it. Everybody ran as fast as possible, but suddenly
a figure shot out in front of all of us. That was Angutidluarssuk, who outran every man in the tribe, young and old,
and got the bear fenced in. Angutidluarssuk then waited
quietly until a young man, who never had caught a bear,
reached him. Angutidluarssuk handed him his gun and told
him to shoot quickly before the others came running.

It was likewise a well-known fact that Angutidluarssuk
was always in the rear when many sleds were traveling together, and he couldn't seem to keep the pace. But when there
was bad driving, and nobody could make their dogs advance, he would always take the lead and guide the others
through pack ice or deep snow. And if they happened to
cross a bear track, nothing could hold back his dogs. They
put up a speed that couldn't be matched by any others.

Angutidluarssuk always reached the bear first—which was not to say that he shot it. It was his great pleasure to leave the honor and joy to others; his own satisfaction was in the thought that he could have felled it if he had wanted to.

It was the same thing when we later began driving big sled loads across Melville Bay up to Thule. When the goods had to be distributed among the sleds, and there was a particularly large or heavy box, Angutidluarssuk always said quietly that it so happened there was room for it on his sled. He put it on, and never drove any slower on that account.

But at this time I didn't know him, and together with the others I entered his rather small hut. I sat looking around me, and the host remarked that he felt embarrassed at my observation of his building, since he never had learned to build houses that didn't make him a laughingstock. To which I said that I was sitting and enjoying how cleverly stone was placed on stone, and everything so well put together.

"For the first time in life somebody hears a little encouragement," said Angutidluarssuk. Then I noticed that his wife had hung some pairs of kamiks up to dry over the lamp. They were made from the finest blue foxes, and I couldn't help expressing my admiration of the precious kamiks.

"Alas, you have come to a poor man who doesn't have the ability to shoot rabbits for kamik skins. In this house, we must be content with the skins of foxes that my useless wife traps, so that also this shame shall come to her bad husband!" said Angutidluarssuk.

We sat a little while talking about the weather and the dogs. When the conversation died down a little, he expressed the thought that possibly his guests would want a bite to eat to pass the time, since he himself was so incapable of telling interesting hunting experiences or worthwhile stories.

We answered that we hadn't planned at all to eat at this particular time, but since we had been told that this was the house where the really good things were served, we wouldn't say no to anything he might offer.

Angutidluarssuk laughed and said that now he would try to forget his shame if it was possible, for he had never as yet had any luck when he tried to bring forth good-tasting food. On top of that, he protested, his miserable wife was completely lacking in all talents. But since his poor conditions surely were known to all, and he presumed that he was the topic of conversation wherever people wished to have a good laugh, he might as well go out and see if any of some poor birds he had collected were left. He would, he said, serve birds because he was incapable of catching seal or walrus or other such animals as manly hunters brought home.

He disappeared out through the entrance while the rest of us expressed our wonder at his modesty and excellent manners. Then we heard his voice calling from the outside. From the entrance tunnel he handed in one end of a long strap. At once several men jumped to their feet and began to pull on it. Outside, Angutidluarssuk was heard chasing puppy dogs away from the entrance tunnel and directing something heavy in through the narrow passage. Inside, the men hauled with exaggerated efforts.

"We can hardly manage this. It is terrible how this great hunter always owns big and heavy things. Do you suppose we ought to give it up?" etc. At last, a huge frozen seal came in through the opening. It was a giviak, the most festive food a Polar Eskimo can treat you to. *Giviak* means something immersed, in this case little auks that have been immersed in seal blubber and ripened through the summer into a delicacy to dream about.

Auks are birds that live by the millions in the bird cliffs along the coasts of Smith Sound. In an indirect way, they were the reason for our being there. For they are the favorite food of the foxes that the Eskimos traded to us in return for the goods we had to offer. They are small birds, no larger than starlings, but tasty to eat, either cooked or dried, and particularly so when preserved in blubber. The birds are caught in nets on long poles as they pass in flocks by the cliffs. What a wonderful time when they arrive in spring! Here it could really be said that "the sun is darkened" by birds.

When you want to make a giviak, you must first catch a seal, which then has to be flensed in a special and very difficult way. You start by cutting around the seal's mouth and let the hands feel their way down along its body inside the skin. The knife must not be too long, and it takes some practice before the hands have the right feel to avoid making holes in the skin. Around the forelimbs it can be particularly hard to find certain joints that have to be cut through. As you continue, both your arms are little by little buried in the seal. Often, big slices of blubber must be cut away and taken out through the opening at the mouth, so as to make room to operate in. When at last the knife has been all over, and the skin is entirely freed from the seal's body, there comes the most difficult part: the entire body has to be pulled out through the mouth opening. As a rule, two men have to pull with all their strength to get it done.

You now have a bag formed of sealskin and lined with blubber. And you are ready to proceed with the next task: the bird catch. A wall of stones is put up to hide behind. The little auks do not nest on the steep cliffs, they make themselves comfortable under the big stones in the scree, and often they crawl into deep holes under these stones. When they then fly out, they amuse themselves by swarming in clouds along the cliff quite low over the ground. Then is the time to let the net dart up and catch it full of birds. The pole has to be turned quickly so as to close the net and prevent the birds from flying out again. The birds are taken out of the net and killed by guiding a thumb up under the breastbone to the heart, which is "displaced," and the bird dies at once. After the wings have been braided together on the back of the bird, it is then put down in the blubber bag. A diligent bird-catcher—the women as a rule—can fill a sealskin in two days. But Angutidluarssuk had filled two sealskins between two sleeps. It must be said, though, that he was famous for sleeping infrequently in good hunting weather.

When the bag is full, it must immediately be put in a secure place and covered with stones. The sun must never shine on it, since the blubber would then turn rancid. The comparative warmth of the summer air makes the blubber seep into the birds and cure their meat. Nothing is quite so delicious, especially the lump of blood collected around the damaged heart, which is almost heavenly to eat.

Now it was winter, and Angutidluarssuk's giviak was frozen. He took his axe and started chopping up the icy stuff. Pink feathers and bird meat flew to all sides, while we watched in pious silence. At last the floor was completely covered with pieces of meat and blubber. Angutidluarssuk picked up a bite, tasted it, and threw it contemptuously away.

"Alas, as I told you: this is inedible! Possibly I have, through an oversight, filled the skin with dogs' dung. Possibly it is only my absolute ignorance about how to make a giviak that has caused this mistake! If you would show me a kindness, you would leave me now so that I could be alone with my shame!"

Upon this invitation, we started in. It tasted good the moment I got it in my mouth. But I had to be taught how to eat this remarkable dish. As long as it is frozen, you just chew away. You get feathers and bones in your mouth, of course, but you just spit them out. Frozen meat always has an enticing taste, and as it dissolves in the mouth, you get the full aroma of the raw fermented bird. It is incredible how much you can down, unbelievable how hard it is to stop. If you happen to come across a fully developed egg inside a bird, it tastes like a dream. Or the liver, which is like green cheese. Breast and drumsticks are cooling and refreshing. It was late before we were full, and there was then about half of the giviak left. This was put up on one of the bunks to thaw for later use.

When we had had some sleep, we started the second part of the feast. The giviak was now so much thawed that the little auks tasted entirely different, and it was possible to eat them in a new way. Whole birds could now be pried loose from the compressed mass, and when that is the case, great elegance can be demonstrated while enjoying them. A man with *savoir-vivre* holds the bird by the legs with his teeth. Then he strokes it with both hands, thus brushing off the feathers that have already been loosened by the fermentation. He brushes his hands together to remove all feathers, whereupon he turns the bird and bites the skin loose around the beak. This can then be turned inside out and pulled free of the bird without letting go of its legs. The eater then sucks the whole skin into his mouth and pulls it out again, pressing his teeth slightly together. In this manner, he gets all the fat sitting inside the skin. Taste is, as we know, an individual matter, but this one—I dare guarantee—can become a passion.

When the skin is free of fat, you bite it free around the bird's legs and swallow it in one piece. The breast is eaten by biting down on each side of the bone, and the bone can then be thrown away. This bares the innards, and you can enjoy the various parts one by one. The blood clot around the heart has coagulated and glues the teeth together, the liver and the gall bladder have a spicy taste, while the bitter aroma of the intestines reminds one of a lager beer. When these parts are consumed, the rest—wings, backbone, and pelvis—is taken into the mouth and thoroughly chewed.

Such delicacies were always served in Angutidluarssuk's house. His meat caches were always filled, and whenever I needed a good feed for my dogs, I went to visit him. He was always my friend. In the spring, he came home with as many seals as he could load on his sled. But he didn't sleep as long as the weather was nice and the seals were basking in the sun on the ice. He just unloaded and went out again to get more. Neighbors and friends had only to take what they wanted. Angutidluarssuk himself was silent and modest and smiled shyly when somebody spoke to him.

His wife was called Itusarssuk. She loved children because once, during a hunger period, she had to kill four of her own to spare them from the death of starvation. The oldest girl was then so old that she already could sew mittens, Itusarssuk told me when I got the sad story from her. This daughter had understood that it was hopeless to try to subsist, for there were no men at the place who could supply them with meat. She had seen that "life was heavier than death" and had helped the mother hang three younger children, whereupon she had placed the string around her own neck so that the mother could pull it and fasten it to a hook. Weeping, Itusarssuk had then left this house of death.

Only an eight-year-old son was left. He had discussed the matter with the others, but he "had no wish to end life." He promised that he would make out by eating grass and hare excrements. His name was Iggianguaq, and he pulled himself through and lived, but he remained small of stature, and he said himself that he was like the dogs which are badly fed while they are puppies, and which never get to be as strong as other dogs.

Itusarssuk was highly respected because of her deed. She had loved her children enough to kill them so as to free them from further sufferings.

Somehow, during my first stay at Cape York, I must have shown that I wasn't yet quite used to good Eskimo food. One evening, I had taken a walk in the darkness to look at a nearby glacier, and when I returned, I heard loud and happy voices from the house of Qulugtinguaq. It turned out that they had prepared a meal from my own travel provisions. All my cans had been taken inside, and everybody was busy breaking them open. Without any discimination whatsoever, they were pouring the contents into a pot that was aboil over the blubber lamp.

"Look here, just look!" shouted Qulugtinguaq. "Now you will be happy. You have eaten our miserable food for several days. Now you shall have a meal of your own kind from your own sled, and the rest of us will eat with you so as to show that we do not despise your food, just as you eat ours."

What else was I to do but to laugh with these innocent

people? The cans were opened, and to the Eskimos it was just as much an honor and a joy to be the guest as it was for me to be their host. That a certain amount of food should be calculated to last for such and such a length of time never occurred to them. They ate for days on end when they had plenty, and starved with good cheer when they had nothing. Besides, they were really making a sacrifice here, for most of the white man's food is distasteful to the Eskimos. It is not only that they could not possibly subsist on it, low in fat as it is, but that they just don't like it. Exceptions are bread, biscuits, and cake, which are considered great delicacies, along with sugar. In southern Greenland coffee is consumed with a reverence as nowhere else in the world; a whole social life —complete, intense, and with its own etiquette—has evolved around the coffee pot. The Polar Eskimos learned to appreciate the brown drink, and they felt very rich and very proud if they could offer it as a treat of the house. Tea, however, they considered an almost necessary drink, as it pepped them up tremendously in the cold climate.

The Eskimos' extraordinary delight at visiting and eating together must be seen against the background of their basic loneliness and isolation. Any conglomeration of people over any extended length of time is impossible in their barren country, since the game of the area will quickly be exhausted or go away to safer places. Since the people are constantly en route to procure the various necessities of life, years might lapse between reunions of relatives or friends. During the summer, a family might be islolated for months, since the fragile kayaks cannot be used for long trips, and there are too many ice- and snow-free places for the sleds to traverse. If the family, moreover, goes on an extended journey, as for instance when a Polar Eskimo family goes to Ellesmereland to get musk-ox skins, it may be a year or more before they see other human beings. No wonder, therefore, that they make the most of the occasion when it happens.

Under such conditions, there has naturally been no formation of societies. The only real social unit is the family, economically sufficient unto itself, and under the absolute rulership of the husband and provider. Most often, though, a few families—not more than four or five—will live together in a settlement. Rarely do they live in their houses for more than a few months of the winter, the rest of the time being spent on hunting trips. An Eskimo is not really regarded as "belonging" to any place until he is buried there.

Formally, the families in such a settlement have not given up any of their independence, since there is no chief. The men hunt together under the leadership of the hunter who is regarded as "the most successful." He is "the one who thinks for everybody"; he decides where and when the settlement is to go traveling, what game is to be hunted, etc. Very often, he is also endowed with the talents of an *angakok,* a conjurer with helping spirits at his command. This gives added weight to his words. You will never find two such strong-men at a settlement. If in the shuffling of families between settlements such a situation should arise, one of them will quickly move away with his family. If not, rivalry and open enmity will result.

Basically, the Eskimos regard the land and the game as belonging to everybody, inasmuch as they are all at the mercy of "the great woman who lies at the bottom of the sea and who sends out the game." Consequently, no hunter is ever spoken of as being good or bad, merely as being "successful" or "unsuccessful," and the unsuccessful hunter and his family have as much right to live as everybody else. The practical advantage of hunting in a group, therefore, is that each man gets part of the proceeds even if he does not actually fell any animal.

I was first introduced to this custom when, after having survived our house-raising celebration at Thule, we went walrus hunting on Saunders Island. Knud and I were in our rowboat with a couple of the men, and we acted as mother ship to four or five kayaks. Even with this unusually large number of hunters present, each man knew exactly which part of each walrus was his, for the old tradition decided it according to his participation in the killing of the beast. The one who was "lucky to get first harpoon" got the best parts, "second harpoons" next best, and so on. The rules were automatically transferred to those with guns. Even the hunters who came up after the demise of an animal would throw their harpoons at it in a token gesture of their claims. Actually, we got plenty of walrus to go round during that excursion, but the Eskimos insisted upon upholding their rigorous code, and the flensing was done in the way that each man cut out his part. They turned out to be fine anatomists: every man knew exactly which joints to cut through and where they were. It was amazing to see them guide their knives down through meat and blood and hit exactly at the designated spot. If a man happened to be a little off, it was taken as a sign that he had lied the same day. Then everybody laughed and said that here was a man who had wasted his thoughts by failing to speak the truth, and so he had forgotten that animals are created with joints that serve to divide them.

Every single walrus we got gave gains to everyone in the party. Big heaps of meat became my property, and with tears in my eyes I would thank the hunter who first had thrust his harpoon in the animal. They laughed uproariously at that, but even the best joke can be repeated too often, and old Sorqaq—who had been a great angakok and chief hunter in his day—took it upon himself to put me straight:

"You must not thank for your meat; it is your right to get parts. In this country, nobody wishes to be dependent upon others. Therefore, there is nobody who gives or gets gifts, for thereby you become dependent. With gifts you make slaves just as with whips you make dogs!"

With these words, the old sage made me understand that we were all human beings helping each other under the hard conditions of the Arctic, and nobody should suffer the indignity of charity.

To own dogs is the sign of manhood, and therefore the only condition for getting game parts is the presentation of dogs. This put the hunters who had half-grown sons at a distinct advantage. They would merely give a few dogs to their sons, who could then claim parts in the catch, and that particular household would get two or three parts. If any doubt was expressed as to the propriety of this practice, the hunter would immediately throw his own part to the complainer, shouting: "Here is something for you!" and then appeal to the rest of the party to do likewise, thus bringing dishonor on the dissatisfied fellow. Nevertheless, the hunters with sons did have an advantage.

It is important to the Polar Eskimo to have plenty of meat. It is a favorite form of bragging, when a visitor arrives, to feed his dogs so that they are too gorged to touch another bite. Shameful as it may seem, I often took advantage of this weakness by letting my dogs go off with me on a visit.

Even a man who was too lazy or too old to go hunting could claim a part in the catch by meeting it when it was hauled in and throwing some kind of weapon on it. Although such persons certainly did not enjoy a good reputation in the community, they were at least never hungry. The aforementioned Sorqaq eventually became too old to hunt, and was lame in both arms. Nevertheless, when a piece of game was hauled up to the beach, he would take some stones in his mouth and spit them out on the animal, thus claiming his part. The younger men would often tease him by placing the catch so far out on the ice that he couldn't get out there. Then they had their amusement listening to his impotent railing. I tried to shame them, but they merely answered me: "Why, we would rather die than to come to such humiliation." I often saw this same cruelty to older persons, but came to realize that it was a matter of necessity in a country where a useless hanger-on can be a hindrance to the maintenance of life. Often, an old father or mother would be left behind on the trek to starve and freeze to death, mostly upon his or her own insistence. And nobody thought the worse of the family for that.

There is yet another procedure established to see to it that riches are properly distributed, and that is another expression of the game being nobody's exclusive property. If, for instance, a hunter has been out alone and has caught a seal, and the other hunters in the settlement got no seal that day, parts of the animal must be given to the other families. This is called *payudarpok,* and responsibility for it rests completely on the women. No man debases himself to worry about the provisions, once the game is killed and brought in. But for the women it is an important matter to have payudarpok with honor—sufficiently to uphold the reputation of the house. It is a woman's pleasure, and her way of boasting a little, to run around to the other houses with her pieces of meat, saying: "My unworthy husband was lucky to get seal today. Please lower yourselves to taste a bite of his catch!"

At Thule, there once lived a man called Ivik. He was a good hunter, but the scarcity of women had forced him to marry a woman from southern Greenland, and she was burdened with the vice of avarice, and more intent upon keeping enough for herself than on giving her husband the esteem of being a great provider and a man who distributed generously. Navarana had several times mentioned to me that this woman, Puto, had come with some miserable pieces of meat, which gave cause for gossip among the women. Nobody understood how she could bring herself to do it, and they laughed much over her practice. The result was, of course, that when we had been lucky, and Ivik had caught nothing, we gave them that much more just to show them payudarpok.

One evening, I was at home; the hunt had been fruitless, but we had a few reserve provisions in the house. There was not much, for it was during the war, and there hadn't been a ship for a couple of years. We economized, but we still weren't destitute.

Then it was rumored that Ivik had caught a big seal, and there was great joy in the settlement. We were five families, all together, so we considered it a sure thing that we would have our fill of boiled meat that evening. After a while, we heard the dogs howl outside, reporting that somebody came visiting. It turned out to be Puto making her rounds and now bringing us our payudarpok. I quickly divined from Navarana's face that a veritable storm was coming up, for it was a wretched piece of three ribs and with the blubber carefully cut off. There were many people in our house, and it was such a ridiculous contribution that my wife broke out in righteous fury.

"Oh no," she said. "At long last, something has happened that we can tell about when we journey out to visit people. The great Ivik has had game, and his wife now takes leave of almost the entire seal without thinking of her own."

There were some women visiting us, so Puto blushed from shame over these words.

"But please let me give you something in return," said Navarana. "For it is impossible for me to accept all this without saying thank-you with a thing or two. Alas, I wish I had something better to give you, but I have only a little bread!"

And then she took the entire supply of the house, namely, one loaf of bread that she had kneaded and baked, watched with great reverence by the entire household, and put it in Puto's arm.

"Please, you shall have that, and it also turns out that I have a couple of cans of milk."

Puto got two cans of milk, out of a store of only five!

"Yes, but please don't think that I would be so uncouth as to let you go away with so little, you who bring such masses of meat that you must have dragged yourself tired to come to our house. There you are, I have a little sugar here, and fortunately there is a pack of tea left; I give that to you who bring such huge gifts of meat!"

Puto was by now completely crushed, and the other women could barely restrain their mirth. But Navarana wasn't finished.

"Oh, how lucky I am that I have a little tobacco," she said. "Here is a pack for you!"

Everybody knew that we had only ten packs for the whole

tribe, about a hundred smokers, until we could bring more up via a long journey across Melville Bay.

"Yes, but if only I had something to really show my gratitude!" Navarana didn't leave the poor woman in peace. "I see that in my misery I still have a couple of boxes of matches. Perhaps a bit of oats would please you, also. Now that you have given all your meat away, it is not impossible that your children need to have their mouths fed with a little porridge. There, I can give you just a little bit!"

And Puto was handed a large tin half full of oats, something precious and completely irreplaceable at that time. Puto reddened more and more from shame, and her eyes shifted helplessly from Navarana to the other women in the room. Then the tears began to trickle down her cheeks. She knew as well as anybody that this event would become a saga that would be told in the whole tribe from north to south. According to Eskimo thinking she had deserved much punishment for her avarice, and now she got it. She couldn't budge for all the goods that were heaped upon her. But Navarana wanted to do a thorough job of it.

"But alas, whatever do I have to offer you? My presents are small and without value, but here are some sewing needles and a piece of linen that I can give you, I who am married to a bad husband, a poor provider, and certainly cannot give away such treasures as your payudarpok without any consideration of what you might be wanting yourself during the winter!"

This was the last straw, Puto broke out in loud sobs. She howled like a dog in clear frost weather, and since she had so much in her arms, she couldn't defend herself when Navarana stuck the needles in the piece of linen and tucked it all under her arm. Then she turned around and pushed the door open with her knee and tumbled out. She had broken the Eskimos' law, and Navarana was a lady who didn't permit that kind of thing to remain unpunished. She ran out after her, telling the other women to follow her. Everybody hurried outside where Navarana was standing, triumphantly raising in her hand the little piece of meat that Puto had payudarpok'd.

"Oh, listen," she shouted after Puto, "wait a moment! Wait, so that you can tell your husband something that I would wish him to know!"

Involuntarily, Puto turned about and stood still. She was still crying, but in her utter humiliation she was hoping for a little rehabilitation, I guess. Now she saw Navarana take the lump of meat that was our only share of the day's catch.

"Look, I have a poor dog that is utterly gluttonous. At last, I have the chance to give it something—if not a meal, then at least enough to make its mouth water!"

And then she heaved the notorious piece of meat into the mouth of the nearest dog, whereupon she turned and went inside, followed by her three lady friends. Inside, they collapsed holding their stomachs, cheering and laughing. They imitated the expressions in Puto's face and repeated Navarana's words so that they could correct each other if they had misunderstood anything, for this case had to be reported! Oh, how happy they were to have witnessed one of the great events of the winter!

I had been in the other room, and now I entered the scene, for in the lonely Polar winter one does not want to miss out on any amusement. Navarana told me the whole story, and I reminded her that now we had no bread that evening, and that we were short of all the other things and all that for a miserable piece of meat.

"Oh yes," said Navarana. "When I think back on it, I really regret it, too, but I was born with a temper—I can't help it, and I got so angry that I thought she ought to be punished!"

The next day, it turned out that two of the women had lost no time in persuading their husbands to go on a journey visiting people so that they could tell what had happened. But we heard from the other houses that Puto had come home with all her gifts and had had to confess her guilt to Ivik, whose house now had been brought in disrepute.

Ivik went hunting and stayed away for a couple of days. He came home with three seals that he didn't flense. In the evening he brought them down to our meat rack and left them there. Then he returned home and beat his wife, the sinful Puto. They left the settlement the next day with their children and all their property and went up north, far, far away, so as not to be near people who had witnessed Ivik's loss of his honor as a hunter.

But for a long time we didn't have tea or sugar. We ran out of tobacco, and we lacked many other things. The result was that we often laughed and talked about the time Puto payudarpok'd. And Navarana said: "Oh, it is my misfortune that I was born with such a temper that I always want to punish people who do not behave right!"

Actually, I guess, she was justified in her behavior. It was not just that she was the first lady of Thule, and had been belittled, but that she had used her people's principal weapon against offenders: ridicule. In a land without police or government, who is nearer to mete out a sentence than the offended one? For a couple of years, Ivik and his family had to live almost in isolation; and what worse thing is there for a Polar Eskimo? In maintaining their code of human behavior, which is so very much based upon—and conditioned by—their merciless country, the Eskimos only rarely have to resort to violence.

6 Polar Justice: Crime and Punishment Among the Eskimos

OCCASIONALLY a criminal becomes such a nuisance to an Eskimo tribe, or his offense is so serious, that a sentence of death becomes mandatory. A great hunter will then take the role of executioner upon himself and mete out justice in the name of the community. Here is a story about how I once met such an avenger.

When the summer of our arrival and establishment at Thule began to change into fall, Knud and I decided that we would each take a trip to publicize our trading post and to tell people that fox skins could advantageously be bartered to us. Knud went south toward Cape York, I went north. I was accompanied by the hunter Asayuk—who had attached himself to me, having been impressed with my luck with a gun during a walrus hunt, and by his energetic little wife, Arnarwrik. Because the ice was shaky, we had to go overland, and we had plenty of trouble since there still wasn't much snow on the ground. Where there was turf we fared tolerably, and several little lakes that were frozen over came in handy. But over rocks and stones it was hell. The dogs struggled, and so did we. Only Arnarwrik's presence made me hold out, for what man wants to give up when a mere woman can stand it?

We came to a glacier, which we crossed via special routes where the cracks in the icecap were known, and arrived in a land called Nunatarssuak where we wanted to search for caribou. We left our sleds at the edge of the glacier and walked for miles, but found nothing. We then shot a few rabbits, and in a lake, where Asayuk chopped a hole in the ice, we discovered salmon trout. Quickly, Asayuk fashioned a salmon spear from an old caribou antler and one of the legs of my kerosene burner. Arnarwrik was left on the lake to fish, and we two men continued our quest for caribou.

We didn't find a single one, but every evening we returned to Arnarwrik, who was catching plenty of trout for our supper. When four days had passed, and our dogs had had no fodder, we decided to leave the place and continue northward. The dogs didn't worry my two companions; it wasn't too cold, so they didn't need much food. We wandered off with big burdens on our backs. Little Arnarwrik took her share, and she scolded her husband constantly without bothering him in the least. To me, this showed that I was winning their confidence: the lady wouldn't act like that before strangers since they should always have an impression of the husband's utter domination of the poor woman.

I had not as yet had a sleeping bag made and was carrying a down quilt—one taken from my mother's best stock. It wasn't practical, but nobody expressed any criticism. I was chilly during the nights while the other two were nice and warm under their cover of caribou skins. Apart from that, I found the traveling life exhilarating.

The dogs followed us with their traces wound around their necks. One evening, at Olrik's Bay, we found them crowded around some meat caches which turned out to contain the meat of quite a few caribou. Great joy, and huge potfuls of boiled meat! The dogs of course still got nothing. Arnarwrik could—from the way the cache was built—see that it was her brother Talilanguaq who had made it. To this day, I don't know how the Eskimos always recognize each other's meat caches, and when I asked Arnarwrik, she answered in great amazement that it was to be expected that a person knew her own brother's way of depositing meat for the winter!

We continued on our way. Asayuk maneuvered us with great caution and ability across the thin new ice of Olrik's Bay, and in the country between the bay and Inglefield Gulf we came to the end of a great long lake, where we camped. At this time a snowstorm unleashed its fury upon us. My poor quilt was covered with ice, but I came through it well enough, and when the weather cleared we started to traverse the lake in all its length. But about halfway out we discovered two people coming toward us. It was a man and a woman who had come up here to fish salmon, of which there was a plentiful supply in that lake.

They decided to go with us to the settlement of Kangerdlugssuak, one of the best hunting places in the Thule district. We realized little by little that we had met a bridal couple on their honeymoon. Of course, my traveling companions knew very well that Meqo wasn't Odark's wife, but with their people's habitual discretion it didn't occur to them to question how the wife-swapping had taken place now, during a season with no sled driving. They knew that Uvigsakavsik, who otherwise owned Meqo, was living apart from the others, though in the same inlet. However, the more curious people in that country are about something, the more silent they are, so as not to seem anxious to hear news.

This was how I met the famous Odark, Peary's companion to the North Pole, later a member of the Explorers' Club and a man honored by both the American and Danish governments. He was also a recognized shaman and the most influential of three brothers who were all great hunters and known for their power and wealth. In due time, we became fast friends and stayed so until his death in 1953. But at this first meeting, Odark became very nervous at seeing me, and his first question to Asayuk and Arnarwrik was: "Who is this white man who is coming with you?" They took that as a sure sign in itself that something unusual had happened, and in Kangerdlugssuak we were finally told that a great drama had unfolded in that inlet only a few days before. Odark and a friend of his, also a North Pole farer, had shot Uvigsakavsik and taken his two wives. Odark had lost his wife the year before, so he needed a woman. But there were other reasons to get rid of the murdered man, who had exercised a reign of terror in the tribe for many years.

He had been an interesting man, as I understood it. Some years before, he had been to New York with Peary, and when he returned and started to describe his experiences, it was soon discovered that he had indeed been far away, so far that he had forgotten to speak the truth. He tried to spread stories about how he had seen houses that drove along filled with people who smiled and looked quite unworried about the fate that awaited them. He had seen people live on top of each other, like birds in the cliffs. Yes, he had seen a lot of things that nobody could take seriously. And when he finally stretched it to the point where he told that he had been standing in a house and talked to Peary himself through a thin thread, although Peary had been in a quite different and remote settlement, then they could no longer recognize him as a worthy co-hunter of the guild. "Go to the women with your lies!" said Sorqaq, as spokesman for the men, and Uvigsakavsik was relegated to a low position in society.

He reacted to his exclusion from good company by moving far south in the Melville Bay area to a hitherto unsettled place. He allowed certain families to take land with him— those of a couple of hunters who, on account of some murders, needed isolation from avengers. Uvigsakavsik was the ruler of this outlaw village and an outstanding hunter.

When he had collected huge stores of skins and other valuables, he moved north again so that it shouldn't appear that he was afraid of other people. But he had already become quite despotic. When his wife died, he stole the wife of a younger and weaker hunter. Not satisfied with that, he desired a second wife to prepare his many skins and do the many chores that are necessary in a great hunter's house. Without ceremony, he therefore took Alakrasina, the wife of the handsome Sigdlu, and forbade Sigdlu to speak to her or even come near her. Uvigsakavsik was so strong that nobody dared intervene, and Sigdlu bided his time while his enemy became more and more arrogant. Uvigsakavsik taunted Sigdlu for his loneliness and openly described Alakrasina's attributes and erotic talents. Sooner or later, Sigdlu would have to take action, for he was a man of some reputation himself. He had just returned from the journey to the North Pole, having made the entire trek to the famous point itself. Consequently, he had rich gifts and great payment from Peary. Such a man could not tolerate having his wife abducted!

Uvigsakavsik went from bad to worse. The stores of crackers and other foods Sigdlu had received from Peary were so bulky that he couldn't store all of it in his house, and some barrels and boxes were standing outside on the beach, covered with skins. Uvigsakavsik now began to supply himself freely from these containers, and finally he went to the extent of forbidding Sigdlu to touch them any more.

His reasoning was that they belonged to Alakrasina and "since she had now changed sleeping place and husband, her food ought to go with her"! Sigdlu wouldn't pay any attention to such nonsense, of course. As if a woman could own anything—in the first place! He continued to go down and get crackers and tea from his supplies every day, as usual. But one day, as he went for his rations, Uvigsakavsik was heard shouting that he should stay away from the barrels. Sigdlu acted as if nothing had been said, but suddenly a bullet whistled over his head. Uvigsakavsik was taking potshots at him from the shelter of his house. Sigdlu took cover behind the barrel, and every time he tried to get back to his house, another bullet rent the air, too close for comfort. And from the house, Uvigsakavsik's jeering laughter was heard. When Sigdlu at last could get out from his humiliating position, he emerged with a pale and determined face. The other members of the settlement, watching from cracks and corners, did not mistake the expression and the tension rose almost to the bursting point. Something had to happen!

At this time, Odark arrived in his kayak at the settlement. This was the opportunity Sigdlu had been waiting for. Not only was Odark one of the champions of the tribe, he was also Sigdlu's old friend and companion from the North Pole journey. Besides, Odark had the purely selfish motive that he was in quest of a new wife—which he could probably get only by violence or through some convenient death, since the tribe was very short of women in those years. The two of them held a council and came to an agreement.

Uvigsakavsik felt the conspiracy against him but he—as well as Odark and Sigdlu—continued to go narwhale hunting with the other men, since an absence would have been interpreted as fear. One day, while they were all out in their kayaks, Sigdlu saw his chance and shot Uvigsakavsik, wounding his left shoulder. Uvigsakavsik almost toppled into the water, but grabbed for his gun with his right arm. However, Odark was quicker on the draw and sent a bullet through Uvigsakavsik's head. The wounded man rose for a moment in great dignity as if to speak, then he collapsed, slid out of the kayak, and sank. Thus the tribe got rid of a very disagreeable man.

Sigdlu took his Alakrasina back, and Odark took the other wife, Meqo, a clever woman, famous for her stamina and good humor, but somewhat at a disadvantage because her one eye was blind and all white.

Since Odark couldn't take his new woman in his kayak, they had walked to Kangerdlugssuak and from his home supplied themselves with the necessary gear for a honeymoon trip. Then they wandered up to the lake to fish salmon.

It was at that time that we met them. In Odark's mind was the knowledge that white men did not condone the killing of adversaries, and he suspected that I had come up to meddle in the affair. But my traveling companions assured him immediately that nobody down south knew anything about these recent events, and that I was of a friendly and peaceful nature. Odark and Meqo did not want to miss out on the great feast that our arrival at Kangerdlugssuak would occasion, so they went with us. In the settlement, we spent luxurious days. I lived with Iggianguaq, Odark's younger brother. He had a big house, and his beautiful wife, Inuarssuk, was used to the ways of white men, after having spent several years on expeditions. We were served the best of foods, caribou meat and mattak, seal liver and birds. Our dogs were fed till they could hardly budge, and never have I seen a more idyllic settlement. Three powerful brothers lived together, and two cousins of theirs had taken land with them. These five great hunters brought in a lot of game, and nobody dared to disturb their peace. Odark expressed his assurance that no avenger would come to molest him.

But at Thule there lived a strange man called Samik, which means "wrong hand," for he used his left hand for everything. His regular name was Angutdluk, but this was never used. He was a brother of the murdered Uvigsakavsik, and when Asayuk, Arnarwrik, and I returned to Thule with the sensational news, everybody expected Samik to take revenge. There was another brother living farther south, but he was known for his gentle demeanor, so everybody looked to Samik.

Now Samik was an out-and-out logician. He announced that since Sigdlu had killed his brother, it was his intention to kill Sigdlu's brother. It was true that Odark had dealt the decisive blow. But as always in this country it was "first harpoon" that gained recognition. So Sigdlu was the one who was responsible, and his brother was chosen to be killed.

This was a convenient piece of logic, indeed, for whereas both Odark and Sigdlu were strong and influential men, the brother of Sigdlu was a young and friendly man who had had nothing to do with the whole case—except that he was now to be murdered.

Knud decided that since we planned to introduce the Polar Eskimos to civilization, this was as good a time as any to intervene. He sent word north that he wished to speak to Sigdlu and his brother; Odark too was to come. They all arrived in due haste, and were lodged with us. Samik was sent for, and when everybody was present, Knud had a big pot of steaming coffee ready. There was also tobacco for everybody's pipes, and the general atmosphere was congenial.

Knud opened the negotiations by stating that it grieved him that his good friend Uvigsakavsik had passed away. But it was clear that sorrowing would not bring him back, and the important thing was to settle this matter once and for all. Of course, it would be quite correct of Samik to take revenge. But the result of that would be that he himself would be shot in due time. Now Samik had two children who would then be orphaned. And everybody knew how sad was the lot of orphans. Why expose them to all this when it could be avoided by making peace?

Knud expressed the opinion that the greatest honor was due both parties already. But to restrain oneself from shooting a man when one had the right to do so was actually the most honorable. For it showed that this person was not afraid, that he could afford to let an enemy walk about freely. Besides, it was now Knud's intention to stay in this country, provided he could procure enough fox skins to pay for ship and supplies. For that reason alone he couldn't stand quietly by while hunters were being killed. This they could all understand, and it was then resolved that no more shooting would be done in this case. They did this very quietly, as if it were a dog trade or an appointment for a hunting excursion. But in the end everybody expressed satisfaction to have peace. To further secure the pact it was decided that Krolugtenna, Sigdlu's brother, should stay in our house for an indefinite time, and his game should go to Knud who, incidentally, was also to receive five foxes from each of the parties. This was not an attorney's fee, merely an expression of joy and satisfaction which they all felt.

This was such a sensational breach of old custom that it was now quite apparent that new times had come to Thule. The report of the peace pact was quickly broadcast in the tribe; and every man, woman, and child felt proud of this omen of modern times to come.

Peary had taught these people manners and self-respect, and they were now eager to learn more of the white man's

ways. Our path was thus prepared before us, which was a
fortunate thing, for we were now expected to make decisions
in all matters of importance and especially to mediate in
strifes.

But since no group of people changes overnight, it was
not always an easy task—like the time, several years later,
when I had to sit in judgment of my good friend Kranguaq.
He had shot Sequsuna and taken his wife. The tribe was
greatly impressed, and I had to take action.

Kranguaq was really a harmless fellow. As a boy, he had
been rescued by old Mequsaq, who found his brother and
twelve other people starved to death at Cape Alexander. Only
Kranguaq and his mother Kullabak survived it. Mequsaq
took both of them with him and rescued both them and
himself at the very last moment of their endurance by catching a walrus. In the meantime, Kranguaq had—as a pastime—
cut both his frozen little toes off his feet. Navarana, who was
then a little girl, had watched this, and memory of it had
"attached them to each other."

This was the binding tie between our families. But Kranguaq had moved up to Granville Bay, together with Sequsuna
—a jocund man, always ready for fun, and well-liked by
all. He was commonly known for the fact that his head was
oblique, as if one of the neck muscles was too short.

Unhappily, Kranguaq's wife died. He was therefore forced
to let Sequsuna's wife sew for him, and the husband's permission to do this was continuously needed. Also, Kranguaq
was quite naturally in regular need of some womanly cor-
poral tenderness, and in this respect also he had to make
application to Sequsuna, who was a passionate teaser; he had
often given permission that something could be sewn for
Kranguaq, only to tear the half-finished piece of clothing
from his wife and put her to chewing skins instead. He would
also give permission for Kranguaq to sleep with his wife for
a night, but when bedtime came he didn't remove himself
from the bunk, as custom and common decency otherwise
commanded. The woman and Kranguaq tried to get back at
him by taking a walk in the hills together, but Sequsuna beat
her cruelly when they came back. No wonder Kranguaq felt
somewhat oppressed at the little settlement, but what was
he to do? It was also said that the woman had incited him.
Navarana told me that time and again, when Sequsuna was
beating her, she cried out, "Toqorale, toqorale! Kill him,
kill him!"

Finally, when they were out hunting one day, the young man lost all patience. Sequsuna was wont to say, when they were returning home in the evening: "Naw, naw! it shall be delightful to get home to the wife!" And he would thereupon proceed to give various sexual descriptions that Navarana found "tending to increase a man's fury." This happened several times, Kranguaq had said; the end of it was that he shot Sequsuna and threw him in the water.

In the evening, he came driving home to the settlement with both sleds and all the dogs, so it was clear to the wife and her old mother what had happened. Kranguaq reported the demise by saying that he had not as yet decided if "a man ought to move into the house he had inhabited heretofore, or if the other one is more suited to fill us both with joy."

The state of things was accepted, as always. When he encountered some relatives of Sequsuna, who were down to trade, he reported that Sequsuna had fallen in the water "without ability to come up again." And that was all he told me. But to Navarana he wasn't at all unwilling to play the role of fearsome murderer and rapacious usurper of a new wife—even if it was the fat hag we knew so well already.

I had to say something. "Listen, Kranguaq, I hear that you have killed your hunting mate!"

"Do not speak to me, I am without decency, not worthy to be addressed by a white man. I am good for nothing. I have killed my hunting mate!"

This set me back a little, so I started a speech about how it gave a feeling of insecurity in the entire tribe when that kind of thing took place. He told me I was right, and he added that he now was the cause of fear spreading to the various settlements. Many would fear him as a murderer, and young men would try to imitate him. To that I answered that his likes ought not to live among the rest of us.

"You spoke true and wisely. I am unworthy to live among others. You had better throw me out!"

We continued in this manner. When I said he was a terrible fellow, he called himself horrible. When I said that in my country such persons were punished, he answered that that was their just desert. He himself ought to have the severest punishment possible. When I extolled the virtues of the demised one, he tearfully regretted having robbed the tribe of this valuable man. "Myself, I am quite impossible, improvement is not conceivable! Decency is not to be found in my body! Ability at hunting I have never shown!"

It is difficult when the one you want to reprimand constantly outbids you. So at last I didn't know what to say. I ended up declaring that it had been better if Sequsuna had shot Kranguaq, since the former had always delivered more fox skins to our shop than Kranguaq, who was a miserable trapper. He gave me right again, and I adjourned the court. That is, the two of us, and our audience, went inside to have coffee and cake. Navarana had acquired great science in cooking and baking from the Danish outpost at Tassiussak, so we always treated royally.

Over coffee and cake, Kranguaq told me that he was faced with an embarrassing duty. He had to bring Sequsuna's son up to avenge his father. But since the murderer was himself, odd situations could arise, particularly since they were very fond of each other.

Strangely enough, I was the one who got the strongest rebuke in this murder case. For the Eskimos had reported it to the missionary in such a way that I was supposed to have said that it wasn't so bad to shoot the unsuccessful hunters—especially bad fox trappers—but the good suppliers should be left in peace. The missionary thought that this was a regrettable standpoint on justice, and it took me quite a while to explain it away.

Eventually we introduced the Eskimos to parliamentary lawgiving. In 1920, Knud called the hunters of the tribe together and said that, having listened to the wisdom of the old ones, he proposed to make some tribal laws. This sounded exactly like what went on in the white men's country, and the idea was accepted with enthusiasm. So, after meetings and festival and fun, the Thule Law was born. Everybody promised solemnly to uphold it, and a council was formed to enforce it.

Soon afterward, in 1921, the Thule district was taken over by the Danish government, which had discerned the superiority of the Smith Sound Eskimos over the Greenlanders of the south. Also, the tribe was rather wealthy; the bird cliffs provided a multitude of foxes, and the people could buy what they pleased. A period of good years began which—without the Thule Law—might not have been. One of the most important reasons for making the Thule Law was the need of game protection. Before firearms reached the country, all animals were tame and could be captured at the close range necessitated by the primitive weapons. With the guns came trouble. Hunters, especially the young men, would shoot at a seal or a walrus on the spur of the moment, and lose it as it sank dead into the water. If only wounded, an animal would swim about in terror, warning its fellows of the hunter. Much damage was done before shooting of game was regulated by law. Most important among the Thule Laws, and instrumental in preserving the game of the district, was the one forbidding a man to shoot a seal or a walrus without first having put a harpoon in it, with a bladder attached to keep it afloat.

The Thule Law stayed in effect until 1950, when all Greenland laws were revised by a Danish commission to better suit the modern times. But the old Eskimo jurisdiction, in which it is sufficient to publicize a crime, remained pretty effective and has partly been inherited by the present generation, although under different forms. No longer do they have song competitions where the offended one challenges his adversary to the beat of the drum and seeks to ridicule him by mocking the man who doesn't have the ability to procure for himself the things he desires, but has to resort to thieving and robbery to get them. One is here faced with the basic rule that to improve the one who shames society one must make him appear ludicrous. No Eskimo—or Greenlander, for that matter—can bear this. He finds it so utterly horrible that people laugh at him that he promptly tries to improve.

At Thule, most things were common property. Besides, the people had—for practical reasons—made it a basic rule that "theft is permitted if a person badly needs what he takes."

All the meat that was brought home from the hunt was laid up on the same meat rack, within a high stone building, where it would be safe from the always hungry dogs. Every man's catch was lying there. We often wondered how each hunter knew exactly what pieces were his. It was dark in winter, all meat was frozen in lumps, and perhaps many huge blocks of meat were at hand, but every man could rather quickly find his game and bring it into the house, where it was to be thawed or eaten frozen.

Anybody at all was allowed to feast on what he desired to eat. He would just simply climb up on the meat rack and sit there with an axe or a knife and hew off what he wanted. Nobody said a word about it. Maybe it wasn't always looked upon with happy eyes, but no hunter would debase himself to protest, because that would expose him as a bad hunter who could not provide all the things he desired.

Sometimes, our wives couldn't help getting excited when we had something particularly delicious lying out there, and other men feasted themselves too much upon what we wanted to reserve for our own children. Then a wife might come out and shout to the gourmands who were sitting up there and stuffing themselves: "Listen, show a little modesty! Please let my little children taste their father's catch! Why don't you provide for yourselves what you seem to appreciate so much?"

Then etiquette demanded that the husband come darting out and chase his wife away. "What words are you speaking to men? Shall a mere woman blame men for their desires? Alas, I am ashamed because I haven't taken care to beat good manners into my avaricious and stubborn wife!"

This was an act, of course, put on to maintain the honor of the house, but it often got good results, and the uninvited guests withdrew.

Semigaq, one of the old women who came to live and serve in our house at Thule, told me about a man named Kayuk who stood his ground against any such hint. He was one of the four husbands she had had, and he was widely known for pilfering for himself all good-tasting things. Modesty was unknown to him, and he was even called a thief. His fellow villagers had much to tell about his behavior; Kayuk was considered dishonest.

Kayuk was very fond of eating newborn dog puppies. He obtained them by visiting a hunter whose bitch had just had puppies. He would first highly praise the dogs; no Eskimo can resist that, he feels extremely flattered. Then Kayuk would pick up a puppy as if to look closer at it. But it always happened that he dropped it rather hard upon the rocky ground, and the puppy died. It was then without value, and Kayuk took it away with him. He sneaked up in the mountains and boiled it in a tin can that he had obtained from some white men. Semigaq told me that she often went up there, when she saw the smoke come up, and saw her husband sitting there and boiling this meal for himself. She felt very ashamed. But nobody could say anything to him, for it might easily be that one of the male dogs had gotten loose and had eaten the puppy.

But justice came to Kayuk one winter. He had a weakness for frozen liver. He himself went out hunting very little, but when somebody else brought home game and reported his catch, Kayuk immediately went to visit that particular house. And when people had seal liver lying on the meat rack to be frozen and served as a special delicacy when they had guests, he would often make himself comfortable upon the meat rack and devour every bite.

One of the hunters got fed up with that. He had a dog that was getting old and useless, so he killed it and placed its liver on the meat rack. It was dark, and liver looks like liver. But dog liver is poisonous, unfit for human consumption. Kayuk suspected nothing, he had been out to look at his traps, and the very same evening he was up there eating away lustily. The other villagers invented excuses to go out and watch him and—for once—enjoy his gluttony.

The next morning he was sick and suffered terribly. He became almost paralyzed, his skin peeled off, and his eyes were very weak for months after. But he didn't die in this round. The next year, when Kayuk drowned, it was naturally considered to be a punishment from Silarssuaq, the great spirit of justice, who hits all offenders.

Here a modern society would find that death for having eaten too much seal liver was too hard a sentence. Kayuk had brought shame upon his family and been a bad example, so they found it better to get rid of him.

Thieving, as such, was perhaps never entirely removed from the Eskimos' thoughts during my time. While it is permissible to take anything edible stored in a settlement, the limit is easily reached. Where is the line where stealing begins? Everybody lives together, everybody knows what each one owns, so there is no possibility of possessing things that belong to others without everybody's quickly knowing it. And to exchange stolen goods is impossible. So it is largely due to dire necessity that everybody is honest.

Nor was there any separate estate in the traditional Western sense. Every settlement had houses to return to for the winter, but they never belonged to anybody in particular. New houses were built, but mostly it was old and even ancient house ruins that were made livable when fall came. The man who repaired a house for his family to live in had a right to it. But if strangers came to the settlement during the winter, they were entitled to move in with any family they pleased. The game they brought in while they were guests went to the common household, and to partake of the meat from people's pots was everyone's privilege. Meat stores put down in stone caches for winter supplies could be opened by any man at his pleasure: he could both feed his dogs and fill his own stomach. Nobody said anything against either. But it was a duty to cover again what wasn't used. To let it lie about unprotected or badly covered so that foxes and bears could get at it was considered thievery and dishonesty.

If a man was hungry, and happened upon another man's fox trap, it was perfectly legal to take the fox and eat it. But courtesy commanded that the skin be brought to the owner. It could happen that this was impossible if the fox was dead and frozen stiff so that it couldn't be skinned. But then, at least, it was an obligation to set the trap again so that another fox might get caught in it.

The feeling of all-inclusive community property was difficult to eradicate. Applied to the civilized state of things, it could often be exasperating. When we first got kerosene burners at Thule and traded them to the natives, we began to notice that the Eskimos freely came up to tap kerosene from our barrel. I explained to them that this was not a thing to do. They understood me only faintly, and they finally told me that surely we had to be paid for the kerosene, but why not then set the price of kerosene burners at such a level that everybody could tap from the barrels when they needed to?

This old code aided the Polar Eskimos to live in relative security even before the advent of the Thule Law, and develop into the noblest strain of their race. Up to modern times they were of course a small isolated tribe in their own corner of the arctic world and were undisturbed by outsiders. When we visited the Canadian Eskimos during the Fifth Thule Expedition, we found many conditions quite different. In Canada there are no natural boundaries between the various tribes, and strifes and warfare were common at that time.

The worst state of affairs was found by Knud when he visited the Netchiliks. This tribe leads an extremely difficult existence in the vicinity of King William Island. Knud found that, of the girl babies born to the women he interviewed, more than half had been killed at birth. The shortage of women was acute; abductions and wife robberies flourished. Because of the ensuing vendettas no man in the tribe knew himself safe. When the families of a settlement undertook a trip, they fared with their sleds in single file. No man dared to step out of this formation, even to do necessary natural business, for the man in front of him would immediately suspect foul play, and being of quick tempers they preferred to shoot first and ask questions later. When the formation came to a settlement where they wanted to visit, they stopped at some distance. Some old woman was then sent to see the chief hunter of the place, bearing gifts and negotiating a truce. Only when she returned, with the assurance that no violence was to be expected, did the sled train proceed in among the houses. For a lone couple to visit a settlement was quite out of the question. At the slightest provocation, the man would be killed and his wife taken by one of the hunters at the place.

Knud once asked an assembly of Netchilik men about their glorious past. Out of twenty-one, not less than fifteen had been involved in one or more murders.

Under such conditions, even the famed Mounted Police had largely to limit themselves to protecting the white man's interests in the country. The white men, themselves, often gave the Eskimos none too good an example to live up to. In Hudson Bay I visited trading stations that competed with each other with methods that in Greenland would have brought the strongest rebuke from the Danish government. Even the missionaries of the various creeds fought each other in a way nobody would think possible. As for the Mounted Police, they were good and dedicated men, but they often lacked understanding of the Eskimos' customs and psyche.

Take the case of the white trader named Janes who was murdered at Igloolik (at Fury and Hecla straits) some years before I visited the place. Janes had an odd method of trading: he would force the Eskimos to give up their fox skins at the point of a revolver. When the Eskimos had had enough of that, they sent for Nuralak, a quick young man who had already distinguished himself by killing a couple of people. Nuralak rid them of Janes, and from their point of view it was a heroic deed for their own protection and fully justified. But the Mounted Police did not look at it the same way. They arrested Nuralak, put him to trial, and he was sentenced to ten years' imprisonment in Ottawa.

On my way from Hudson Bay back to Thule, I visited Igloolik and met Nuralak's father, Umilik. He was as proud as a Spanish noble because his son had reaped such reward for his heroic deed from the white men; they kept him in a big house at one of their huge settlements and supplied him

An Eskimo camp on the move across the ice of Pond Inlet in the Eastern Arctic

Peter Freuchen with young explorer, Knud Rasmussen

Eskimo mother and her child

An Eskimo beauty,
16-year-old Elizabeth, of
Frobisher Bay

Top: An old Eskimo settlement near Thule, Greenland, where summer homes are made of sod. Below: Eskimo couple at home

Top left: Navarana, Pipaluk, Peter Freuchen and Mequsak. Bottom left: Pupils at the Resolute Bay Eskimo School. Above: Eskimos establish summer encampment on the shores of Eclipse Sound

Top: Inspecting a harpooned seal at Pound Harbor. Below: Building an igloo on Baker Lake near Hudson Bay

Top: Boys dance to concertina music, Resolute Bay. Below: Searching for seal asleep on the ice, White Bay, Baffin Island, on Eclipse Sound

Peter Freuchen leaves Copenhagen in 1930 for Greenland as a Secretary for the Prime Minister

Eskimos return from hunting. Float attached to harpoon line is made from air-filled sealskin

with food and clothes without any effort or payment in return. To the poor Eskimo, with his existence at the brink of death and starvation, this must indeed have seemed like a paradise. He ascribed the success of his family to the fact that they had adopted the Christian faith, because such things had never happened in dark pagan times. There had been some tendency to return to the beliefs of the forefathers, for the weather had been bad all summer. But Umilik and his reference to the triumph of his son always made the apostates return.

As was bound to happen, Nuralak later got tuberculosis in prison. He was released and sent back to his tribe, where he soon died. He was one of the many cases which demonstrated how utterly fruitless and meaningless imprisonment was in dealing with the Eskimos.

Some years after the Fifth Thule Expedition, the Canadian government sent for Knud Rasmussen. It had finally become clear to them that it was necessary to deal more effectively with the Eskimos by getting to know them better and taking their ways and beliefs into account. Knud became their counsel in this new development that has now given the Canadian Eskimo both wealth and security.

Even in Greenland to this day there are no prisons, although the economic expansion of the last years has made it as modern a country as any. By and large, the old Eskimo way of advertising a felon's shame is still pretty effective.

7   Eskimos as Servants

WHEN I LIVED at the edge of Hudson Bay, I had a manservant named Inuijak, which means "the doll." He was not especially easy to look at, but his inner virtues were marvelous in every way. The most noticeable thing about him was his almost unbelievable endurance and constancy. What he began, he finished; whatever he did, he did with all his heart and soul.

When, for example, he lay down to sleep, he *slept*: long

and deeply, and deaf to all sound, sunk in realms far removed from his workaday life.

Knud always felt a great desire to do those things no one else could accomplish, and he had often boasted that he could easily wake Inuijak, if he had to. He didn't understand why I found it so difficult.

One day I wanted to go on a trip. Inuijak had slept for seventeen hours, and surely should have had enough sleep by now. But no matter what I did, I couldn't waken him. So I called Knud and told him that here was his chance to show what he could do: would he please waken my man? Nothing easier, said Knud, and he began to tickle Inuijak in all those places where people are ticklish, but to no avail. Then he pulled a handful of hair out of the head of the sleeper. But Inuijak merely scratched his head a bit, turned over on his back and slept on with open mouth—snoring like a walrus.

Inuijak was a great lover of sweets. So Knud emptied the sugar bowl into his mouth in the hope that this would waken him into activity. But no, Inuijak slept.

Knud then took his shotgun, opened the door, sat down a couple of feet from the head of the sleeper, and fired. It made a frightful noise in our little hut, and shook it from one end to the other. The only one who didn't hear it was Inuijak. Knud tried in many other ways to wake Inuijak; he used fantastic ingenuity and expended all kinds of energy. But when Inuijak wakened of his own accord four hours later, he had slept peacefully without even a disturbing dream.

In addition to being a good sleeper, Inuijak was also a good trencherman. When we were on the hunt, and lived on the catch, it was impossible to control his appetite. He ate until there was nothing more, or until he was taken forcibly from the food, or until he fell asleep.

But of course at home in our expedition-headquarters, we always had civilized—or at least nearly civilized—manners. We ate at a table and we used plates, knives, and forks. The whole outlay had a most cultured appearance. Inuijak, however, didn't fare so well there; his food was dished up for him, and even though he always had the hugest helping, a plate could hold only so much. So after Inuijak had emptied his plate, he emptied the bowls; and when there was nothing in them, he then went after the cooking pots. Even after that, he would still look mournfully about him, and with a most reproachful look, would lick the pot and bowls and plates so clean that it wasn't necessary to wash dishes. At least he saved the cook a great deal of inconvenience.

I don't want to give a misleading picture of this worthy man. So I must admit that his working ability was, if not excellent, at least marked by perseverance. When he was on the hunt, he hunted until he had a bag, although it might take days to get one. In this way he sometimes went without food for a considerable length of time. Perhaps it wasn't so strange, after all, that he sometimes took his revenge for forced hunger.

But work in the usual sense of the word was unknown to him. One day I decided that the time had come for him to learn about it. The snow was just beginning to melt, and I gave him orders to shovel it away from our huts and to make paths through it. Inuijak was a man of the great open spaces, so he energetically tried to convince me of the foolishness of my request; in a little while the weather would be warm and the snow would melt, he argued, so why take the trouble to toss it around?

No, I replied, it must be taken out of the way.

Well, he shot back, he and his people weren't afraid to crawl over a snowdrift, and if *they*, who lived their whole lives up here, could put up with the snow, he supposed I could do as much—I, who intended to remain only a few years.

Nevertheless, after all the debate, I put an end to our discussion by stating that the snow must be shoveled away. "Now you begin here," I said, "and shovel a path along the house, and I'll come out and tell you when you've gone far enough!" Then I went indoors to my own work.

Soon it was time for supper. The hungry were called, and we ate. But Inuijak didn't show up. I had forgotten all about him, and as people often happened to miss a meal, having gone on a trip or on the hunt, no one thought of Inuijak that evening.

When the meal was over, and we'd talked a while about the events of the day, I worked out some astronomical observations which occupied me for some time; with that finished, I suddenly became sleepy, so I went to bed and slept well into the next day. After breakfast, I went outdoors to take a look at the weather, and to see what might be going on in the village.

There was not a disturbing thought in my mind, when

far, far away I spied the figure of a man who shoveled snow furiously. It was Inuijak. The snow was piled high about him, and he had shoveled a long trench from the house and way out over the hill for more than two miles. I hurried out to him, and asked what in the world he was doing there.

Well, he replied, he was shoveling snow as I'd told him. And while we talked, and while we ate and slept, he had continued shoveling energetically.

"But," I said, "can't you see that it's absolutely idiotic to shovel snow out here on the cliff where it won't do any good?"

Only now did Inuijak stop his work, set the shovel from him and look me right in the eye. "I never could see any reason for it. *But you ran around here and insisted on my doing it!*"

Inuijak never shoveled snow again.

8   The Eskimo Mind

Life and Death

THE ESKIMO is generally pictured as good-natured, amiable, and obliging. But few people have gone beyond this very superficial description of his nature, and there are none who claim to have reached an understanding of his psyche. Though I myself spent more than half a century with the Eskimos, I do not believe I ever completely understood them. On the contrary, I know less now than when I first went to the Arctic, believing in my youthful inexperience, that after a year or two I would have the logical explanation of all arctic phenomena. I gradually began to see that there were many things that I had misunderstood in the beginning. And after ten or fifteen years among the Eskimos, I finally realized that problems deepened into mysteries; and that I knew practically nothing about them. Their souls had depths almost impossible for a white man to penetrate.

Partly out of contempt and partly out of fear, Eskimos made it a habit not to confide too much in the white men.

They had contempt because they saw how helpless white men often were under arctic conditions. How often did I hear them say: "They are like newborn children in our country, and it would be below one's dignity to contradict a senseless child." So they did not contradict the white man and his willful spirit, but let him think and judge as wrongly as he pleased. But Eskimos also feared white people because of their power and riches and concealed their deeper reasonings from them, especially when whites scoffed at their beliefs and traditions or tried to change them overnight without trying to understand the circumstances that conditioned them. Navarana, during our eleven years of marriage, told me many things that otherwise would never have been disclosed to me.

If, as a stranger, you come to an Eskimo and ask his help for some task or other, he will almost always receive you kindly and promise his assistance. He will usually answer yes to anything you ask him, and inexperienced people have often taken this for dishonesty, whereas it is really a wish to please. If you ask him something, he tries to find out what answer you want and then proceeds to give it to you. Suppose that you want to ask him if a certain road can be traveled, and you say: "I want to go that way; do you think it can be done?" He will reply, as a rule: "Yes, the road can be traveled." It is not in his mind to deceive you, but if you should then happen to ask him to accompany you, there will be something wrong which prevents his going with you. He may claim that his dogs are in bad condition if it is a sled journey, or that his kayak has holes in it, if it is a rowing job to be done. If you insist, he may finally promise to undertake the trip with you, but the next morning he will withdraw with the excuse that his wife is ill, that his child will miss him, or some other such thing.

It must also be considered that the Eskimo never thinks much beyond the present, and it usually wouldn't occur to him that his little pleasantry might have disagreeable consequences. He takes care of his problems for the day and trusts that he can do likewise tomorrow. When you learn to know him better, you may be able to distinguish between his yes and his no even if—philologically—the words don't convey the meaning. Sometimes his answer to your question is "Perhaps." The intonation or the accompanying gestures will tell you whether it is yes or no. Peace is all the Eskimo wants. His whole life is a fight against nature, a fight in tension where life itself is often at stake, and therefore—in his home and in his associations with other people—he tries to have the peace and quiet that is his desire.

It is easy to see how white men, having only a superficial knowledge of the Eskimo psyche, would give them a reputation for being lazy and unreliable. A famous example is that of two American scientists, Radford and Street, who in the year 1913 were stabbed to death by Eskimos of the Musk-ox people. They were making a journey across the Barren Grounds to the Arctic Sea coast. At the head of Bathurst Inlet, where they wished to obtain helpers for the rest of the trip westward, they had a quarrel with the natives—one which ended fatally. It has been reported that Radford was a fiery-tempered man who whipped the Eskimos who wouldn't accompany him. So he not only had himself to blame for what happened, but he also misunderstood the nature of the Eskimos' resistance. The fact is that Eskimo hunters—if they had gone on the trip—almost surely would have been trapped by the spring thaw, and their wives and children would have starved to death over the summer. It is therefore interesting to read the testimony given about the Eskimos by the leader of the Mounties patrol: "They are all born thieves, awful liars, and so absolutely untrustworthy that I would not be surprised if I heard before long that more murders have been committed, as every one of them is willing to sell his soul for a rifle."

Denmark has the distinction of having been associated with the largest group of Eskimos for the longest time. I shall always maintain that Greenland, as a colony, got a better deal from Denmark than other European countries gave their colonies. But I have always been struck by the complete lack of confidence which the Danes showed in the natives. When I started traveling in Greenland, the Eskimos were allowed to have muzzle-loaders only. It was too dangerous, really, to let these people have breech-loaders. It was commonly supposed that they immediately would begin carelessly to shoot each other down. "Believe me, we know them," an experienced hand told me.

In time, of course, these worries turned out to be unfounded. Even so, I remember when Dr. Deichmann brought the first motorboat to Greenland; he, and other physicians after him, had to take a course at home in tending a motorboat, and they had to promise solemnly that they never would let a Greenlander get near it. It was believed with absolute certainty that each Eskimo would forthwith rush up and stick his fingers into the motor. No one ever explained what it would be that could tempt the Eskimo to do that.

The telegraph came to Greenland. This was assumed to be a decidedly difficult field which these low-cultured people couldn't master. But today all radio stations are served by Greenlanders.

And so it was with almost all things. It took some doing before we were allowed to have kerosene in Greenland. I was informed by people in the government that if the Greenlanders were given kerosene, they would surely amuse themselves by throwing burning matches into the barrels. I tried to assure my informant that if you throw a burning match into a barrel of kerosene, the match will go out, and besides, I couldn't see what should give the Greenlanders such inclinations. I was then told that I was a disagreeable person who would be best to shut up when my betters were speaking.

The Danes in Greenland have never been malicious. But many of them came up there imagining that Greenlanders were big children and had to be treated as such. These same people had never tried to sit in a kayak or stand by a blowhole or fish cod in order to provide for a family at the incredibly low prices the producers were offered at that time. They had no occasion to see how a hunter or fisherman had to brave the world's hardest climate and most inhospitable conditions of nature and come out ahead.

Also, many Danes had the idea that the Greenlanders were lazy, or uneconomical and lacking in energy. It was argued that they didn't use "every opportunity" to go hunting. But in the first place those who said that kind of thing knew nothing of the life and treks of the game. In the second place, there was absolutely nothing in life that could tempt a hunter to provide anything more than what was necessary. The articles on sale at the colony trading stations were good, but dull as dishwater. There were some tools and a little cotton goods, etc., but nothing tempting. There was nothing to look forward to, nothing to rouse the enthusiasm. That is why the natives must be admired for pitching in as they did. They worked as *kivfaks* (servants) for starvation wages, they had to be at the beck and call of young and inexperienced government assistants. That they didn't lose patience shows more than anything else that the Greenland Eskimos had a large spiritual reserve.

There was prejudice against Eskimos on the part of white men. I saw it clearly myself when I married Navarana. Danes wrote to me pleading with me not to do it. I would put myself in a lower class. It was a disgrace to my name as a Dane, etc. During trips, I stopped overnight with Danes who invited me to their table but said: "There is something provided for your wife in the kitchen." When I then told them that I would prefer to eat with the Greenlanders, because they had the good grace not to look down upon me because I was born in another country, they just said: "Well, but we never take Greenlanders into our apartment." I hasten to state that such experiences were exceptions.

But since I witnessed a smiling tolerance on the part of my wife when people tried to make her feel that she was "only" a Greenlander, I came to understand what a fine and tactful people the Greenland Eskimos really are. Time and again, their integrity was violated, they were exposed to obscenities and impertinence, but they always had the serenity to be silent and think. When I myself felt angered at hearing a Dane address a Greenlander impertinently, I perceived a little glint in the eyes of the latter and understood that this Greenlander was often more dignified than the one who was debasing him.

I remember my friend "Little Jonas," in Proeven. Once, I heard the wife of the colony manager use coarse and obscene language on him who, as a master hunter, often fed the whole settlement. Little Jonas stood there quietly and let her rave for a while. Then he said: "Alas, you are a child in this country, and a child in your thoughts. It is impossible to be angry with a child; it would be a loss of dignity!"

It must not be presumed that Eskimos are never highstrung, never suffer from nerves, or the like. Quite the opposite is true. As with other primitive people, their nerves are always just below the skin. Their indifference to death may often give them a tranquility that Christian people can envy, but they are afraid of all inexplicable things, and they have no organized religion as a guiding line for their daily lives. They explain all phenomena by populating nature and lifeless things with spirits whose malevolent or benevolent intentions determine what happens. Otherwise, they are really individualists in their beliefs; they let everybody believe what he pleases. Their religion is really only a set of rules to help them in their fight for existence, and their clergy—the angakoks—are only intermediaries between them and the spirits of nature. Thus, when you penetrate a little below the smiling amiability of the Eskimo, a deep violent fantasy is revealed, a profoundly reasoned speculation on the conditions and circumstances of his life.

Eskimos have many strangely naive and beautiful beliefs about death. In general, though, they merely say that death can either be the end of it all or a transition into something new, and that in either case there is nothing to fear. It sounds strange to get such an agnostic answer from the very same people who—five minutes before, perhaps—told you that the aurora borealis is the souls of deadborn children who dance and play football with their umbilical cords. Or they may have told you about angakoks who have descended to the underworld and met the souls of people who had committed crimes. It is as if they one day believe in the continuation of life after death, and the next day don't take it into consideration. Life is their essential concern. The thought of death is remote.

But suicides are numerous among them. If they are hit with sickness, if great human sorrows weigh them down, when—as they express it—"life is heavier than death," then no man hesitates to make an end of his torment and cross into the distant land. In many places, voluntary death is normal for old men and women who are burdened with the memories of their youth, and who can no longer meet the demands of their own reputation. Old people kill themselves to avoid being a hindrance to their kin.

Fear of death is unknown to them, they know only love of life. The Eskimos are themselves unaware of the difficulty of their existence, they always enjoy life with an enviable intensity, and they believe themselves to be the happiest people on earth living in the most beautiful country there is. When an old man sees the young men go out hunting and cannot himself go along, he is sorry. When he has to ask other people for skins for his clothing, when he cannot ever again be the one to invite the neighbors to eat his game, life is of no value to him. Rheumatism and other ills may plague him, and he wants to die. This has been done in different ways in different tribes, but everywhere it is held that if a man feels himself to be a nuisance, his love for his kin, coupled with the sorrow of not being able to take part in the things which are worthwhile, impels him to die.

In some tribes, an old man wants his oldest son or favorite daughter to be the one to put the string around his neck and hoist him to his death. This was always done at the height of a party where good things were being eaten, where everyone

—including the one who was about to die—felt happy and gay, and which would end with the angakok conjuring and dancing to chase out the evil spirits. At the end of his performance, he would give a special rope made of seal and walrus skin to the "executioner," who then placed it over the beam in the roof of the house and fastened it around the neck of the old man. Then the two rubbed noses, and the young man pulled the rope. Everybody in the house either helped or sat on the end of the rope so as to have the honor of bringing the old suffering one to the Happy Hunting Grounds where there would always be light and plenty of game of all kinds. There a man can decide whether he wants to go bear hunting, caribou hunting, or fight the walrus in a kayak.

Old women may sometimes prefer to be stabbed with a dagger into the heart—a thing which is also done by a son or a daughter or whoever is available for the deed. There is absolutely no cruelty connected with this. They just believe that life has come to an end. The many suicides and murders among the primitive Eskimos must be seen in the light of this intimacy with death.

Take, for instance, this imaginary account of a hunter, Mala, his wife Iva, his two sons, and his mother, old Naterk, on a sled journey to the faraway trading post.

They had to continue after their rest. Everybody had slept a lot, and Naterk had been happy to rest. Her old legs were sore, and the air whined in her chest.

It was strange when they started again. The others were rested from lying still, but old Naterk had become more tired, it seemed, and when the sun had turned a little, she was almost exhausted.

"I forgot something on the sled!"

And she walked slower than the others and let them pass her, and the dogs caught up with her. She walked for a little while by the sled and supported herself on it, but soon she lagged behind, so they had to wait for her by a ravine. When she reached them at last, she was quite red in the face, as if she had been running very fast on a summer's day.

"Let us try with a cane," she said, and pulled a harpoon stock out of the load.

"Sit on top of the load and rest," said her son.

"As if the dogs don't have enough to pull and you not enough to guide along. Since I am a human, it is best that I walk."

And then she took the lead, such as she was used to, and
Mala restrained the dogs, so that they wouldn't catch up
with her. Every time they stopped, he examined the sled
runners, repaired the ice layer on them, and was slow to
get started again, so that old Naterk could hold her lead
for most of the day. But she was too weak to feel any pleasure. The effect was so great that it was a pity to behold. And
Mala stopped early in the day out of pity for his old brave
mother.

"She is tired, and the going is rough," he said. "Grandmama has difficulty walking. The snow is high."

The children didn't understand it and began to boast a
little about how fast they had walked, and their father lauded
them. They were good boys, and swift at walking, he said.

In the evening, Naterk wasn't hungry and just lay there
panting, like a walrus lying on the surface collecting strength.

Pualu took a marrow bone that his father had split for
him and extracted the marrow like a long fat worm, held
it up to Grandmama's mouth and buttered her lips with the
delicious tidbit.

"Eat," he said. "I shall go out and shoot a great caribou
for you. I shall catch good things."

The old woman was touched and said that he was a great
hunter who brought delicious things home to his old grandmother.

"No," said Pualu, "but I am one who wants eating to be
done where I am, for those who don't eat cannot say amusing things."

"Yes, come then, your grandmama shall eat of your game."

While the others slept, Naterk couldn't find peace. She
was hot in her head, it whined in her chest, and her whole
body ached. She chopped some lumps of snow out of the
bunk and put them upon her forehead, and she thought of
some powerful magic formulas that had helped many before
her. But the words had no strength; perhaps she shouldn't
have said them while she was not alone, but she was afraid
she would wake the others if she got up and went out. She
really wanted to stay in bed and sleep, anyway, only she
couldn't sleep. She thought of all the happy talk she had
heard in her youth, of all the men who had embraced her,
but everything started to run in confused circles, and she
was happy when the others started to get up.

Naterk took her time getting out Upik's clothes, boots,
and mittens that morning. She rubbed them as usual, but it

tired her. She then put her fur coat on and crawled out through the entrance, out into the fresh air. Her old spine hurt when she stood up and smelled the air. She went over to the hill neighboring the igloo and sat down there, looking out over the country. She took off her chest strap and wound it tightly around her left foot. Out there Naterk sat without people around her, and she wanted to summon the spirits to hear her fate. All her life, her foot spirit had answered obscure riddles, and now she was trying to call it, but it didn't want to emerge. One has to be strong and believe in order to have power over the helping spirits, or else they stay away.

She returned while Mala was fixing the sled to continue the trip. With his mouth he sprayed water over the runners to smooth them out.

"I have something to say, and my words are strong," said Naterk. And her son understood that this wasn't ordinary women's gossip. There was an expression on his mother's face that made him little again, and he bent down to her.

"I am tired, and I am old. You must build me an igloo, for now I must travel alone."

"Don't say that, Mother. We still want to see your face among us, and I will not build you any igloo. Let us go down to the white men and the ships, to tea and tobacco!"

"Oh, my son Mala, I am tired. Therefore I have to rest."

"Mother," answered Mala, "think of the children. They will miss you, they will cry, and Iva will lack your help and good advice. As for myself, I have always had your face before me, and I cannot be without you."

Naterk said nothing for a while. Her mouth trembled a little as she glanced toward the horizon. Far away, she saw the domed mountain where the mountain spirit sucked caribou in through his nostrils when he drew his breath. Here she had lived as long as she could remember.

"Hand me my cane," she said to her son. "I'll walk ahead." And nothing more was spoken.

Mala hurried over to his pot, from which he drank the water to spray over the sled runners. His face became quite black when he drank from the pot, for the soot from the blubber lamp sat thick on it.

The old one waddled along and made headway; it was a little while before the rest of them caught up with her. They were talking about some caribou tracks they had seen and some lemmings that had run past in the snow.

In the middle of the day, the old one was tired again, but

now Mala insisted that she sit down on the sled, and she sat there freezing while the others worked hard for her.

Now Iva took the lead. Iva was young and strong.

That night, Naterk groaned a lot. Her back was aching, and she had violent pains in her limbs. She wasn't aware that Iva lit her lamp, but the others saw that the perspiration was trickling down her face, and she thought strange thoughts and spoke mysterious words. She imagined she was young again, and that it was summer, and nobody understood her speech.

Iva put her clothes on, sat down by the old one's side and called her, but Naterk didn't answer. Then Iva took hold of Naterk's hair in the middle of her forehead and pulled it out in small wisps. The wisps were put in the fire. The smell would drive out the evil spirits, and the seat of the sickness would be burned up. It helped, and Naterk became able to think again. She got hold of a couple of pieces of dried caribou meat from last year. She scraped the hairs and mold off them with her nails, and treated the boys to them.

In the morning the sun was shining, and they continued their journey. But about noon, Naterk pulled up her fur hood and went to speak to Mala.

"My son, now I have words that are firm, and which you must not contradict. My years are many, and my legs are tired. Build me an igloo. When I asked you, you didn't want to. If I now must say it again, then it becomes a command, and don't let it be that I must give my son a command to get my way."

She stood there for a moment arranging something in the sled load, then she brushed the snow off the oldest boy, who had fallen during the game.

Mala said nothing, he took his snow gauge, felt the snow, and began building the house.

"Are we stopping already?" said the children.

"Yes," said Iva. "Your father has decided to stop."

And Mala built the igloo.

The two women took their baggage off the sled as usual, they tightened the cracks in the igloo and poured snow over it. The boys took a sealskin, tied a strap to it, and made a toboggan out of it.

Pualu was so big that he wanted to help in building the house, so Upik was alone and without a dog to pull him. So he called his grandmother. "Come and pull me. I want to drive."

Grandmother came.

"You must run fast."

But the legs were weak. Suddenly she let the strap fall and just stood there with trembling lips, and the tears rolled down her cheeks.

"Grandmama cries. She is no fun to play with."

And then he thought of some other game.

They took possession of the finished igloo, and they sat still without talking much. Grandmama was sewing a pair of mittens for the little one. He threw so many away.

Mala went out and built another igloo. Nobody helped him, and he didn't call anybody. When he had finished it, he came back in and brushed the snow off his clothes.

"Has something happened?" said Iva.

"Nothing has happened. An igloo was built."

And then he went out again. He mounted a hill to look for caribou.

The old woman took her things. She turned up her hood, though she was inside the house, and looked for something on the bunk. One skin after the other she picked up, looked at it, and put it aside again. At last she took an old worn skin, almost without hairs, rolled it up and started to go out. At the entrance she stopped and turned around. Emotion flooded her. She was about to leave life, to abandon the world that was so beautiful. The children were sleeping; she went up and grasped their heads, put her mouth to their noses and sucked them clean. Pualu woke up. What was that for? He could blow his nose himself, he was no little boy any more. But Grandmama was so strange today, so determined. The boys were lying in their undercoats, and she tucked their hoods away so as to bare their left shoulders. She put her teeth in them and bit down hard, for the bite of an old woman brings good luck to children. It didn't hurt, for the old teeth were worn down completely from chewing skins. Even so, the boys woke up completely and cried uncontrollably.

Grandmama was so strange today, and there were a pair of new mittens and a pair of new pants at her place on the bunk. They were meant for the boys, but she didn't mention them.

"It so happens that one is leaving," she said, then took her old skins and crawled out.

"Are you leaving now?" said Iva, and she continued sewing.

The boys lay down to sleep again, and life in the igloo was the same.

Outside, the old woman looked around her, but her back yearned to lie down, so she crawled into the new fine house that had been built for her, and there she lay down upon the worn skin, and she stayed thus.

A little later, Mala descended the hill. He had seen her go inside. He took his knife and cut out a block of snow which he put in the entrance hole, walling it up. They didn't speak, there was nothing to say. The house was closed.

There the old one lay, waiting for death. It was long to lie, and her thoughts were not tired. She heard the children come out and heard them ask about the new igloo. Their father told them not to go too near it.

She tried not to think any more. But the boys were dragging their toboggan around, they came so near to her igloo that she heard their footsteps in the snow. Oh, now Upik fell and hurt himself, and he screamed unrestrainedly.

"It bleeds, it hurts. Mama, Grandmama."

Then it was hard to stay there quietly. But she was not alive any longer. She was gone.

Then Iva came out and shouted: "Come in and eat. Here is boiled meat."

"Where is Grandmama?" cried Pualu. "Doesn't Grandmama come to eat?"

When she heard that, tears welled up in her, and the saliva ran down her chin. Now she was lying here, so tired, and life was heavier than death, but the transition was so difficult.

Night passed, and when it was dawn she was still thinking. She heard them get up out there, heard them prepare the sled, and she followed everything in her thoughts. Now the dogs were rushing into the deserted igloo to eat the garbage. Now they strapped down the load on the sled, and the children wanted to know if Grandmama had walked on ahead. She heard that, too, and she heard the sled drive away. Finally, she didn't hear anything more.

Oh, they were driving away from her, they had left her behind. Oughtn't Mala to have prevented her in this?—he who always was so good. Now he let her stay behind. She got up and wanted to get out of the igloo, but the old limbs were weak. Now her feet were not freezing any more, though, and when she pulled her arms out of her sleeves to warm them on the body, she felt that she was cold all over. She wanted to follow the others, yet she also wanted to stay and rest.

And darkness came, and night closed about her. Old Naterk had been born, and had lived, and now her life had come to an end.

In the evening, the little family was quiet in its igloo. Upik asked why they had built a house before catching up with Grandmama. They told him to be still, and nobody said anything but what was necessary. Then he cried a little before he fell asleep. The next day they didn't travel. Mala went hunting that day, and the next day, and the next again, and the boys asked if they shouldn't hurry down to the ships.

One day, after a long time had passed, Mala went away from the camp. He had been driving in a ring and had come back to the place where his old mother had entered her igloo. Snowdrift had covered the landscape and also the house. No animal had been there, and all was quiet. He took his knife and made a hole in the roof of the igloo so that the soul could get out.

When he returned to Iva, he had no game with him, but said that he had been away to a place where it was painful to go.

"The roof was opened," he said, and he sat down on the bunk without eating.

For five days they sat there without traveling. The sun shone, and the weather was beautiful. The children were not permitted to play and not allowed to talk. Iva cut snow out of the side bunk to melt for drinking, and it was she who cut up meat for the pot as if she were a man. Mala didn't stir. He sat with his hood up in the house, and slept in his clothes at night, and the boys were not undressed, either. It was so strange.

"The lice are eating me, the lice are eating me," they called out during the night, and scratched their bodies, but they were still not allowed to take their fur coats off.

At the end of the five days, Mala and Iva went away, leaving the boys behind. They went to Naterk's igloo, Mala first, Iva exactly in his footsteps. He cut a hole in the backside of the house, and they entered. The old woman was lying stiff and bent with her hood pulled down over the face and her knees drawn up. He remembered her when she was a young matron, and he himself was a boy. He remembered many things about strange men who came to fight for her, but never won her or made her come along with them. A clever mother, a wonderful mother. And now she was lying here.

They carried her out and took her up to a place where the stones were lying loose around a rock. There they built a grave, and then old Naterk was gone from this world. She had lived, and now she was buried. Her name was not to be mentioned any more. It is only those who are drawing breath who are human and are to be of any concern. Because they had touched a corpse, they took off their mittens and put them down among the stones.

When they returned home, they used the same footprints in the snow, and they kept their hands inside their fur coats so as not to freeze them. Once in a while, Mala turned around and erased their tracks with his knife, so that death shouldn't find them and follow them.

For it is a well-known fact that the spirits of the dead envy the living for the gift of life, and unless all the prescribed rituals are followed and all precautions taken, they may take a terrible revenge.

In the Hudson Bay area, I once arrived at a village at Wager Inlet in the midst of great commotion. Just before my arrival, an old man called Oomilialik had been found hanging from the ceiling of an igloo. He had climbed up on top of the snowhouse, drilled a hole in the roof, and lowered a rope down to serve his purpose. Fortunately, just after he had hanged himself, the oldest of his four sons returned home from the hunt and came in in time to cut him down. The old man was furious. At this stage, I arrived and saw the father fight his four sons with his cane in a manner which didn't indicate any weakness at all on his part. The fight calmed down a little when I entered, and they told me what had happened. All four sons assured me and their father that they did not consider him a nuisance or burden at all. They had plenty of meat and good game, and they wanted to see his face among them for a long time yet and take advantage of his renowned experience.

I expressed agreement with the four sons, but the old man said that he had been the greatest caribou hunter ever known, and now his knees were too weak to walk across the hills. So life had no more to offer him. Besides, he had no more tobacco, and without that he found it too hard to sit at home instead of accompanying his sons out hunting.

While our discussion took place, the two women in the

house had boiled some meat, and we all had our fill. I brought in some tea and sugar, and after this treat the old man forgot his anger and talked pleasantly with his sons. They discussed hunting and even future travels, and a little later in the day we all decided to go visit Captain Berthier, whose ship was frozen in a few miles from there. We knew that there was going to be a dance the same evening.

We went there, and nobody was happier than the old Oomilialik, who laughed and shouted and enjoyed himself. The festivities lasted a couple of days, and I found a chance to tell Captain Berthier about the old man and make him sell me some tobacco, which I gave to Oomilialik when we departed. In return, I got his promise that he would not try to hang himself again. He came down to my sled to see me off and waved and laughed.

The next year I passed by Wager Inlet again, and I went to visit Oomilialik's house. I found only his sons at home, and I asked them how their father was. They answered me that he was all right, doing well, because he was now dead. He had hanged himself again, and this time with greater success. Only a little boy had been in the house when he made his preparations, and to him Oomilialik made it a point to state that he now had no more tobacco, and therefore was under no obligation to stay alive any longer. Then he chased the little boy out of the house, and when the men came home in the evening they found him hanging dead and cold.

Matter and Spirit

For the Eskimos, a human being is made up of a body, a soul, and a name, and is not complete without each of the three. This belief, even if it is not clearly formulated by all Eskimo tribes, still has its effects on daily actions and reasonings and runs like a golden thread through Eskimo life and culture.

As for the soul of man, the Eskimos claim no exact knowledge—but then, who does? They see it however as the origin and principle of life, the prime mover of all activities within a being, and the energy without which life cannot continue.

The name of an Eskimo is believed to have a life of its own independent of its bearer. It combines the good qualities and talents of all the persons who have been called by that name, and one may imagine it as a procession of ancestors stretching into the dim past and surrounding the

present bearer of the name with a sort of magic protective
aura. When a person dies and has been buried, the name
may not be mentioned again until it has been reborn. Many
Eskimos believe that a newborn baby cries because it wants
its name, and will not be complete until it gets it. Immediately after the birth, therefore, the angakok or some wise
old ones of the village are called in to determine the name.
It has to be the name of somebody who has died recently, of
course, but otherwise it may in some cases call for much
conjuring and soothsaying, and in other cases be a self-
evident matter. When my son was born, it was quite apparent
to everybody that it was his great-grandfather, Mequsaq,
who had died a few months before, who had been reborn in
him. He had a slight squint in the very same eye that old
Mequsaq had lost to the cannibals in Baffin Land; this was a
sign from the name spirit that here it wanted to belong. So
Mequsaq was his name.

When, in 1927, I returned to Thule for a visit, I found
that not less than five little girls had been named Navarana
after my dear late wife. So great was the confidence in her
ability and character that there was believed to be enough
for all five. It was thus a beautiful kind of memorial they
had made her, though a slightly expensive one for me since
I had to give all the little girls presents.

Most often, though, the baby was given four or five names
so as to have the highest possible protection, and certain
names became great favorites. With so many individuals
called by the same names it was often very confusing. Even
in Christianized Greenland this custom was continued. In
the little settlement of Kook, in the Upernavik district, all
five hunters were called Gaba (i.e., the archangel Gabriel).
I was informed that some years before, a great man called
Gaba had departed from this earth, but several unmistakable
signs made it apparent that this spirit was very much active,
and to please it they had named so many baby boys after
him. In order to distinguish between them, they called them
"Fat Gaba," "Little Gaba," etc.

A Polar Eskimo would never mention himself by name.
Doing so could break its magic protection. And since the
ever jealous spirits were always listening, it could cause
great affliction. It was often disconcerting to me in the beginning, when meeting somebody in the dark of winter, that
I was never able to get any other information than *"Oanga"*

(it is I). Eventually I learned to know them all by their voices.

Something similar to the name concept and its magic is found in the use of amulets. Contrary to what most people believe, it is not the amulet itself that is thought to protect its possessor, but rather the fortuitous properties it represents. Navarana carried a little ball of polished wood; wood cannot feel pain, and possession of it means great wealth. For it can ensure a rich and painless life. One of the most popular amulets was the foot of the raven, which was put in a string around the necks of newborn babies. No bird can get along under hard conditions like the raven. It is so clever that it often finds food where all other animals starve to death, and it can subsist on almost nothing when need be. At the end of my first walrus hunt at Thule, Ayorsalik decided that raven meat was to be eaten in my honor. This man was not a good hunter, but popular and a bit of a comedian, and he now conceived the idea that my good record from the hunt ought to be extended indefinitely into the future. Two young men were ordered to shoot three ravens that were hovering expectantly near our campfire. Ayorsalik put the pot to a boil, and the ravens were skinned and cooked. Their taste was revolting, and later I ate that bird only in times of great hunger. On this occasion, Ayorsalik handed me all three hearts and three livers with his sooty fingers. They went down, but almost came up again. I don't know if they had any real effect. But later on, when I had game parts of any size, Ayorsalik always recalled his art and expressed his anxiety that I would lose the power I had received from the ravens by not giving him a little share.

It is always the boys and the men who are given amulets, for they are the ones who expose themselves to all the dangers of nature while the women stay at home. When a girl is given amulets, it is mostly with the purpose of giving her strong sons.

On the rock of Agpat, behind Thule, where the dead ones were stone-set, I often saw men and women sit in quiet meditation. On these occasions they would dress in their newest and most beautiful clothes, and then sit quite still, staring out over land and sea for hours on end. They believed that during this stillness they received the wisdom of the ancestors. It is the only thing approximating religious devotion I have seen among them, but also—I think—the most beautiful form of devotion I have ever seen.

For this is no benevolent deity. The protective spells of the names and the amulets and the helping spirits of the angakoks are man's only defense against nature, which otherwise is populated with numerous spirits who always are ready to work their evil against mankind if sin or breach of taboo is committed. With his happy-go-lucky mind, the Eskimo believes that the good is sufficient unto itself and takes care of itself. But living in a barren and perilous nature, he believes that the evil must constantly and vigilantly be placated and kept at bay.

So, when—after having obeyed all rules of good behavior and broken no taboos—a tribe is still afflicted with sickness or bad weather and starvation, it is up to the angakok to find out how people have, knowingly or unknowingly, offended the spirits. He can summon his helping spirits, he can travel to the underworld, under the sea, and through the rocks, and thus find out where the trouble is.

Essentially, angakoks are people who are experienced in the state of trance, without therefore having any monopoly on it. I have often observed even the people serving in our house at Thule in a state of trance, sometimes for days on end. It is necessary to bring to mind the long depressing winter with its black darkness and its aura of evil lurking around, and the summer with its perpetual sunshine that wearies the mind and confuses the senses. Every year, in the fall, we had a veritable epidemic of evil spirits materializing among the houses when the storms and darkness set in, and panic ensued. Sometimes nerves would reach the limit of endurance, consciousness would be canceled out, and the individual in question would become senseless and hysterical, doing and saying incomprehensible things. However, the Eskimos regard this as a sacred state. The afflicted person is temporarily given the same respect as is shown the angakok, and after his seizure he is invited to interpret what has been revealed to him. His revelations can sometimes be startling.

When Knud was on his second trip across the icecap, we sat one evening and talked about him. Suddenly one of the old women, Inaluk, slipped out of the door, and five minutes later we heard her singing outside. We went out and found her standing there in the moonlight, without her coat, swaying from side to side, and her long black hair switching around her face:

"Those who have been on the east side are back,
Those who have been on the east side are back.

Satok and his wife will visit us too,
His wife is preparing by taking off her pants."

As she emerged from her trance, she went on to say that Knud and his party were returning home, but that two of them were missing.

"Is Knud missing?" I asked.

She made a pause in her conjuring to jeer: "Who suggests that the icecap can get the better of Kunuk? Perhaps somebody else had difficulties up there."

When the various visitors had gone home, we went to bed. I was a bit disturbed by Inaluk's augury and couldn't fall asleep. All of a sudden, Knud stuck his head in the door! Great joy to see each other again, but the look of the icecap was upon him, with months of starvation and hardship written on his face. It was several minutes before I asked: "Are all of you here?"

"No, two are missing," answered Knud.

That was the end of the ill-fated Second Thule Expedition. Our dear Eskimo friend, Henrik Olsen, was eaten by wolves, and the Swedish scientist Dr. Wulff had to be left behind to die on the icecap!

Just to complete Inaluk's record, Satok and his wife did come visiting, although a whole month later.

The state of unconsciousness is so important and so familiar to the Eskimos that even the children play at it. It is a favorite pastime of theirs to hang themselves by their hoods. When these tighten about their necks, the blood is kept from their heads, and in time they lose consciousness. The other children in the house take them down when their faces turn purple. But they say that the state of unconsciousness is so delightful that they play this game over and over again.

I have personally met many angakoks in my time, and I am convinced that there were no charlatans among them. They train themselves to enter the state of trance whenever they want and to interpret their visions when they return to consciousness. It is not possible to reduce them to mere magicians, as has sometimes been tried. I would rather say hypno-suggestion and mass hypnosis were the tools that they unconsciously used. Also, they actually do not wield very much influence in the Eskimo society except in cases where they also are chief hunters; but even if this happens, quite often it still remains the exception. For a great hunter and outstanding provider is such because he is quiet and sober, while an angakok most often is a less successful hunter, a man who suffers under the monotony of daily routine, and who is only called upon in the hour of need. It is a special trait of the Eskimos that they can very well pay homage to a man for a short time, without looking up to him throughout their whole lives just because they accepted his help at one time or another.

When a young man wants to become an angakok, he will usually attach himself to an older man of the profession and learn from him. There are various systems and schools of thought, and the means of slipping in and out of trance are many. One way is to starve and thirst until the feverish mind starts the proper hallucinations. Another way is to obtain concentration and paralysis of the conscious mind by, for instance, going to a lonely place and rubbing a stone in a circle on a rock for hours and days on end. This was the method used by the great Odark when his two helping spirits, two little men as high as his thumb, showed themselves to him.

When the apprentice has learned the trance, his next task is to procure his helping spirits. Again, the various systems differ: he can, for instance, divide the spirits into classes, and demand a helping spirit of each class and for each field of his activity, usually at least five or six. He must—during his trances—make mental journeys to find them, and when they reveal themselves to him, he must touch them—then they become his. They could be the spirits of the sun and the moon, or those of his ancestors, also those of powerful animals, or they could reveal themselves as utterly unknown and horrible monsters.

To illustrate how the spirits and the angakoks influence the daily lives of people, let me tell about the strangest case ever. Pakitsoq, a cave between Thule and Cape York, was often used for overnight stays. Once it was huge and housed more than all the other caves in the country. It was possible to have a tent standing inside it and from it to have a view over the sea.

But, I am told, people abused the liberty which the spirit of the cave gave them, and performed impious deeds in the cave itself. It had been revealed to them that a bit of meat had to be left for the spirit who, incidentally, was none other than Tornarssuk, master of the earth. It was only reasonable that he receive a small thank-you present for his hospitality. But Sorqaq and his friend Krilerneq, who both

were great angakoks, had once held a big seance in the cave.
And there they had opined that "The Big Meat Dish,"
Neqivik, who lives at the bottom of the sea and sends out
the game animals, was more powerful than Tornarssuk, who
hides in the mountains, and has to swim through rock when
he wants to get to people. To follow up on these potent
pronouncements from her favorites, Neqivik sent the great
sea quake that was felt by all and killed many people, to
prove her strength. The whole coast trembled under her
wrath, and Tornarssuk had to bore himself deep into the
earth from where, for many winters, it was impossible to
conjure him out. All this indicated how great was his fear
of the big woman at the bottom of the sea.

When the sea was frozen over again at Pakitsoq, it was at
first impossible to find the place again. Otoniaq, who used to
set his foxtraps right outside the cave, came and found that
they had quite disappeared. He thought that some malicious
person had removed them, and he decided to drive up to the
cave and sleep there overnight. But great was his astonishment when he reached the place, for it turned out that there
was no cave at all. Then he had to laugh, although he was
all alone, for he discovered that he didn't know the very
place where he had been so many times. He drove out on the
ice a bit, but thus he saw that the contour of the mountain
was the same against the sky, consequently Pakitsoq had to
be right at that place. He drove up to it anew, but such
a great fear caught hold of him at seeing the cave closed
that he jumped up on his sled and drove home to Parker
Snow Bay, where he had taken land, at the top of his speed.
On the way, he felt malevolent spirits in his tracks, so that it
became necessary for him to employ all his best formulas of
evasion in order to speed his dogs up enough.

Since it is a fact that magic formulas lose their potency
by being used, and Otoniaq repeated his over and over again,
he lost all his abilities as a conjurer in that one night. And
after that, Otoniaq was not quite as successful on hunting
trips, and he always had to be content with game parts
from the skill of others' harpoons.

Later, hunters from Agpat and Umanak came to Pakitsoq, but they also came back with tales about how the cave
was closed, and thus it appeared that powerful angakoks
had done harm to people by robbing them of a useful shelter
in bad weather, when there wasn't snow enough to build an
igloo.

When the little auks returned in the spring, Oolulik went up to the place to survey it. He found the cave entirely filled with stones thrown up by the sea, and they even lay spread along the coast on both sides.

Since it was quite evident that it was Sorqaq and Krilerneq who had caused all this by challenging Tornarssuk's power, it was now thought that it was safe to try to reopen the cave. Oolulik and another man removed so many stones that it was possible to enter it. It was spacious as before, but low to the ceiling, because the floor was filled with stones. As people now began to use Pakitsoq for sleeping again, they built a bunk to sleep on. Qisunguaq spent several days collecting big stones so that the bunk became fairly smooth to sleep on. Every year, the first party to come to the cave collected withered grass from the bird cliffs and spread it out over this, and together with your own sleeping skins that makes a nice bed.

But one more tragedy had to take place in Pakitsoq before the spirits were quite appeased. Oolulik's father-in-law, Miuk, visited it once, together with some other hunters, and while he was there he suddenly got the feeling the *pibloktoq* was about to come over him, and therefore he said to the others that his breath was about to leave him.

He began to chant louder and louder, and nobody dared to come near him. How could they know if it wasn't one of his helping spirits who wanted to give predictions to people. If this was the case, it would be dangerous to touch Miuk. For spirits who want revenge do not consider whom they punish. They sometimes chastise even innocents who know of nothing.

So they let Miuk sing. But in a short while he grew quite violent and began to shout instead of singing, such as pibloktoq people are wont to do.

Then he bent down and took out the pointed knife he kept hidden under his bed skins, and he whetted it until it was very sharp.

He called out that it was desirable to test his ability at whetting. Then he stuck the knife into his wrist so that the blood sprayed out. But Miuk laughed and carried the knife up along the arm, ripping up the skin. A long, long gash he cut in himself. At the same time he shouted that his skin was tough and would be good to make kamik soles from. But he continued with the knife. Up to the shoulder and across the chest. Now he took the knife with his left hand and carried it down the right arm. When he came to the wrist, where the blood is right under the skin, it spurted out in a long red jet. Those who saw it said it looked like when a man lets his water. But a little later, Anaugark, who stood close by him, said that this was now so dangerous that it was best if somebody tried to stop Miuk in his wanton self-destruction. Then they took hold of him, and his blood colored them quite red.

They got the knife away from him, and immediately it was as if Miuk's pibloktoq had spent its strength. He collapsed on the floor and was very weak.

Soon he got back his thoughts, but when he saw how he had molested himself, he said that he didn't know what moved him to use the knife on himself since—after all—there were enough game animals in the sea that he could bring home to cut into.

When he had said this, his voice left him, and in another moment he was dead. They set him in a stone grave in the scree, and for five days they didn't leave Pakitsoq. This was done because for five days the spirit of the dead hovers around his corpse, and if any taboo is broken during that time, it becomes an evil spirit, a *tonrat,* that wreaks terrible revenge upon mankind. In order to give the spirit peace in the underworld, all kayaks and tools were turned inland as a sign of no activity, and nobody stirred for anything unnecessary.

The hunters present exchanged dogs with the dead man and killed some of their own somewhat slow ones in return for his renowned bear dogs. After that, they killed many bears. Anaugark especially became famous as a bear hunter, because he took three dogs from Miuk's team. Also, they used some of the time to carve some miniature hunting tools out of a little wood, which they took from Miuk's sled. They exchanged these toys for the dead man's very clever harpoons and other weapons. For he had been much more skillful than the other hunters in shaping handsome and ingenious hunting tools. He was of course to use these things in the underworld, but he would be a powerful spirit there and he would have the ability to shape things according to his needs.

Since they all shared in his funeral feast, the sorrow over the lost hunting mate diminished somewhat. And from that time on, people have slept in peace in Pakitsoq.

One of the most important tasks of the angakok is to cure sickness. In doing so, he cures the soul, never the body. The body has no life of its own. It is the soul that—because of some sin, or influenced by an evil spirit—creates suffering and expresses it through the body. It is up to the angakok to undertake a journey to the realm of the spirits and find out where the affliction originates. When he comes back, he prescribes the cure.

Having studied medicine myself, I can only say that I have the highest regard for the angakoks in this activity. I think, for instance, of Greenland as it was before the advent of the most modern development, with its small settlements and outposts. It was not possible for the doctors there to be present at more than about five per cent of the sick cases; the great distances and traveling conditions forbade it. Conscious of the fact that they had a physician, the patient and his family would wail because he couldn't be there, and all would look hopeless.

It was different with the Polar Eskimos, who were not yet baptized. They got immediate help from their angakok. His influence was naturally of a suggestive sort, but he could sometimes bring the sick man to believe in him. In this way pain frequently disappeared, as the patient was hypnotized into feeling well.

More than once I have seen a man who actually was fatally stricken, but who had been convinced of his cure, sustained in his faith in the angakok until the very moment when his body refused to function any more and he collapsed in death. But at least hope was maintained, and the patient suffered none of that fear for the fate of his family that is a dying man's greatest misfortune.

On the other hand, of course, it could happen that the angakok pronounced the doom of the patient—who would then succumb very soon. The presence of a doctor who was many miles away from his patient was no match for the direct hypnotic influence of the angakok.

I have also seen samples of how the angakok's magic formulas could encourage the patient, to the extent that he had faith in them. Once, when I was assisting in the amputation of some broken fingers, the injured man felt no pain because an old sage sat by him speaking pain-dulling magic formulas during the operation.

I should like to tell about an experience I had with such a medicine man. This was in Hudson Bay, in our winter quarters on Danish Island, where we were one day visited by a big party of Netchilik Eskimos. Among them was a

man named Anaqaq ("The Little Excrement"). His story was
quite remarkable. His homeland was suffering under an
acute lack of women, and many women had two or even
three husbands. Anaqaq had been a member of such a tri-
angular marriage, which could have been harmonious enough
if only his co-husband had not turned out to be wily and dishonest. Anaqaq was quite an angakok, his specialty was
digestive disorders, and during the time when there were
many caribou and people ate themselves sick, he was in
great demand and often away for a long time.

But he always brought his honoraria, consisting of caribou
tongues, lumps of marrow, and other delicacies, home with
him. The three of them together enjoyed them in concord
and harmony. But then unfortunately it was discovered that
the co-husband had rented the wife out to strangers, and the
payment received was divided by the two conspirators, who
deprived Anaqaq of his rightful share. This guile overcame
Anaqaq so completely that he left the home forever. What
was the world coming to if people couldn't trust each other
in a marriage?

Anaqaq wandered far away. It took him two years to reach
Repulse Bay, for he was poor and had no dogs or weapons.
Often he had been at the point of starving to death, but his
conjuring had helped him to find dead animals and unexpected fish, and he had survived. And he joined a party
that now came to visit us. It was our principle to keep visitors
for four days; then they were politely—but firmly—requested to leave. Anaqaq left with the others. But since he
was on foot, he had plenty of opportunity to meditate over
what he had seen and heard at our place. He arrived at the
conviction that it was us he had dreamed about his entire
life. He wished to be back, and one day he reappeared again
and said that he wanted to see our faces for a while longer,
yes, he would feel it as the greatest sorrow of his life if we
threw him out. I was flattered by his petition and took him
into our service. I figured that he could always catch enough
for his own food, if nothing else. But here I met a barrier.
When I had seen him walk about and admire us for some
time, I thought that the hour of work had come, and I gave
him a job to do.

He then informed me that this was wrong. Anaqaq was
a holy man; it was forbidden him to work with anything but
his brain and his helping spirits. For once I was quick to find
a way out. I explained to him that we also were religious

people. We had had reports of his arrival long ago by spiritual communication. To prove my words, I showed him a photo of himself, which he recognized. He understood immediately that absolution was assured in this case, we got him started, and he rendered us quite good service while he was with us.

A good year later I met him again. With my servant, Inuiyak, I was crossing from Danish Island to Repulse Bay when a storm forced us over toward Vansittart Island. Near the beach we saw a tent, and it turned out to be none other than Inuiyak's brother and my good friend Oosugtaq with his family. Since they were far from their usual hunting grounds, they had thought that they needed extra protection against the evil spirits, so with them was Anaqaq as a kind of house chaplain. We were all pleased to see each other again, but none of us had any provisions. Oosugtaq found a little flour, and it was decided to make pancakes.

The preparation was not the most appetizing, for the whole family, and especially the children, had terrible colds, and mouth and nose were running on them. Their mother put them to chew caribou tallow to fry the pancakes in. The result was some slimy lumps, and for the first and only time in my life I found myself disinclined to eat pancakes, and tried to postpone the actual eating as long as possible.

In the middle of all this, the youngest boy, aged about four, had to perform a duty on behalf of nature. It was evening now and dark, but even so his parents thought he had better go outside, for it was a well-known fact that white men didn't like little boys to pee in their drinking cups. That was exactly what the brat wanted to do, and a discussion ensued. Reluctantly, the boy finally went outside, but a moment later he came back in with mission uncompleted and in a state of tears. He had seen a horrible sight outside, which frightened him.

The others got scared, and Oosugtaq took the little one on his knee and questioned him closely. It was—it seemed —a beast like a snow owl, only much larger and with terrifying glance. The boy refused to go out there again; he would be eaten.

The situation was serious, and Anaqaq prepared himself to do his duty and fight the enemy who had shown up in spectral form. He collected his hair in a knot, turned up his sleeves, and wound his torso tightly in a harpoon line. He began to bite into leather and say mysterious words, and while the women groaned and the men mumbled, his face darkened, and a berserk rage came over him. With a roar he rushed out of the tent, and we heard the din of battle. It sounded like the noise of several parties, and it was clear from their hoarse roars that they had hold of each other's throats. I couldn't sit still and wanted to go out there, but Oosugtak mustered all his authority: "Nobody must leave the tent and contribute to the damnation of our friend." Through holes in the tent wall I tried to spy something, but this too was forbidden me. They informed me that it had blinded several men to see the spirits materialized; we should be happy that the boy's sight was spared.

Then we heard the rumble of the fight draw down toward the beach, where sleds were overturned and dogs howled. At last, the noise pulled out over the ice—the danger had been averted, and Anaqaq had saved us. Soon his footsteps were heard in the snow nearby, he howled like a wolf and seemed weak. Now he was just outside the tent, and Oosugtaq and Inuiyak took position on each side of the entrance to receive him. They told me not to be afraid, they would manage him alone, and we should trust them even if it would take time to subdue his powers.

Anaqaq's howling was weaker now, but suddenly he gave a roar and jumped into the tent, where the women yelled and the children screamed and took cover. The two brothers caught him and fought against his supernatural strength. They wrestled and fell in a heap on the floor, the three of them. It looked as if the angakok was going to get the upper hand, in which case it would have been the end of us all. So I sprang up and grasped his shoulders to hold him down. I noticed that his hands were all smeared with blood from the finger tips to above the wrists, and blood was coming out of his mouth. We overpowered him easily now, and he became weak in our hands. This was our chance to derive a little advantage from his seizure. Willingly he let himself be led up to a corner of the tent, where he lay down and curled up. They covered him with skins so that nothing of him was seen, and now they directed a series of questions to him, in order to find out about various things. In this particular state, an angakok can only answer "yes" or "no," so that it may often take a long time to extract all the information desired. It was revealed that it was an evil angakok from Netchilik, a notorious robber of souls, who had come flying through the air down to here to devour their little boy. We were also informed that this same enemy already had killed two little girls on his way to this tent. But now he had been subdued and forced down into a crack in the ice. Then it was disclosed that the caribou were on their way north, and that the sea catch at Tayarnak would be good that year.

We now let the boy pee in his cup, we all went to sleep, and the next day we broke camp. Oosugtaq and his family could easily be pursued by the same evil man, who perhaps wanted to revenge his defeat of yesterday. Anaqaq was highly honored and enjoyed his victory. But he was still a little weak from exhaustion and loss of blood. The others explained to me that he had had his hands in the jaws of the enemy and thrust them down his throat, the blood on his hands being the lung blood of the evil angakok.

An angakok, or evil spirit, can rob a person's soul. When that happens to a person he withers away gradually and finally dies. The only remedy against it is that another angakok might see his way to get his soul back for him. Some people among the Hudson Bay Eskimos take no risks of this kind. When a boy baby is born, they send for the angakok to exorcise his soul and tuck it away under the mother's blubber lamp, which is the one place where it is safe. No matter how far the son should stray away from this lamp later in life, the soul has power enough to radiate all its faculties to him at all times.

Another method for an angakok to do evil to an enemy is that of creating a *tupilaq*, a hell animal. He does that by collecting bones from various animals and putting them together into a skeleton, which he then wraps in a skin. He puts it at a prescribed place, and after much conjuring it becomes alive and swims across the path of the hunter who is to die. As soon as this hunter has harpooned it, he is doomed. Thus I was told that the great angakok Kritlaq, who led the immigration from Baffin Land, once wanted to harm his rival Sorqaq. One day Sorqaq's son, Tatterat, harpooned a seal which aroused his enthusiasm in a quite unnatural degree; he hopped and danced and almost went berserk. And sure enough, when the seal was brought home and cut up, it turned out that all the bones were wrong; it was a tupilaq fashioned by Kritlaq. A short time later, Tatterat began to develop stiffness in his legs, and in time he became completely paralyzed so that his mother had to feed him like a baby and take care of him. How this injured Sorqaq can be seen by the fact that he came to great poverty and indignity as an old man, with nobody to provide for him. As for Tatterat, he lived for some years with us at the Thule Station. Eventually, even his jaws were paralyzed, and I had to knock his front teeth out with a hammer so as to provide a hole through which he could be fed. But he always chattered a blue streak and demonstrated the Eskimo's usual happiness at being alive.

The first seance that I ever witnessed was performed by Sorqaq, when we had been at Thule for hardly a year. That period had been marked by many strange accidents and tragedies, and finally Sorqaq announced that he would attempt a journey to the underworld to try to find the reason. And he proved his good intentions by fasting for several days, and frequently looking at his excrement until it appeared satisfactory. He then went up to the cliffs to meditate and prepare himself for the travel through bedrock, which he would surely have to swim through in order to find Tornarssuk.

A huge igloo was built for the occasion and draped inside with old tent skins. Along one wall it had a ledge that was to serve as a stage. On the appointed evening, the settlement gathered in the igloo. There were also many visitors from other settlements, and Krilerneq, Sorqaq's assistant, arranged the seating.

Sorqaq was the last man to enter the igloo, and he was announced three times before he finally arrived. He greeted us all by saying that we were all a bunch of idiots to have come to see a thing that didn't have a word of truth to it, and which he was incapable of doing anyway. The audience answered his modesty with shouts of praise and encouragement. He then walked up to me and asked me to leave: "This is nothing for the great white man to look at. I am a big liar, and even if these fools are stupid enough to believe me, I could never deceive you, and your presence will embarrass me. What happens here has nothing to do with the truth."

"I should like to listen to your great wisdom."

"Naw, naw," he said. "That goes to show you that even a white man may be born foolish."

I concurred with him in that, and he went over to his ledge. There he took off his clothes, which were removed by Krilerneq, and sat stark naked. Then Krilerneq took several sealskin lines and bound Sorqaq tight, tying his arms to his body and binding his legs together. The thongs cut into his muscles, but he kept himself rigid.

Next, Krilerneq placed the drum, the drumstick, and a piece of dried sealskin beside him on the ledge. Then he joined the audience and put out the lamps, except for one tiny flame; the light was so faint that we could barely see each other's faces.

Sorqaq's voice began to chant. First it was his usual weak old man's voice, then it grew stronger and stronger and seemed to emanate from different parts of the igloo. Then we heard the sound of the drum, muted at first, but it too growing in volume until the igloo reverberated from the banging of the drum, the echoing voice, and the rattling of the sealskin, now over our heads, now beneath our feet.

I do not remember how long this infernal din lasted. I do remember taking hold of Krilerneq's arm to see if he was helping. Apparently, he was not! All of us joined in Sorqaq's song, but Sorqaq's own voice became fainter after a while, gradually it seemed to come from outside the igloo, and finally it was gone.

Suddenly Krilerneq put on the lights. Sorqaq had disappeared. There was only his drum and the sealskin on the ledge. Senseless as I was from the bedlam around me, I remembered to look behind the draperies. He was definitely gone!

I looked around at the audience, and I could hardly recognize the calm quiet friends who had come down to us to trade. Their faces were ecstatic, their cheeks swollen, their eyes bright and unseeing. Naked from the waist up, they swayed back and forth to the rhythm of the song. In the middle of the floor, Krilerneq was writhing and twisting like a dancer, driving the men and women into a higher and higher frenzy.

One of the men, Krisuk, had a seizure. He stood up howling like a wolf, and people around him had to defend themselves against his attacks. He came at me, but I pushed him aside, and he fell over Ivalu who sat beside me. With one move he tore her pants and kamiks off, but in her frenzy she hardly noticed it. No longer able to contain himself, Krisuk dove straight through the wall of the igloo, creating a much-needed breathing hole.

But everybody began to shout in a language I didn't understand. It was not the usual Eskimo language, but they all seemed to understand it. During their seances angakoks are not allowed to mention any objects or beings by their regular names, since it could bring disaster upon the ones mentioned. They use other words and paraphrases. But this tongue seemed utterly strange.

The song continued and tore me along with it. I lost all sense of time and place. Ivalu lay naked across me, and I could feel others chewing my hair, clawing my skin.

Suddenly everything changed. Krilerneq stopped his dancing and proclaimed that Sorqaq was trying to return. He begged everybody to return to their original places and sit there and sing, concentrating our minds on the angakok who was at this very moment fighting his way up through the rock under the igloo. He—who had made the journey himself several times—impressed upon us what sufferings Sorqaq was undergoing, having to swim through the rock like it was water.

Krisuk returned, naked and shivering. He pressed himself down among the perspiring women, who screamed when he touched their hot bodies. Ivalu started calling him by a series of unquotable names, but she was cut off by Krilerneq's booming voice: "The shadow is ripening! The shadow is ripening!"

In the seance language, "shadow" is "man," "ripen" is to "arrive." We listened for a few moments, and now Sorqaq's voice was heard faintly in the distance. Krilerneq extinguished the light completely, for in order to travel through the rock Sorqaq had had to shed his skin completely, and the one who sees an angakok "muscle-naked" must die.

Krilerneq told us that Sorqaq had trouble returning, because somebody had left the house and returned, which made it difficult for him to find it.

But presently his voice grew until it almost drowned the chant from the audience. Again his drum made the igloo tremble, and the crackling sealskin flew through the air. I tried to grasp it, but received a blow that almost broke my arm. Hell had broken loose!

Then it all stopped. Krilerneq mumbled a long tirade, and the igloo became quiet save for the crying of the children. In a droning voice, Krilerneq implored the angakok to tell what secrets he had learned in the underworld. Sorqaq's voice came from the ledge:

"The Great Spirits are embarrassed by the presence of white men among us and will not reveal the reason for the accidents. Three deaths are still to come. So as to avoid more tragedies, our women must refrain from eating of the female walrus until the winter darkness returns!"

Those poor women! The taboos were almost always directed against them, because they were considered unclean. But the angakok had done his duty; the performance was over, and all the lamps in the igloo were lit.

Sorqaq was sitting on the ledge, strapped tightly in his sealskin lines. He was obviously exhausted, perspiring profusely, and foaming saliva ran down his chest. I approached, but Krilerneq warned me not to touch him, since the fire of the earth was still in him. Krilerneq untied the sealskin lines, and Sorqaq fell into a coma for a few moments. When he opened his eyes, he saw me and tried to smile: "Just lies and tricks. The wisdom of our ancestors is not in me. Do not believe in any of it!"

I wonder! My point of view has always been that there is nothing supernatural, only things for which we so far have no scientific explanation. So I just relate what I saw and heard, and I have heard other people—wiser and more sober-minded than I—recount similar experiences.

The Eskimo Idea of the World

Another thing that makes the angakok interesting is that many of them are treasure houses of old fables that give us the Eskimos' ideas of the world. Not that other Eskimos couldn't tell you these same fables, for they learn them in the cradle from the old women. But since angakoks usually are people who think deeply over things, they have put more order into it and can give you a more complete picture of Eskimo beliefs.

Here, then, is how the world and the things in it came about:

The Beginning. In the beginning there was nothing but water. But then suddenly one day stones and rocks began to rain down from the sky. And land was created.

But there was darkness, and animals and humans lived promiscuously among each other, copulating as they pleased, and assuming each other's shapes without order or reason.

But in this blessed darkness words were born. And since words were new and never had been used before, they were as powerful as magic formulas. And strange things began to happen in the world because words were pronounced.

The fox met the snow hare.

"Dark, dark, dark," said the fox. He wanted it dark so

that he could easily steal from the meat caches of the humans, among the cliffs.

"Light, light, light," said the snow hare. He wanted it light so that he could see to find a bit of food in the grass.

And at the same moment it became as the snow hare wished. It became light. And since then light and darkness have alternated upon the earth.

The First People. The first people were much stronger than people are now. Thus, they could with their magic make their houses fly, and a snow shovel could move by itself and shovel snow. People lived on earth, and when they wanted new nourishment they just sat in their houses and let them fly to new places.

But one day a man complained over the noise the houses made when they flew through the air. And his words were powerful, and houses lost their ability to fly at that moment.

And since then houses have been stationary.

At that time new snow could burn like fire, and often fire fell down from the sky. There was no ice either, but one day the great hero Kunuk was pursued by a witch woman whom he had teased. And she threw her scraping knife after him, so that it danced "ducks and drakes" upon the water. And the water froze to ice at that moment.

The people were also more powerful in their evil. It is a well-known fact that a dead one may become a tonrat when we break a taboo or do evil to somebody. The first people created the most powerful spirits there are with their evil.

The Sun and the Moon. Sun and Moon were sister and brother. They always took part in the copulation games in the young people's house. But one night, as Moon was trying to decide which girl he would try to find when the light was dimmed, his eyes fell upon his sister, and he thought she was the most beautiful of all. He noticed how her clothes were made, and when the lamp had been put out, he found her by feeling his way.

He did this many times. At last, Sun became suspicious, and she took a little soot from the lamp upon her fingers. During the copulation she pressed her fingers against the forehead of the man who took her. And when the lamp was lit again, she saw her brother Moon with soot on his face.

Sun became red and hot with shame. She took a whisk of moss from the heap by the lamp, dipped it in the blubber and lit it, and she ran out.

Moon wanted to follow her, but he was in such a hurry that he didn't get his moss lit very well.

"We must run far away and never see each other again," said Sun. And at the same moment they became spirits and were lifted up in the sky, where they continued their flight.

But Sun has the stronger warmer light, because her whisk of moss burns clearly. Her brother Moon, who pursues her but never can catch up with her, has the weaker colder light.

Thunder and Lightning. There were once two orphans who lived in a settlement on an island. Nobody cared much for them, and they had to take food where they could find it.

One day, when they had been sleeping in the corner of an abandoned house, they woke up and found that the settlement had been moved. The people had deliberately not taken them along, since they were only a bother. And they went for a long time without food, for there was none around.

One day they found a piece of dried sealskin and a flint-stone.

"What shall we be?" they asked each other.

"I shall be thunder."

"I shall be lightning."

They did not know what thunder and lightning were. But at the same moment they were lifted up in the sky and became thunder and lightning, and from there they punish people for the evil committed against them, by releasing their fury against them.

The Bear that Became Fog. Once a family was living near a burial cliff. They began to notice that whenever a dead one from the settlement had been set in his grave there, he always disappeared the next day. Finally, the man decided to find out what caused this, and he put himself in one of the graves as if he were dead.

When night had fallen, he suddenly heard someone say: "Ah, here is a corpse again!"

And he felt himself being lifted up and carried away. When he dared to open his eyes, he found that it was a bear who was carrying him. He then amused himself by catching hold of bushes and branches they passed by, and the bear thought that the burden was very heavy. He was quite exhausted when he arrived home, and he lay down to rest while the little bear children gathered around the corpse to look it.

"Papa, the corpse is opening its eyes!"

"Be still, children, the road was long and heavy for me!"

In the same moment, the man sprang up and took an axe that was lying there to cut up game with, and he killed the bear and all his children. But when he came outside, he saw the woman bear returning from her fishing. He started to run, and she pursued him.

They came to a river, and the man spoke a magic formula and jumped right over it. The woman bear asked him: "How did you get across the river?"

"I drank it dry," said the man.

And the woman bear lay down and began to drink the river. And she drank so much that she burst wide open, and all the water she had drunk became fog.

Sila, the Weather. In the old days there were giants on earth. Once it happened that some people found a giant baby lying abandoned on the ground. His mother had lost him from her amaut while she was collecting grass. And the people gathered around the giant baby to have some fun out of the situation.

The women showed how its penis was so big that four of them could sit side by side on it; yet they fell down when he had the slightest convulsion.

As the people now continued their wickedness, the giant baby was suddenly lifted up into the sky, and there he became Sila, the weather. When he loosens the caribou skin that is his diaper, he lets loose the winds and the rain.

And when an angakok will appease Sila, he must travel up into the sky and tighten the carbou skin that is his diaper.

Neqivik. There was once an orphan girl named Neqivik who lived in a big settlement by the coast. Nobody cared for her, and she had to fend for herself, and her clothes were poor and worn.

One time they decided to move the settlement, and the people tied their kayaks together, loaded their things together on them, and prepared to leave.

Neqivik came running down to the scree, she wanted to come along, but the people forbade her to come into the kayaks. And they told each other that if they left her there she would starve to death, and they would be rid of her.

Then they sailed out, and the desperate Neqivik had no other choice than to jump in the water and swim after them. She became cold and tired, and she tried to pull herself up into one of the kayaks. But one of the people chopped her fingers off with his axe, and she sank back into the water.

But so great was the evil now committed against her that she became the most powerful spirit there is. Her chopped-off fingers became seal and walrus and other animals, and that is how the game animals were created. She herself sank down to the bottom of the sea, from where she rules all the animals in water and on land. She sends them out to people when they have been good and obeyed all taboos. Jealously she watches for breaks of taboos or other things that can insult the souls of the animals, and when people have been wicked she closes up the animals in the water basin in her house.

Then people get no game, and they must starve, maybe even die, until she has been appeased. Angakoks who have traveled down to appease her say that she lives in a big house that is made just like people's houses. A giant woman, she lies nude on her bunk with her long black hair flowing over her shoulders.

There are also some who say that all the errors of people collect in her hair and her house like grease and dirt, and since she has no fingers she cannot comb her hair. An angakok who wants to appease her, therefore, must clean her house and comb her hair. When he does so, she is pleased, and sends the game out again.

Man and Woman. We do not know how the first people became numerous and how their women were created. Some say that they went out and found that babies had grown out of the earth and lay there among the tussocks. The women just picked them up and took them inside.

But then came a great flood, and the whole world perished. Everybody drowned except for two men, who then moved together into the same house. And they lived together like man and wife.

At last, one of them became pregnant, and since they were both great angakoks, they conjured until he could absorb his penis and become a woman.

And it was from this couple that the people living now are descended.

The Girl Who Married a Dog. There was once a girl who refused all the men who wished to marry her. At last, her father became angry with her, and he took her and his dog with him out to an isolated island. The dog took the girl to wife, and they lived together on the island. In course of time, the girl wore off all the skin from her elbows and knees, so often she had been forced to go down on all fours when the dog wanted to have its way with her. Finally, she became pregnant and brought forth a number of whelps. The girls' father brought meat to them, that they might not starve.

One day, when the young ones were grown up, their mother said to them: "Next time your grandfather comes out to the island you shall swim out to him and overturn the kayak."

The dogs did so, and their grandfather drowned. Thus the girl took revenge for having been forced to marry a dog.

But since she did not want her brood to stay on the island and starve, she then cut the soles off her kamiks. And she put some of her young ones on one sole, and the rest on the other, and worked magic over them, so that they sailed out into the wide world.

Over one kamik sole she said: "Be skillful in all manner of work you undertake." And it drifted out from the island. A little way out it turned into a ship, and they sailed away to the white man's land and became white men. It is said that from them all white men came, both good and bad.

Over the other kamik sole the girl said: "Avenge me on your grandfather, show bloodthirst as often as you meet with human beings." And the kamik sole was washed ashore, and the dogs with it wandered into the country and turned into *Itgitlit* (the Indians).

How Big the World Is. Once there were two young couples who had taken land together. The husbands were good hunters, the wives clever and beautiful, and they stayed together.

One day, the men sat and talked together about many things, such as people do when they have eaten their fill and their thoughts can occupy themselves with something other than food.

"The world is big," said one of them.

"Yes, but how big?" said the other. "No matter how long a time you drive with your sled, you can always see land in front of you."

"Let us find out," they said as with one mouth, and so it was decided that they should depart and travel to where the world meets itself, taking opposite directions.

Right away they prepared for the journey, and the women cried when taking leave of each other, such as women are wont to do, for they knew it might be some years before they would see each other again.

Then they traveled. Every year when the ice broke up, they took land and stayed there over the summer. They always caught enough game to keep them going for the winter also, and when the ice was firm again, they started out and kept traveling for the whole winter, on and on.

They went on year after year. The children of both couples grew up and married people from the settlements that they visited. They too grew old and their children married, and at last there was an entire tribe traveling in each direction.

At last, the old couples were weak. The men could no longer drive their own sleds, and their wives had to sit on the sleds instead of running alongside them. But they never forgot their old idea, and they went on. After many years they grew blind and had to be led by the younger ones, but they could not die until they had met their old friends.

One day, both parties eyed in the far distance another group moving toward them very slowly. It was the two couples who finally met. Very slowly they walked up to meet each other, and they recognized each other's voices.

They had been so long on their journey that their cups made of musk-ox horn, with which they scooped water up from the river, were now so worn that only the handles were left.

They greeted each other and sat down.

"The world is very big."

"Yes, even bigger than we thought when we parted!"

Then all four of them died, and here ends their story.

That is how big the world is.

These fables certainly tempt us to analytical thought. For if there is any such thing as racial memory, we meet it here in the flesh. And as long as the mystery of the origin of the Eskimos is not quite solved, it is worth considering that many of their tales may trace back to an incredibly distant past.

Notice, for instance, that there is talk about snow burning on the ground and fire raining. Then remember that there has been no volcanic activity in North America for millennia. The Alaskan Eskimos have stories about animals that—by their description—can only be mastodons, animals that have been extinct for ten thousand years! We are told that the first people lived on earth and that there was no ice in the land. Is this a memory of the ancestral country in Central Asia?

Of more recent origin are the memories of many bloody fights with the Itgitlit. In Greenland the Itgitlit are understood to be people with dogs' bodies and human heads and hands, living on the icecap. But it is still the memory of the Indians that lives on in this form.

As a whole, the stories have a common basis and they have—with variations—developed along the same lines. From eastern Greenland to Alaska the folklore is the same, the variations and foreign influence only emphasizing the common source. The tales and fables have been handed down through the generations, and as for the Eskimos, there is no doubt in their minds about their veracity. They have no concept of fiction and cannot question the truthfulness of a storyteller. Their reasoning is quite simple:

"It is said to be so, therefore it is so!"

So from their point of view their folklore is really their history, and all the magic and mystical happenings are explained in the introductory phrase: "In the old days, when people were different from now———." And the teller believes in the tale as much as the listener.

Just like the primitive Indians, the Eskimos have the greatest respect and love for the animals they live on. They imbue them with souls, and it is their great concern that they shall feel good about being hunted and killed. Therefore, the animals play a big role in their folk stories, in the little fables as well as in the long winding epic tales that often take more than one evening to render.

Here is my rendition of some typical epic tales:

The Story of the Woman Who Adopted a Bear. Once long ago, when people were stronger than now, there lived at Cape York a man called Angudluk. He was a famous chief hunter, and many sleds came visiting every winter because it was known that there was never any lack of food in his house. He himself was a modest man who only rarely put on important airs, and they could never induce him to take the lead in group hunting, whether it was for sea animals or for caribou.

He liked to go hunting alone, and usually he would come home with his sled so loaded with seals that his wife and his mother couldn't get enough sleep because they had to sit and scrape blubber off and tan the many sealskins he brought with him.

Then, when strangers came to his village, and they had not been successful in their summer hunt, he would roll some skins up in a bundle and say that he was very sad that he didn't have anything of value to give them, but that he would be glad if they would accept his miserable skins that were of bad animals and very badly prepared.

Sometimes it annoyed his wife that she had to toil so hard, and she said to her mother-in-law that she envied the wives of the unsuccessful hunters, for they didn't have so much work to do preparing the skins, and they made out anyway. And why should we sit and scrape blubber off for those women whose husbands cannot bring enough seals home to their houses?

"Oh, Angudluk just happens to be such a great hunter that he has his pleasure in giving away his excess," said old Iterfiluk. And so they went on scraping sealskins, which the man gave away without any thought that it might vex the women. But with all the wealth there was in the house, the wife became very fat and attracted the attention of men wherever she went.

One day they were visited by a hunter from another village who recently had lost his wife and had journeyed out in quest of a new one. Since he had touched a corpse so recently, it was thought that it would be best if he stayed away from the game animals for some time, at least until the next change of the moon.

"Possibly here are some bits of meat for your mighty dogs to have a meal on," said Angudluk. And then he drove out for big game as usual.

The stranger stayed at home and courted the great hunter's wife. He told her that he only regretted that she didn't have time to take part in the other women's play down on the ice. They were playing football there.

"Much pleasure would have come from seeing you hop about with pretty movements," he said.

"Alas, since I came to this house my fingers have been worn shorter and shorter from much work. I have forgotten what it is to play, and I recall the sweetness of leisure only from when I was a child."

Thus she lied. But now the stranger knew that she was dissatisfied, and in the evening—when Angudluk could be expected to return home—he took his harpoon and followed his sled track from the morning so as to meet him.

When the hunter finally came driving, it was at a slow pace, for his sled was so heavily charged. He had felled and skinned a big bear, and its meat and two whole seals weighed down the sled. When the stranger reached him he started to shout so as to get his attention. It was dark, and Angudluk jumped off the sled and went up to the man to see what was the matter. The stranger took his harpoon and thrust it violently right into Angudluk's heart. Angudluk collapsed on the ice.

"Your wife is overburdened with work, I will revenge that!" the murderer yelled, and aimed once more for Angudluk's chest.

"She will possibly get less to do with scraping skins in the future!" said Angudluk, and then he died.

The slayer took his sled and wanted to drive home, but the dogs obeyed him only reluctantly, and he wasn't used to transporting such heavy loads, therefore he discarded the two seals and came driving home with the bear meat.

When people in the village saw that he came alone with Angudluk's sled, they understood that violence had taken place out on the ice. But they were afraid to go visiting the widow and find out what had happened.

The next morning they found only old Iterfiluk and Angudluk's little son in the house. The wife had gone away with her husband's murderer, and the sled tracks pointed north.

The mother wept a lot, but the little boy had no idea of what he had lost, so he played with the other children on the ice.

When now the villagers saw that there was only an old woman in the chief hunter's house, they started to supply themselves from all the meat in the meat rack. It used to be that there always was plenty, so that nobody noticed when boiling meat was taken, but now they started feeding their dogs with the dead man's meat.

Iterfiluk remarked to the other women: "Alas, if only my little grandson's food could be left in peace, then we would have enough until spring, when I can go up to the cliffs and catch little auks for him."

The women didn't answer her, but they repeated it to their husbands at home. These became ashamed over her words, but also angry and revengeful. Some time later the murdered Angudluk was found on the ice. And also the two seals his slayer had thrown off the sled.

So as not to be bothered with burial or give other villages reason for gossip, the men decided to put the dead one down in a crack in the ice; but since his corpse was frozen now, it floated on the water and wouldn't sink. They had to thrust their harpoons into him to get him in under the ice so that the current could carry him away.

While they were doing this one of them said, "Now we got second and third and fourth harpoon in the killed game!"

The others didn't answer, but their thoughts grew heavy, and they regretted what they had done. Still, they took the two seals on their sleds and brought them home to the village.

"Somebody had luck at a blowhole," they said when the children crowded around their sleds.

"It is strange that the seals come frozen stiff to the blowholes!" a little voice said. That was Angudluk's son, he was only a child, but he already had the ability to think like a great hunter.

This made the driver of the sled so irate that he took his big snow knife and struck the boy on his head so that his forehead was split and the brain matter welled out, and the boy was dead before he hit the ground.

"Alas, now you have robbed me of all I have in life," said Iterfiluk. She brought the dead boy into the house, where she sat for five days on the bunk without eating anything and without sleeping. For she had lost her only relative.

When the five days had passed, she carried the corpse out and put it on the little toy sled on which the boy had so often brought ice to the house. She pulled it up into the mountains and set the corpse in stones without help from anybody.

When she came down to the village again, the hunters had just come home with a female bear they had killed and a small bear cub. They had brought the cub home alive so that their children could have the amusement of killing it and playing great hunters chasing bear.

The old woman went up to the sled and saw the cub lying tied on top of its own mother's meat.

"You could give me the poor bear cub instead of what I have lost," said Iterfiluk. And the men thought that it might be a good idea to let her feed it and then kill it when it had grown big and would fill up the pots.

Iterfiluk carried the cub into her house, and there she fed it well and got it so tame that it followed her where she went and lay by her side at night. And she talked to it a lot, so that it developed the ears to hear her speech, and it understood everything that was said.

One day Iterfiluk went down to the meat rack to get meat for her pot, and there she heard the hunters say that now there wasn't much left of Angudluk's catch, it took too much meat to feed that bear also. "It is perhaps best that we kill it soon, so that it won't use up our stores any more."

Iterfiluk became afraid, and during the night she rolled up some skins and went with her bear over to the other side of the cape, where she knew that her late son had caches from the spring catch on which she could live.

She collected a lot of grass from under the bird cliffs and made herself comfortable in a cave, but she didn't dare to light a fire lest the men should discover her and come to steal the bear cub. Therefore, they ate only frozen meat, and she began to yearn for some warm food.

"Oh, if we only had a little boiled meat," she said one day to her bear. And a little later it left the cave and stayed away for some time. Iterfiluk felt uneasy and went out to look for it, and while she was standing there in the beginning light, she saw it returning with a newly caught seal.

Oh, she was so happy, she hurried to flense the seal, and she ate steaming warm liver and drank blood, and soon she felt her old limbs warm up again.

After that the bear went hunting every day and came home with seals. In the manner of bears it ate only a little of the back blubber; the rest of it was therefore left to its foster mother. And a big heap of frozen carcasses of seals grew up outside her cave. One day, when her former village mates happened by, their dogs discovered the many tracks leading up to the cave, they rushed up there, and the men were highly astonished to see great numbers of seals lying about with only the liver and the heart and sometimes the brain taken out:

"It appears that somebody who knows the good-tasting things lives here!" they said. And then they saw the old Iterfiluk and her bear sitting side by side and looking right at them.

"An old woman has taken land for herself, since she is not fitting company for men," said Iterfiluk.

But they hurried to tell her that they would be happy to see her face in the village again. The thing was that there was no more meat at home, and for several years the hunters had been used to what Angudluk provided and were no longer in the habit of going on long hunting trips to feed their families. They saw readily that the bear was a mighty hunter and that it was well worth getting for a village mate. Iterfiluk was invited to get on one of the sleds, and the bear trotted along back to the village.

But for many days the men drove seals home from the cave, and the bear's catch filled the meat rack so that it looked as it had in Angudluk's time.

Every day, the bear went out hunting and came dragging home game. But sometimes it happened that it came home with nothing at all; that was when it had met other bears at the seals' blowholes. It didn't want to take the quarry away from them, but sneaked home, because it was ashamed over having taken up with people. When this happened, it stayed in the house for a few days without stirring, and then it started going hunting again.

When the spring came and the ice broke up, the bear had grown so big that it could manage both narwhales and white whales. It went up to the cracks in the ice and sat there waiting until the narwhales came up to blow. Since its patience was enormous, it just stayed there waiting. If the narwhale came up a little in front of it or a little behind it, it didn't move, but the moment one came up to breathe exactly where it was sitting, it landed its huge paw in the head of the whale, killing it. It was easy for the bear to pull the whale up on the ice, and then with its claws it tore a long gash in the whale's back and ate a little mattak and a little blubber. Then it resumed its waiting. When it returned home it would drag the whole narwhale after it and place it on the ice just outside Iterfiluk's house. Then all the hunters came running up. They threw harpoons without points at the unflensed whale and shouted and carried on as if they were whaling on the sea:

"I was lucky to get first harpoon!" yelled one.

"Yes, but I was second!"

And thus they continued announcing their skill as if it was their own game. And they flensed the animal.

Iterfiluk was given only a small piece, such as is given to women without husbands, and she had to be content with that. She often sat in the house with a very narrow flame on her lamp, because she didn't have blubber enough to let it burn in its full width.

One day she had the ill luck to break her lamp when she was rearranging her bunk. It fell on the floor and went to pieces. Iterfiluk started to cry, for she had no husband who could chop out soapstone for a new lamp, but then it occurred to her that her son Angudluk had had more lamps than the ones his treacherous wife had taken with her when she fled north with the murderer.

But so great was her respect for her late son that she didn't dare go and request them from the other villagers, for then it would look as if she was referring to the dead one and dishonoring his memory.

Therefore she said to her foster son that if she could only get the tusks from a couple of the narwhales he caught, then there was perhaps a possibility that she might give them in payment for one of the lamps that she once had taken care of herself in the great hunter's house.

The bear understood what she said, and next time it came home with a narwhale it broke off the tusk and carried it up to its foster mother.

She was sitting and weeping over her sad fate, that she could get boiled meat only when she went visiting the neighbors. At home, she ate only frozen meat and such things as could be consumed raw, but she missed the smell of hot soup and lamp smoke which is necessary to feel comfortable in a house.

Then one day, when the bear came home with a narwhale, Iterfiluk came out to meet him with her curved knife in her hand.

"It so happens that somebody got an irresistible desire to have a piece of tail fin," she said, and the bear turned the narwhale so that the tail was in front of her. With a couple of swift cuts she started to separate the tail. But so as not to be thought immodest, she took only the one side of the fin and carried it into her house, together with the tusk which the bear had broken off for her.

At this moment, the villagers caught sight of the great fish lying on the ice, and they came running out.

"What has happened?" they shouted angrily. "Again he brings home a narwhale without horn, and it seems that the sea animals must be insulted by having women cut their tail fins off."

Iterfiluk said nothing, for her desire to eat the narwhale's fin was greater than her shame over having broken good customs.

Now some days passed without any of those things happening that are remembered and mentioned in stories.

The bear took care of the hunting, and the men stuck to home. And since they in their great idleness used up the day going on visits to each other's houses, they were infected by women's desire to gossip, and while the meat was being cooked in the pot over the lamp they bragged of their great deeds.

At last, their speech was so trivial that the women began to mix into the conversation. The men lost their dignity to such degree that they listened to the women and answered them as if it were sensible speech they came out with.

When the men then came out of the houses, they saw their dogs lying well-fed and rested in front of the houses. They fed them every day, so as to enjoy the sight of the great quantities of meat that disappeared into their jaws. But because the dogs looked so impressive, the men began to show arrogance, and when it happened that the bear returned home late, or maybe stayed away a whole day because the game animals were rare or shy, then they reproached it and shouted to it thus:

"It would appear that somebody has forgotten to hurry! It might easily happen that people in the village became tired of waiting. And strange it would seem if people were forced to show anger because kind speech retards somebody's luck at hunting!"

And then the fattest one of the hunters said that it was sad to see how the bear ruined the sealskins when it clawed a couple of bites off the back and ate the seal with blubber on!

"It will be necessary to stop that kind of thing," he said. "And a bear's teeth are strong, it can do with a couple of the bones which it can easily chew. But since spring is coming, we shall need many skins for tents. Therefore no more may be ruined!"

Then they took all the meat and brought it into their own houses, but they gave nothing to old Iterfiluk, who had to go hungry into her house. There, in the darkness, she fumbled her way up to her foster son and found a little warmth for her old limbs by pressing herself up to him. She started to cry during the night, partly from hunger and partly because of her village mates' evil actions. Also, the loss of her son and the little grandson, who both could have been alive and kept the house in great wealth if only they had not been killed through the evil of other people.

As she had always been good to the bear, it became very upset over the old woman's sad fate, and when she had finally fallen asleep, it silently slid down from the bunk and quickly ran out on the ice so as to procure something delicious to comfort her with. It didn't take long before it heard a snort from a crack by a stranded iceberg. The iceberg rested on a cliff deep in the sea. The ice around was lifted and lowered with the ebbs and tides, and this caused big cracks in it. Therefore, seals and white whales gathered there to breathe and to rest in peace when they wanted to sleep.

The bear took its position astride an open crack, and there eyed a fat white whale shining up through the dark water and rousing a powerful urge for food in the bear. It was so eager to get game that it hit a terrible blow down on the head of the white whale just as it was coming up to blow, and the whale died instantly. The crack was quite narrow, but the bear stuck head and forelegs down through it, got hold of the white whale and pulled. And so great was its strength that it could haul the entire animal up through the crack. All the whale's ribs broke, though, and its intestines were pressed out through its rectum, before the bear could get it up on the ice. It was therefore a strange-looking whale the bear came dragging up to the village. All the men watched it when it arrived, and as usual they came running to stick their harpoons into the already dead animal so as to secure parts in the game.

"What kind of ruined animal is being brought here?" yelled the fat hunter. "Again you have spoiled good things from the sea. And it is a big question if the sea beasts will not be insulted over this treatment. Other people usually chop a hole in the ice when a killed animal must be hauled up."

But the bear took no notice of him. With its teeth well clamped down on the whale's head it passed right by the man and walked toward Iterfiluk's house.

"What strange thing? Oh, the impudence seems to grow in this village!" shouted the fat hunter. "It is required that you stand still and let people do certain things to the whale!"

But the bear continued up over the beach.

"This impertinence must not be tolerated, we had better kill the bear!" they said to each other.

"Yes, and it is growing so big that it can be dangerous!"

In this manner they excited each other, so that they quite forgot that if the bear wasn't there, they would themselves have to drive long distances out on the ice to get their daily sustenance. Because they had for such a long time been out of the habit of making decisions, all wisdom left their thoughts, and they rushed upon the bear and thrust their spears in between its ribs. One of them hit its neck, another drove the sharp point in through the kidney and the gut.

The bear sank down dead, and the men were completely flushed and frenzied.

"It was I who first put spear in it!" yelled the fat one.

"Oh, I hit almost at the same time!" said another.

"No, the two of us threw in unison, and it was our spears that reached the bear's skin first!" protested two of the others.

While they were quarreling like this, they suddenly saw the old Iterfiluk standing and crying by the dead body of her foster son. She lamented that she now had nobody at all to help her, she thought that life had become too heavy to bear, and they would do best to kill her at once.

Her tears and wails made a little shame return to the men. They didn't answer her at all, though, but ran up to get their knives and start flensing.

Now it appeared that in their excessive leisure they had forgotten the ability to flense, and they all started in with untrained hands. At last they managed to split the skin open down the chest and belly of the bear, and along the four legs.

But before they had gotten the skin off the body, a man—eager to get to the heart and eat it—had started cutting into it without anybody else noticing it. And no sooner had he opened the body than he gave a loud yell of dismay and horror. For now Angudluk's little son emerged from the dead bear and stood with wrinkled brow and irate face in the middle of the group. So terrible did his wrath appear that two of the hunters sat down on their behinds, because their legs refused to hold them. But the boy showed no pity with the people who had killed his father and himself and in their senseless avarice had tortured him when he—in the shape of a bear—wanted to help his grandmother.

He grabbed the harpoons and spears lying by the bear-skin, and with his first throw he pierced two of the men. Then he hit a third one, and the blow was so powerful that he crushed all the bones in the man's head and body, and the harpoon stock was shattered to pieces on the ground.

At once they were all beset by terrible fear, and they started running toward the houses while they wailed loudly to the pursuing boy: "Oh, spare our lives, please spare our lives. We had no evil intentions! You know our inclination to joke a little! Let us show our joy at welcoming our dear little village mate!"

But the orphaned boy spared nobody. He killed all the

men before they could reach their houses, but, not content with that, he kicked so violently at the roofs that they flew off the houses, and he went on killing women and children until nobody was left. He went from one house to the other, and his fury was so violent that the lust to kill increased with every person he slew. At last, all the houses were sundered, and the enemy lay spread about pitifully massacred. Then he started in on the dogs who had so often growled at him and shown angry teeth when he lived in the shape of a bear.

They were all killed. And in his powerful rage he dashed wildly all over the settlement. The blood pressed out in his eyes, because his wrath pressed from within. And suddenly he discovered that there was yet another living being in the place. That was Iterfiluk, his grandmother, who now came walking toward him to welcome him and thank him for getting revenge. But such a senseless fury as possessed the boy now was not stilled in such a short time. With a crashing blow of his fist he smashed his grandmother's head and she fell over.

"But a great joy appeared at last!" said Iterfiluk, and then she died.

But the boy had now got relief for his thirst for revenge, and he began to mourn the death of the grandmother. And he didn't dare to go to see other people until he was quite sure that he was peaceful. Therefore he went out hunting alone and built huge meat caches in the mountains.

Not until spring came did he wander out to visit other villages.

Since he arrived without dogs, he was not considered to be a man of importance, and he was given the side bunk to sleep on in the houses; but he didn't show any displeasure.

It happened one day that he came to the house of a chief hunter whose son had gone up the fjord to fetch a wife. He came driving proudly home with her; he had taken all his weapons with him, and there were many dogs for his sled. This was done to give a good impression when he came courting.

When the boy saw this wealthy young hunter come driving back with his newly acquired woman, who was very beautiful, he went to meet them. When the dogs saw him they increased their speed and ran eagerly toward him. When they reached him they stopped, and the arrogant young driver called out to him to get out of the way: "What kind of fellow are you that you dare stand in the way of a man who is driving his wife home?"

The boy didn't answer, but strode up to the sled and grabbed the groom. He took the whip out of his hand and handed it to the bride, asking her to hold it for a moment. Then he wrung the head off the boastful young man and threw it out behind the sled. The body he left on the ice.

"Hand me the whip again!" he said to the young woman, and then he gave the starting signal to the dogs. He directed them away from the nearby houses and continued on until they reached his home village.

"Oh, what a miserable place you have taken me to!" said the bride, and began to cry. He didn't answer her, but showed her the big piles of meat he had collected. Then she understood that she had come to the domain of a great hunter, and she stayed with him. They lived for many years, and the boy became the ancestor of a famous family who to this day show great ability and never have known poverty. But also they are feared because they are quick to get angry, and do not tolerate affronts of any kind.

And here ends the story of the orphan who took the shape of a bear.

The Story of the Two Sisters Who Married Abroad. It is said of a man called Tulimaq that he had taken land on one of the islands north of Svartenhuk. He lived there alone with his family, and since he was a successful hunter he brought seals home every day, and they never lacked meat in that house. But even so, he was not a happy man, for his wife had not borne him any sons who could brighten his old age by bringing home game. They had only two daughters who grew up to become clever girls, but it didn't look as if the young men from other settlements were going to come to see them. No kayaks brought visitors to stay overnight.

Every summer, when the skins from the spring catch had been finished, and the sun had thawed the ice in the fjords, Tulimaq used to go caribou hunting deep into that fjord that cuts near to the icecap. He used his daughters as rowers, he himself directed the course and spoke angry words if they didn't row fast enough.

Since his legs were a little weak, he had trained his daughters to pursue the caribou in a swift run and drive them toward a ravine, at the end of which he was waiting with bow and arrow.

So fast were the girls at running that fire shot out from

the tips of their long hair when they took off over the cliffs.

Tulimaq felled many caribou, and his daughters dried the meat in the sun; the tallow they preserved in caribou stomachs, and the marrow they melted into big cakes that they gorged themselves on during the winter. When they had dried as much meat as the skin boat could hold, their father would tell them that they should kill another few animals, so as to come home with fresh meat, and so they did.

One evening they were sitting by the fire, and the daughters were looking at the terns that were diving for fish. The old ones had already entered the tent to go to sleep.

Then said the elder sister: "How unfortunate it is that our father has taken land at a place where there are no other people. Now we could have been married and had our own tents, if we had only known some men."

"Yes," said the younger one. "It is unfortunate!"

Tulimaq, in the tent, heard what they said, and their words infuriated him.

The next day they broke camp to return home, and he had not forgotten his ire. When they came to a place where they used to get fresh water, he directed the umiak to the coast and said to the daughters: "Fetch water!"

They each took a scoop and jumped onto the beach. There was a little lake behind a ridge, and there they went to get water.

As soon as they had disappeared behind the ridge, Tulimaq commanded his wife to row away from the daughters. His wife pitied her two children and started to cry, but Tulimaq raised his spear, threatening her, and she didn't dare to protest.

When they had gone a little away from the beach, they heard the girls laughing, up in the hills; they didn't suspect that their parents would abandon them. The mother couldn't hold her sobs any more, but her husband put on a grim face and raised the spear again. She became very afraid and swallowed her tears, and they rowed away.

And when the daughters came back down to the coast, they saw that the umiak was so far out that their shouts couldn't reach it. They sat down on the beach and were very sad. Suddenly they discovered a small ice pan floating nearby them.

"Let it be our boat!" said the eldest. "Come, jump aboard, and we'll sail home!"

And they stepped onto the ice pan, and they started to run

in circles on it, faster and faster. They were so fast that the
ice pan began to turn like a top, and it was set adrift. They
drifted rapidly out to sea, and after a while they passed by
their home island, and they saw their father repairing his
kayak, and their mother sitting and scraping skins. But the
girls sailed on and came out on the great ocean.

Out here, the younger one began to cry from fear, but
her sister comforted her and said that they were not going to
suffer any hunger. And just as she said that, a seagull came
flying with a fish in its beak.

"Kitekee—kitekee—kitekee, here is something to eat for
you!" it said, and it threw the fish down on the ice pan.

The daughters divided the fish between them, and they were
satisfied for several days. When they finally became hungry,
the younger began to cry again, but the older sister calmed
her down.

"We shall not starve!" she said, and a walrus appeared.

"Uik-uik-ah-ah!" it said, and then it threw a heap of clams
up on the ice pan. They ate as many as they could, and kept
the rest for the next day.

In the meantime, a storm had come up, and the waves
crashed on the edges of their little ice pan. The younger
sister started to cry, for she feared that the pan would break
up.

"Don't be afraid," said the older. "We will reach land."

The ice pan drifted on, and soon they saw something black
on the horizon. The younger sister thought that it was storm
clouds drawing up, and she started to cry again.

"We are going to drown, anyway," she said. But the older
one quieted her down and said that surely it was not storm
clouds. It grew before them, and finally the sisters saw that
it was a high country they were drifting toward.

"Let us jump ashore!" said the older sister. "But you have
to close your eyes until you feel that you are on firm ground!"

And so they did, both of them. When they opened their
eyes and looked around, the ice pan had disappeared. Only
a little foam was bobbing in the waves.

When they mounted the coast, they saw a huge number of
narwhale tusks spread out on the beach.

"I want to stay here. These narwhale tusks can be used
for trading when ships come!" said the younger sister. But
the older one said that they had better go inland to look for
people. They walked and walked for many days, and one
evening they came upon a house, and they sneaked up to look

in the window. Inside two men were sitting, each on a bunk, and each one had a lamp that they were cooking by. But in the manner of men they tended the lamps so badly that the sisters couldn't help laughing, they were so clumsy.

"It sounded as if somebody was laughing at us!" said one of the men. "Let us hurry out, perhaps it is enemies who want to attack us!"

But when they came out, they saw the two girls, and they looked so scared that the men took pity on them. They went up and took hold of them, but then they discovered that they were very lean, and since they were cannibals, they decided to take the girls in as their wives and use them to take care of the household, and fatten them up for eating.

The two girls entered the house, and there were a lot of chores for them to do. The cannibal brothers felt very pleased to live in a house where the lamps were tended so well that they never sooted, and the lice were picked out of their hair so that they never needed to scratch themselves, their kamiks were dried and mended so that they never froze their feet. The sisters had learned to be clever and helpful in their father's house.

"It is very strange," said the younger sister to the other one day. "Every night when I am asleep, I am awakened by my husband's poking me in the ribs with his fingers."

"He does that because he wants to feel how fat you are. We are married to cannibals."

And then they started to poke around behind the house, and there they found human bones that had been split, which showed that the marrow had been sucked out of the bones so that those who had been eaten shouldn't become ghosts and take revenge.

The younger sister was terribly scared and began to cry. She suggested to her sister that they should run away before they became so fat that they were to be slaughtered.

"There is no haste right now," said the older sister. "We had better wait, for I am with child, and until it is born there will be no big feast!"

When some time had passed, the older sister bore a son. Then one day the younger sister heard her husband say to his brother: "I am very sad that only you have got a son. I think that I had better slaughter my wife at the next full moon, then we can ask our relatives to come visiting and enjoy her fat meat, for she is well-fed now and bursting with fat."

When she heard that, she feared much, and as soon as the

brothers had gone out hunting, she told her sister what she had heard.

"It is a long time yet until the full moon. Bring me a little of his urine so that I can tame him," said the older sister.

In the evening the brothers returned. The younger sister's husband had felled a great bear.

"If you would please me, give me the membrane that is around the bear's heart," said the older sister. So he did, and she made a little bag out of it and dried it by the lamp in the evening. When they were about to go to bed, the younger sister's husband went out first to let his water, and his wife sneaked after him. When he had gone back into the house, she cut out the snow where he had been standing with a knife. She brought it to her sister, who put the snow in the small bag and hung it over the flame so that it would thaw. In the morning the bag was filled with a black fluid.

"What is it you have hanging there?" asked the younger sister's husband.

"Oh, that is the contents of a ptarmigan intestine which I have emptied out in water. If you put it in your soup you will get great strength and be able to resist cold just like the ptarmigan," she answered him. And the man, who was often cold, was eager to try it. So he poured the fluid from her little bag into his soup. And then he went out hunting.

When he returned in the evening he was sick. They fetched an angakok from the nearest village, and he summoned his helping spirits, who revealed that it was the two sisters who had used their magic to make him ill. As soon as the two sisters heard this, they ran away so as to avoid revenge. Now it was to their advantage that their father had trained them to run so fast, for the pursuing brothers were soon lost from sight. But when evening came they were tired and had to sit down to rest.

In a little while they heard their pursuers come nearer, and they knew nothing better than to hide themselves in a crack in the rock nearby. They crawled down in it, and the older sister said to the other: "Lick the edge of the crack on the one side!" And she started licking the other side herself.

They had hardly finished this when the two brothers were upon them. But the two sisters pressed themselves deep into the fissure, which immediately closed above them. Only a small opening to look through remained, and they could hear what was said: "Naw, I thought I saw the two sisters."

"You must have been mistaken, it is your wish that is so strong!"

"If we only had eaten them both at once!"

And then they continued their pursuit. When they had disappeared, the older sister said that they should blow on the rock which had closed itself over them. So they did, and the fissure opened up again, and they crawled out.

They walked on and came down to the beach. The younger sister despaired, for there was nothing but open water in front of them. The sea roared, and large specks of foam danced along the beach.

"Close your eyes and jump for the large speck of foam!" yelled the older one. And so she did, and jumped as far as she could. She expected to fall in the water, but she thought that it was better to drown than to be eaten by cannibals. To her amazement, she felt firm ground under her feet, and when she opened her eyes they stood on an ice pan which already was drifting away from the coast.

Now the older sister hurried to take the thong that supported the amaut in which she carried her little son. She swung it in a circle in front of them, and just in the nick of time, for now the men were on the beach and began to shoot arrows at them. And when she swung the thong the arrows dropped down, and the sisters picked them up. Then the two men threw their harpoons after them, and they also fell at the feet of the two sisters.

"They will be good to have during the voyage," said the older.

When they came out to sea they began to feel hunger, and the younger sister started to cry.

"It is better to be hungry than to be eaten!" said the older sister, and immediately a walrus appeared in the water.

"Uik-uik-ah-ah!" it said, and just stared at them. But the oldest sister grabbed one of the harpoons and lifted it to throw. The walrus got so scared that it vomited in its fear, and it spat out a great number of clams, which they picked up and ate.

The next day a seagull came flying above their heads.

"Kitekee, kitekee!" it cried, but the older sister took one of the arrows and threatened to send it at the bird, and it got so scared that it dropped a fish on the ice pan.

The sisters laughed and ate the fish. Then they lay down to sleep, while the ice pan sailed on at high speed. When they woke up the next morning, they were close by their little

home island. When the ice pan hit the beach, they jumped off
and approached their parents' house.

Old Tulimaq came out, and he feared that they had come
to take revenge. But the sisters entered the house and presented the little boy to his grandmother, who immediately
began to play with him, and when Tulimaq entered he found
them thus.

"You have been away a long time!" he said. And nothing
more was said about that.

They lived quietly through the fall and all of next winter,
and then one day the younger sister was reminded of all the
narwhale tusks that were spread on the beach of the country
they had visited. She talked so much about them that her
father felt a desire to go and fetch them. When the ice broke
up, he ordered his wife and his daughters to sew a new
cover for the umiak. Seven ribbon seals went into it. When the
women prepared to go to the fjord to hunt caribou as usual, he
didn't mention to them that he had decided differently. He
let them take a lot of provisions on board, and then they
rowed out to sea. Instead of turning east toward the fjord,
he turned west and commanded them to row on.

When land was lost from sight, Tulimaq told them to pull
in the oars and lie down in the bottom of the boat with closed
eyes.

So they did, but they felt distinctly that the boat cut
through the water at high speed. After a while, the younger
sister got tired of lying with closed eyes, and she opened the
left eye a little bit. At once their speed was slowed so suddenly that Tulimaq tumbled down from the thwart he was
sitting on, but the younger sister hurried to close her eyes
again, and soon they resumed their speed.

"Maybe we hit an ice pan," said Tulimaq. "A good thing
that we have two layers of skins on the boat!"

Soon he saw land before them, and he called to his wife
and daughters to open their eyes and look around them. The
daughters recognized the country, and they landed on the
beach where all the narwhale tusks were. They decided to see
if the umiak could hold all those tusks, and they took every
last one of them and loaded them on. It now turned out
that the umiak sank halfway down into the water.

"It appears that a poor boat has great loading ability!"
said Tulimaq. "Lie down in the bottom of the boat and close
your eyes well!"

They did as he told them, and immediately the boat took

off at great speed and sailed out to sea. The women lay trembling in the boat for a long time. Tulimaq didn't speak to them until suddenly he shouted to them to open their eyes and lift their heads. So they did, and they were home again.

Tulimaq sold the tusks to whalers when their ships came near his settlement. Their wealth increased, and soon both sisters were married to great hunters.

The older sister's son grew up to become a famous chief hunter whose descendants are still living among us, and they are all easily angered, because they descend from cannibals through him.

And here ends the story about the two sisters who went to Baffin Land and married cannibals.

The Story About the Hunter Who Married a Fox. In the old days, when people had remarkable experiences, there lived a hunter in Hudson Bay who had no wife. He was not a bad hunter, but he could not hold his own in fist fights with the other men and get himself a woman. Every time he tried to get near a girl, other hunters came and took her away from him, and he was much too good-natured to try to take revenge.

Because he was a man, he did not know very well how to scrape skins and tan them, but somehow he managed to get along until the time came to sew some clothes. He could never make them fit right, and his kamiks especially were a sorry sight. At last, he felt that he could no longer stay in the sight of other people, for they made a laughingstock of him because of his ridiculous clothes. He left his settlement and wandered into the bottom of an inlet, and there he built himself a house and stayed all alone. For he was ashamed to show his misery to other people.

One day he saw a little fox whelp nearby his house. It didn't seem to be afraid of him, and he didn't kill it because it was in the summer, and fox fur was without any value. He took it into his house and amused himself by watching its funny jumping around. In the course of time it became very tame, and it would come up to lick the blood and blubber off his hands when he had flensed some game. For since he had no woman around, he didn't think of washing.

The hunter grew more and more fond of his fox, and he was afraid that when it grew up it would run away from him. So he tied a string around its neck and tied it to the housepole.

Sometimes he didn't catch much game, and then the fox had to be content with the bones from his own boiled meat, which he threw to it.

One day he was out hunting and stayed away longer than usual, and when he came home he was utterly surprised to see that some sealskins he had started to scrape were now finished and stretched out with sticks in front of the house, as women usually do it.

He was a bit uneasy, since he was quite alone; but he couldn't see any other people anywhere, so he just went inside to eat, and then he lay down to sleep.

The next day he went out hunting again, and when he returned, steaming hot cooked meat and fresh ripe berries, with seal oil poured over them, had been prepared for him. The hunter was mystified again, of course, but he ate with good appetite and lay down to sleep.

The next day, on the hunt, he was too excited to catch any seals, for he couldn't help wondering if there would be any more strange presents for him when he came home. And sure enough, when he entered the house his eyes fell upon a beautiful pair of kamiks that had been placed on his bunk. He was overjoyed.

"Perhaps one might approach people again!" he said. Then he went to sleep, but his consternation was by now so great that he dreamed powerful visions, and he did not rest very well.

The next day he decided that he would try to find out how these things happened. He rowed out in his kayak as usual, but when he passed behind a rock, he left his kayak and climbed up so that he could see his house. He waited there patiently until it was almost evening, but when he almost despaired and wanted to return home, he suddenly saw a beautiful woman step out from his house, throw out some garbage, and go in again.

The man hurried down to his kayak and paddled home. When he entered the house, there was nobody there, yet the house was swept and cleaned out.

He was unable to think of anything else but the beautiful girl, and he laid a plan to trick her. The next day he rowed out in his kayak, and when he got behind the rock he pulled it up on land. Then he walked in a great circle so that he came up behind his house and hid there to watch.

Then he saw the beautiful woman come out from the house, like yesterday, and his desire overcame him completely. He ran up and caught her and pulled her into the house and made her his wife. She did not resist him very much, either, but seemed to like him.

They lived happily together for a long time, and she proved to be clever at all household chores, and since the man really was a good hunter who brought many skins home, he soon became as well-dressed as he before had been ragged. She also sewed him a new skin cover for his kayak, and now he could go on longer trips than the old water-soaked skins allowed him to do.

One day he rowed far away to a place where there used to be many bearded seals, and there he happened to meet a former hunting mate and they talked with each other.

"You must surely have a clever wife!" said the friend to him, and looked him over. "Such handsomely sewn clothes and well-fitting kamiks!"

"An unusually beautiful wife appeared!" said the hunter. And since he had not seen other people for so long, he became too talkative, and he boasted so much of his wife and her talents that the other man was embarrassed to listen to it.

"It might be amusing to learn to know her," he said, "since she seems to be so perfect in all respects!"

And then he proposed to exchange wives so that her reputation might spread and her honor increase. The hunter could not refuse such a request, so he paddled home to his friend's house while this latter rowed the long distance to the isolated dwelling in the inlet. He was very eager to have this experience.

When he reached the house, the woman had already gone to sleep, and he crawled in through the entrance tunnel to find her. Then he noticed a rather strong and distinct odor from within.

"It is terrible how it smells here of foxes," he said.

When the woman heard this said in a strange voice, she began to cackle like a fox. "Ka-ka-ka-kak," she said, and then she turned into a fox and hopped down from the bunk, and she slipped out the entrance past the stranger and disappeared before he could catch her.

When the hunter came paddling home the next morning, his guest told him what had taken place. And only then did the hunter remember that he had been in such an ecstasy over his little wife that he had completely forgotten about the fox that he had tied to the housepole. But it occurred to him that one night, when they were lying side by side on the bunk, that he had seen that her gums were bloody, and he had asked her why.

"It was caused by the hard bones that you sometimes threw to me so that I had to gnaw them," she said. And then they didn't discuss that any more.

But now the hunter was very sad, because he had lost his wife and made himself ridiculous in his friend's eyes. The fact was that he had become so used to the smell of fox that he didn't notice it any more.

As soon as the guest had left, he went up into the hills to find his wife and bring her back. Following a fox track, he walked for many days in the mountains. Already on the first day he saw that one side of the track turned into a human footprint. A little while later he saw the prints of two human feet, but soon after the right side track turned into a fox footprint again. Then there were two fox tracks, and in this way it changed for several days, turning from fox into woman and back again.

The hunter yearned so much to see his wife that he forgot to eat and sleep, he just went on walking. Finally he came to a cave, and the tracks led into it. But the entrance was too small for him to get through. Then he heard his wife talking inside.

"Come out to me, do come out to me! I am here to take you home!" he shouted to her.

"I am not coming out to you, since you traded me away to another man!" she answered.

Then she said to some other woman in there: "You go out to him."

The other woman came out. But she was terribly ugly, she had such long legs and such a short torso that the hunter would have nothing to do with her.

"I want to be your wife!" she said.

"I don't want you; your legs are too long!" said the hunter. For it was a spider that had taken the shape of a woman. The spider went back into the cave and told the woman: "He didn't want me, my legs are too long!"

The hunter called his wife again.

"I am not coming out, since you traded me away to another man!" she said again, and then she told somebody else to go out.

Presently another woman came out, but she had two horrible bulging eyes that were hanging down over her cheeks.

"I want to be your wife!" she said.

But the hunter said that he could not even look at her, she was far too ugly with those big eyes. In fact, it was a blow-fly that had turned into a woman.

The blow-fly went back inside: "He did not want me, my eyes are too big!"

"Come out, I am here to take you home!" called the hunter to his wife.

"I don't want to return to you, because you traded me away!"

And again he heard her tell some other woman to go out in her stead. And now a woman came out who was even uglier than the two others.

"I would not mind being your wife!" she said.

But the hunter saw that she had long rows of protruding bones up along her sides, as if her many ribs were sticking through her clothes. It was nothing but a centipede who had turned into a woman.

"I don't want you, you have got far too many legs!" he said.

And the centipede returned to the cave, very sad.

"He didn't want me because I have too many legs!" he heard her say.

And now he cried out once more to his wife: "Let me take you home!"

But she answered: "No, you have heard what I said, I don't want to live with you any more, because you traded me away. You come in to me!"

"How can I get through that narrow hole?"

"Just shut your eyes and bend down and bore yourself forward!"

So he did, and he managed to crawl through the hole. Inside he opened his eyes and saw that he was in a little house, and his wife was sitting on the bunk. He was so happy to see her that he forgot his anger and that she had run away from him. He wanted to show her his joy so that she might share it, and therefore he lay down on the bunk and placed his head in her lap and said: "Oh, what a long time since you have picked the lice out of my hair. My head is itching all over. Please rid me of my lice!"

And she started picking the lice out of his hair. And while she did so, she sang to him:

"Just lie quiet—

Go to sleep—
Go to sleep—
Until the spring when the blow-flies fill the air,
Then you can wake up.
Go to sleep—
Until the spring when the terns are back,
Until the spring when the ice breaks up,
Then you can wake up."

Her song sounded so enchanting that he fell into a deep sleep. He slept without dreams, and when he woke up and looked around, he saw that his wife had left him. He called her, but nobody answered. Far up in the mountains, though, he heard a fox cackle at him. "Ka-ka-ka-kak," it said, and then all was silent again.

The hunter crawled out, and he was amazed, for when he went to sleep, fall was turning into winter, but now it was high spring. The blow-flies were swarming in the air, and when he went down to the coast he saw that the ice was gone, and the waves crashed on the cliffs. As he walked along, he saw the terns swooping down into the water to fish for shrimp.

After walking a long time he reached his house. There he saw a woman sitting on the roof, and he became very happy, for he was certain that it was his wife sitting and waiting for him to return. He shouted to her, but she kept turning her back to him. Finally he reached her, but as he tried to embrace her, the clothes collapsed in a heap. Only some old bones had been put up to support the garments.

In this manner his wife told him that she had no more need of clothes; she had abandoned her human shape!

The hunter had to resume his old way of living, preparing his skins and sewing his clothes himself. How he regretted that he had traded his little wife away just to gain some reputation. For he never saw her again.

And here ends the story about the man who married a fox. This is the end of this story, for what later happened to the man people have forgotten to tell, and to this day nobody knows what became of him.

Since all stories are based on real or supposedly real events, the telling of stories and the reporting of news become one and the same interpretive art. This art has been developed by some Eskimos, notably the angakoks and the old women, to its highest potential. The best storyteller I have ever known was Tatterat, the lame one. Before he came to live with us at the trading station, his devoted mother pushed him around on a small sled, and he talked to people and got their news. Even the most inconspicuous event he could turn into a news item of considerable interest. Everywhere he came, people flocked around his little sled to hear the latest; his art and finesse in holding their attention and amusing them were incomparable. He was a veritable living newspaper, and his store of tales and gossip seemed inexhaustible. People gave him bits of food and clothing because he entertained them so well, and it is no doubt on account of this artistic talent that he survived at all.

It was also because of this talent that Knud decided to have him live at the station and to keep him happy with all the tobacco he could smoke. For Knud was an eager collector of Eskimo folklore; he had already published two volumes of Greenland stories, and he was now planning a similar volume dealing with the Polar Eskimos. I always used to say that Knud collected old women! But this of course was not so much a collector's mania as it was a means to get tales and stories of the old times out of them. In this, he succeeded brilliantly.

During the Fifth Thule Expedition, Knud completed his unique record of Eskimo folklore that spans the whole Eskimo world from Greenland to Alaska—traditions that are forgotten by the newer generations, and which therefore are available only through his work.

Eskimo Music and Poetry

But since the Eskimos have no concept of fiction, their creative art is contained in their drum dances and poems. The drum, as a matter of fact, is the only Eskimo musical instrument. It is called the *ayayut*, and consists of a circular framework of bone or wood over which is stretched a skin of some kind—walrus throat, caribou stomach, or the like. The drum has a handle to hold it by, and it is beaten with a short, thick stick of bone or wood. It is always the frame that is beaten, not the skin, and since the drum is often more than two feet in diameter, it takes both skill and strength to handle it.

If it is only a matter of making music, it is usually done by a team of two. They stand opposite each other on the little floor of the house or igloo. One of them beats the ayayut, boom-boom-boom, always three beats in succession;

the other one sings and dances while he sings—that is, there isn't much room for hopping around, so usually he doesn't move his feet at all, but sways from side to side with gyrating hips, his body, head, and face emphasizing the rhythm. The tunes are quite simple, moving up and down a short scale in half and quarter tones, and we would hardly call it music at all. Often there are no words to the song, either, so that the artistic creation consists in mood and expression alone. The audience is grouped around the two performers on the bunks, and as they are caught by the mood of the tune, they join in with a refrain: Ay-ay-ay-aya, or some such thing. The singer gradually forgets everything about him and falls into a kind of trance, the rhythm becomes more violent, the pitch of his song gets higher and higher, until it seems to end in a scream.

At this moment, his partner stops him by brandishing his stick in front of him, and then he takes over. He sings one, then the first singer sings three, the second sings three, then the first sings seven, and so on, until saliva and perspiration flow richly from both of them. When they finally collapse with exhaustion, there is always somebody else who jumps onto the floor, asking permission to sing and challenging another man to be his partner. In fact, it was never difficult to start the Eskimos singing, but it was quite a problem to make them stop again. I have often seen a songfest go on for eighteen or twenty hours without any sign of anybody getting tired.

Sometimes you may see two singers who actually compose songs together, with text and all, and such a unison is considered sacred, almost like a brotherhood. These two poets will never sing together with anybody but each other, they hunt together, they exchange wives, and they marry their children to each other.

Among the Polar Eskimos, it was usually believed that women should not participate in the singing, except in the refrain, but this rule was not enforced, and among the Hudson Bay Eskimos I saw women participate in the songfests on a completely equal basis with the men, some of them being both fine singers and poets.

The real creator of songs would usually sing without a partner, so that he was poet, dancer, and drummer all by himself. But he could still surround himself with the chorus. As the chorus caught the mood of his poem, they would fall in with the refrain at certain places: Unaiya—

unaiya, or: Hey—hey—hey, just some sounds that could be varied gaily, sadly, or jeeringly. And nothing in such a performance would be haphazard. The song had a tune; the words had to follow the drumbeats and also the dance that was bound by a certain rhythm. Even if there was no scanned rhythm in the songs—which would probably be impossible, anyway, because of the polysynthetic language composition—there was respirational rhythm. If not, the dance became uneven, and trance didn't occur. There was no rhyme, but frequent repetitions aided the memory.

In most cases, then, it was only people who were trained in the composition of words who could create a song, and we are here faced with art creation that is far from primitive. Most songs created on the spur of the moment would be quite simple:

The Old Man's Song

I have grown old,
I have lived much,
Many things I understand,
But four riddles I cannot solve.
Ha-ya-ya-ya.

The sun's origin,
The moon's nature,
The minds of women,
And why people have so many lice.
Ha-ya-ya-ya.

The Old Woman's Song

Since I am no angakok,
I cannot reveal hidden things.
Ha-ya-hey.

Virtue is only to be found in old women,
And therefore it is my sorrow,
Oh, I am so sad,
Because I am old.
Ha-ya-hey.

The Father's Song

Great snowslide,
Stay away from my igloo,
I have my four children and my wife;

They can never enrich you.

Strong snowslide,
Roll past my weak house.
There sleep my dear ones in the world.
Snowslide, let their night be calm.

Sinister snowslide,
I just built an igloo here, sheltered from the wind.
It is my fault if it is put wrong.
Snowslide, hear me from your mountain.

Greedy snowslide,
There is enough to smash and smother.
Fall down over the ice,
Bury stones and cliffs and rocks.

Snowslide, I own so little in the world.
Keep away from my igloo, stop not our travels.
Nothing will you gain by our horror and death,
Mighty snowslide, mighty snowslide.

Little snowslide,
Four children and my wife are my whole world, all I own,
All I can lose, nothing can you gain.
Snowslide, save my house, stay on your summit.

The Mother's Song

It is so still in the house.
There is a calm in the house;
The snowstorm wails out there,
And the dogs are rolled up with snouts under the tail.
My little boy is sleeping on the ledge,
On his back he lies, breathing through his open mouth.
His little stomach is bulging round—
Is it strange if I start to cry with joy?

The angakoks were usually the best poets, not because
they were familiar with the state of trance and the "inspiration" coming out of the trance, but because they more
than anyone else were experienced in the composition of
words. As mentioned before, they had a special seance language in which all things and all beings were called by other
names than the usual ones or by circumlocutions. This im-

mediately put a whole new set of images at their disposal. But also, their trade required that they always have numerous magic formulas ready for use when needed. These formulas would lose their power if used by anyone else. Therefore, within the rules of the polysynthetic language, they would make their own word compositions, not understandable to other people. Since the formulas lost their power after too much use, they had to be constantly renewed, and the anga-koks thus trained themselves in new and unusual word com-binations. As a result they could write many poems.

For no matter how great and noble the primitive inspira-tion may be, it is of no use if the tools are not available to the artist. The case is completely analogous to that of a modern artist who learns his trade carefully, "from the bot-tom up," then promptly forgets it all. Down into the sub-conscious with it so that it can weave its spell when inspira-tion occurs!

Here are two magic songs in which inspiration plays a part. The first one is recited when in sudden danger of death:

> You earth,
> Our great earth!
> See, oh see:
> All these heaps
> Of bleached bones
> And wind-dried skeletons!
> They crumble in the air,
> The mighty world,
> The mighty world's
> Air!
> Bleached bones,
> Wind-dried skeletons,
> Crumble in the air!
> Hey-hey-hey!

The Hudson Bay Eskimo, Padloq, who sang it, said that his father had composed it. One day the father had shot a raven, and while he was contemplating its death agony he had recited the song. The words had come by themselves. But Padloq characterized his father as a man who liked lone-liness, a description which—in Eskimo usage—is no doubt equivalent to the man's being a poet or angakok.

A bit odder is the case of the woman angakok, Uvavnuk, because it is so grotesque in its mysticism. One winter eve-ning, Uvavnuk had gone outside her igloo, when suddenly a ball of fire showed in the sky. Horror-stricken, she wanted to flee, but before she could move the meteorite hit her, and everything inside her became flaming light. Half unconscious, she had run into her igloo, and immediately she started to sing the following ecstatic stanza, so singularly pure and great in its line:

> The great sea
> Moves me!
> The great sea
> Sets me adrift!
> It moves me
> Like algae on stones
> In running brook water.
> The vault of heaven
> Moves me!
> The mighty weather
> Storms through my soul.
> It tears me with it,
> And I tremble with joy.

And it was said that whenever she sang it again, everybody who heard it became senseless with joy and cleansed their minds of evil.

Yet, the Eskimos were often completely aware of the phenomenon of inspiration, as shown by the words of the poet Kilimé:

"All songs are born in man out in the great wilderness. Without ourselves knowing how it happens, they come with the breath, words and tones that are not daily speech."

The Eskimo word for "to fill the lungs with air" can in English just as well be translated by "to concentrate in the hope of being inspired." And does Kilimé not—when he says "in the great wilderness"—describe the condition we call "concentration"? There may be no reason to attribute more mysticism to the working methods of a primitive poet than to those of a modern artist. Consider the unfortunate experience of Sadlaqé:

"Once, when I was quite young, I wished to sing a song about my village, and one winter evening when the moon was shining, I was walking back and forth to put words together that could fit into a tune I was humming. Beautiful words I found, words that should tell my friends about the greatness of the mountains and everything else that I enjoyed every time I came outside and opened my eyes. I walked, and I continued walking over the frozen snow, and I was so busy with my thoughts that I forgot where I was.

Suddenly, I stood still and lifted my head up, and looked:
In front of me was the huge mountain of my settlement,
greater and steeper than I had ever seen it. It was almost
as if it grew slowly out of the earth and began to lean out
over me, deadly dangerous and menacing. And I heard a
voice from the air that cried out: 'Little human! The echo of
your words has reached me! Do you really think that I can
be comprehended in your song?' I was so scared that I almost fell over backward, and in that moment I forgot all the
words I had been putting together for a song, and I ran home
as fast as I could and hid in my house. Since then, I have
never tried to put words together."

The sound hallucinations and the sudden panic are primitive enough; but the concentration is no more primitive than
it is modern. We are faced with conscious art.

The Alaskan Eskimos even have a word for artistic concentration; they call it *qarrtsiluni,* a word that literally
means a waiting for something to break. But a better explanation of its meaning is given us by Mayuark of Little
Diomede Island:

"Listen now, all you who would compose in words, paint
on canvas, or carve in stone; listen to what an old, primitive Eskimo woman has to say about your business:

"In the days of old, every fall, we held big festivals for
the soul of the whale, feasts which should always be opened
with new songs which the men composed. The spirits were to
be summoned with fresh words; worn-out songs could never
be used when men and women danced and sang in homage
to the great beast. And it was the custom that—during the
time when the men were finding the words for these hymns
—all lamps had to be put out. Darkness and stillness were to
reign in the festival house. Nothing must disturb them, nothing distract them. In deep silence they sat in the dark, thinking; all the men, old and young, yes, even the youngest of the
boys, as long as he was only able to speak.

"It was this stillness we called *qarrtsiluni,* which means
that one waits for something to burst.

"For our forefathers believed that the songs are born in
this stillness, while all endeavor to think only beautiful
thoughts. Then they take shape in the minds of men
and rise up like bubbles from the depths of the sea, bubbles
that seek the air to burst in the light!

"That is how the sacred songs are made."

One of the great difficulties in translating Eskimo poems

is the polysynthetic language with its long yet clearly defined word-phrases, that have an altogether peculiar impact. But I should like to give an example of the work of a
skilled poet under the influence of strong emotion or inspiration. The following song was made by Uvlunuaq, a
kind of first lady in the Netchilik tribe, the wife of a great
angakok, and herself an angakok and poetess of great re-
pute. The family was rich and influential, but now it had
the great sorrow that the young son, involved in a strife,
had killed his adversary. Out of fear, partly of the Mounties,
partly of the family of the slain one, he then had to flee
with his wife to a lonely place in the hills and shun the
company of other people. Uvlunuaq, his mother, sat for
many days in the tent in silent and tearless grief. Finally,
she took her ayayut and found relief in her sad drum song:

Eyaya-eya.
I recognize
A bit of a song,
And take it to me
Like a fellow human.
Eyaya-eya.

I should be ashamed
Of the child
I once carried proudly
In the amaut,
When I heard of his flight
From the dwellings of people.
Eyaya-eya.

They who think so,
Right are they.
Eyaya-eya.

Right are they.
Eyaya-eya.
I am ashamed,
But only because
He didn't have a mother
Who was blameless as the blue sky,
Wise and without folly.
Now, people's tongues will instruct him,

And gossip complete the education.
Eyaya-eya.

This have I—
His mother—deserved,
I who brought forth a child
That should not become the refuge of my old age.
Eyaya-eya.

I should be ashamed!
Instead I envy those
Who have crowds of friends behind them,
Waving on the ice,
When after festive leave-taking their journey begins.
Eyaya-eya.

I remember one spring
We broke camp at "The Squinting Eye."
The weather was mild.
Our footsteps
Sank gently creaking
Down in sun-thawed snow—
I was then like a tame animal,
Happy in the company of people.

But when message came
Of the killing and the flight,
Earth became like a mountain with pointed peak,
And I stood on the awl-like pinnacle
And faltered,
And fell!

II

ADVENTURES WITH
THE ESKIMOS

1 Lootevek: Casanova of the Ice Floes

LOOTEVEK CERTAINLY considered himself in luck. He was at the end of a long, unprofitable winter, and also—what was more important—at the end of his tangible resources. He was also in a bad way as far as credit at the trading post was concerned. I had been there myself on the previous day when he had come in and, in his usual glib manner, tried to charge some tobacco and a few groceries. Mr. Nielsen, behind the counter, did not even remove his pipe from his mouth to shake his head at the young Eskimo.

But now everything had cleared up, and here he was, paddling his kayak over the water to what he hoped was plenty of easy money. And as he glanced over at the beautiful white skin boat of Orfik, and his eyes took in the three girls who were rowing the older man, other ideas of what the journey might hold for him entered his carefree mind.

Only a man in Lootevek's desperate straits, perhaps, would consider his present connection enviable. My old friend, Orfik, had come to him that morning, squatting in front of Lootevek's mean little house and talking, presumably, to the air.

"One contemplates a small journey to some island," he said, "and one needs a young man as a helper."

Lootevek also spoke to the air. "Good luck in one's difficulty," he said, and then was silent, but thinking rapidly.

He knew Orfik well. The older man had no reputation whatsoever as a hunter, but was considered shrewd and well able to provide for himself and his family. And this, in a community where a man's worth was judged solely on that basis, was enough for the adventurous Lootevek. He was to get all his food on the journey, and a share of the profits from the venture. When, in addition, he found that Orfik's daughter, Sara, and two other women were to go along, the balances were definitely swung. If he had known the chain of circumstances in which he was shortly to become involved as a result of these three females, he might have hesitated before accepting the proposition.

But now a strong wind was behind them, speeding their trip westward to a small group of islands typical of those with which the coast of Greenland is dotted. As he paddled alongside the larger boat, Lootevek's glances further appraised the three women.

Sara, Orfik's daughter, was actually as ugly as a daughter could decently be, in spite of the fact that her father considered her a miracle of feminine beauty. So far did his paternal blindness extend, in fact, that he forbade her to go to the dances at the post, for fear that she would turn the heads of the young men to a point where they would become uncontrolled. The other two women were, certainly, vigorous rowers, but the fact that they were older than Sara, yet still unmarried, indicated that they were by no means considered the belles of the settlement. But to Lootevek, against whom many doors were closed—since he was not considered a serious prospect for marriage—they seemed sufficiently desirable.

The islands which they reached were seldom visited, and as a result of this isolation were a haven for birds, whose nests were thick and easily accessible. The quantities of down with which these nests were lined had great commercial value—and the gathering of it was the purpose of Orfik's little expedition.

In the weeks of continuous, blinding sun which followed, they worked ceaselessly. They stuffed the down into all of their belongings which could be used in any way as containers. The bags which they had brought were full; their blankets, underwear, stockings, pants—even their tents were crammed with the fluffy white substance. They snared many of the birds, and ate well. Crammed with food, Lootevek again considered himself to be very fortunate. He thought of the large cash share of the profits which would be his when they returned to the post; and despite his arduous labors, he found an astonishing amount of time—when Orfik was taken to another part of the island—for delightful and indiscriminate love-making with the three females of the party.

Finally, as the summer was ending, Orfik decided that they had gathered as much down as they could possibly carry home, and he was impatient to make the trip back to cash in on his efforts. The return journey was made in high spirits. The girls laughed and sang as they rowed; Lootevek, in his kayak, feeling himself a great man, a Caesar, paddled around them in circles, played tricks, capsizing his small boat and righting it to the delighted shrieks of the women.

Impatient as Orfik was to get home, he could not resist one stop on the way so that he could show off a little, and start talk in a strange settlement about his prowess as a provider. So when they reached Itooisalik, he decided to land and visit his friend, Itooi, an old bear hunter who lived there. It saddened him a little to find Itooi away on a trip of his own, but when the small party had entered the hunter's house and found it well stocked with the rare delicacies of coffee and sugar, their dampened spirits immediately revived. They brewed and drank as much as they wanted; ate as much of Itooi's food as they could hold, and felt that life was very good, very good indeed.

This apparently small incident might have passed off as merely a pleasant interlude in the life of Lootevek—except for the aftereffects of one small circumstance. When Orfik had again herded his party back into the boats, he suddenly had the thought, that they might, perhaps, have forgotten something. He sent his daughter, Sara, back to the house of Itooi to make certain, and Lootevek, seizing what might be his last opportunity, went with her. Orfik was in a hurry to be away, and when they did not immediately reappear he shouted to them from the beach. They came out and ran down to the water—but in their haste they forgot to lock the door behind them. Before they were out of sight Itooi's dogs swarmed into the house, and started to finish off whatever the party had left. Eskimo dogs can, and do, eat everything. Itooi's dogs were no exception.

Lootevek's entrance into the trading post, loaded with bags of down, brought the pipe out of Mr. Nielsen's mouth.

"Well, Lootevek," he said, "I can hardly believe it, but it looks as though you might have been doing a little work."

"Oh, one has made a small trip," Lootevek said, "and one has been fortunate."

Orfik nodded his head at the trader. "A few small bags of down were found by me and my helper," he said modestly. "Nothing much of great value."

As the women brought in additional bags Mr. Nielsen set his pipe on the counter and swept off the large scales, those which were used only for the weighing of heavy articles, like blubber. Bag after bag was weighed, and the astonished trader jotted down the totals. The stuffed clothing was put on the scales; the blankets; even the tent cloths, bursting with the down. The loiterers in the store crowded around, and Orfik had a difficult time to keep from smiling immodestly at his large haul. Finally, Mr. Nielsen added up the column of figures and turned to the Eskimo.

"Later, when it is unpacked, I will weigh the bags and clothing separately, and then deduct their weight from the total and figure the exact weight of the down," he said. "However, as an advance, I will give you fifty kroner, and we can straighten the rest out this evening."

Orfik was very pleased. Fifty kroner was not an inconsiderable sum. It meant that now, tonight, he could realize to the fullest the joy of being a rich man. He could give a party for the entire settlement. He could hold a huge dance in the carpenter's workshop, and supply coffee, and tea, and sugar, and even the fancy biscuits with which the post was stocked. It would not merely be a duty, but an extreme pleasure.

Lootevek drew the older man to one side. "One has worked hard," he said, "and one would like very much to have a few kroner in order to buy tobacco."

"Yes," Orfik said. He gave Lootevek three kroner. "Later," he said, "you will receive the rest of what you have earned."

The party certainly did Orfik credit. The carpenter's shop was crowded to the doors; the little phonograph whined and scratched, and the atmosphere got thick with smoke and the smell of gallons of coffee. Lootevek danced and danced. He danced with Sara, he danced with the other two women of the party, and now he could even dance with the girls who formerly would not look at the lazy young man who, they had thought, could never make them a respectable husband. Lootevek, as well as Orfik, felt himself to be a very important figure in the community.

In the middle of the gaiety a message came that Mr. Nielsen would be very pleased to see Orfik in his office, immediately.

"One is honored," Orfik said, importantly. "And one will be equally pleased to see Mr. Nielsen."

But when he reached Mr. Nielsen's office his pleasure was somewhat clouded. Mr. Nielsen's expression was one of sorrow, but also unmistakably one of anger. Mr. Nielsen's Eskimo wife was also in the office, as were her son and the local school teacher. Mr. Nielsen pointed silently to a pile in the middle of the floor. Stones, whole eggs, gravel, bits of wood, formed a small mound under the overhead light.

"I am ashamed," Mr. Nielsen said, coming right to the point. "I am ashamed for you, Orfik. I considered you an honest man. And when I unpacked the down and found that these things"—he pointed at the pile—"and not the down itself, were what weighed so heavily on my scales, I could not believe my own eyes. You have cheated me, Orfik."

Orfik's eyes were wide, and suddenly he felt proud no longer. He stuttered and stammered.

"One is not—one did not think—one can—"

But the anger of Mr. Nielsen's Eskimo wife cut him off.

"So!" she said. "This is the way in which you repay my husband's trust! For this you take young Lootevek along on a trip! To gather down, is it? You are not only a stupid man, you are a blind one! Your daughter, Sara, and those other two! It is all common gossip, what went on on that journey, Orfik! Love-making and eating and pleasure—and now thievery besides! You and that Lootevek—you are as bad as he is, and you are much too old to behave in this fashion!"

Mr. Nielsen was more concerned with business than with morality.

"Furthermore," he said, "consider this. I gave you fifty kroner as an advance against the total—and now I find that the total is worth scarcely twenty-five! It would take me a long time to make any profit on that basis, Orfik!"

The betrayed man could not get in a word between the shouting of Mr. Nielsen and his wife. This was Lootevek's doing, and if what the woman said was true, then his daughter and the other two girls had served really only as added sport for the young man on what he had taken for his holiday. And he had fed Lootevek, too—and even given him three kroner in cash not many hours before!

He made his way back to the dance, no longer the proud host, his mind full only of dark thoughts against Lootevek. He found the young man whirling Sara around the dance floor, and Orfik looked at his daughter more closely. Yes, Mrs. Nielsen had been right—and he saw now that the little down which had actually been gathered served only as a bed for Lootevek and his daughter—not to mention the two other women. He accused the young man directly. He had cheated him out of labor, out of three kroner, and had amused himself with his daughter with no intention of marriage!

Lootevek hung his head as the older man berated him. The three girls huddled into a little knot, as though to seek protection from Orfik's rage, and cried as they and their betrayer stood helpless under the torrent of words. They were all disgraced in front of the watching dancers—not one of them could defend her behavior. And Orfik shouted and raged to such an extent that the dance broke up and the people all left.

And the same night, Orfik took his skin boat and the two older girls, and sailed for his home settlement. But he left Sara behind, confiding her to the care of an old aunt who was, supposedly, experienced in necessary and secret rites.

The next day Lootevek found that his position in the community had been swept back to the status he usually enjoyed. No longer was he the triumphant companion of Orfik. No longer was he envied as being one of two men who could give a party. Mr. Nielsen's opinion of his credit was no better than it had been at the beginning of the summer—and Mrs. Nielsen's opinion of his conduct was not in the least complimentary.

News travels swiftly through these northern communities, and Lootevek found himself friendless and an object of ridicule. Thinking to let the matter blow over for the moment, he took his kayak and started to paddle away from the post. But Lootevek was, in a sense, to find himself powerless to leave the scene of his treachery and exposure.

He had not been gone an hour when he saw a boat coming toward him, headed for the trading post. As it drew nearer he recognized it as being the impressive whaling boat of the itinerant minister, and it was an exciting and seldom-seen spectacle. It was handsomely and fully equipped, even to being manned by six young Eskimos splendidly dressed in white anoraks and blue cloth trousers. Its arrival at any port was an event of momentous importance, and Lootevek could not bring himself to miss out on the excitement it was sure to occasion. So he turned his kayak around, and headed back.

"With such a boat ahead of me," he thought, "a little man like me cannot hold the attention of these others who want only to laugh at me."

And he was right. The people all ran down to the landing place at which the minister stepped out of his boat, and did not notice Lootevek, who beached his kayak around the point and made his way to the settlement.

But even more was to happen that day. An hour behind the whaling boat of the minister came two more boats. In one of them was myself, and a friend of mine—and in the other was the irate Itooi, the man at whose house Orfik's party had stopped on the way home. My friend and I had met Itooi while out whaling, and he had asked us to come home with him for a few days. So we had been present at his homecoming, and had witnessed the scene that met the returning hunter's eyes! For the dogs which Lootevek and Sara had carelessly allowed to run through the unlocked door had torn Itooi's house almost apart. Skins were eaten, the stores had been broken into and eaten, whips, spare harness, bed covers—the dogs had ruined everything!

Word got to him almost immediately that it had been Orfik's party which had permitted this to happen—and with rage and revenge in his heart Itooi started for the post. I must confess that my friend and I went along to see the fun. Fun? I had reckoned without Lootevek!

He, meanwhile, had again met Sara, and the two of them, welded together by their common fear, wondered what to do next. Itooi was in a rage against them; the minister would hear of their sinful conduct and would shame them into further disgrace; and I, as a white man with whom they would want to curry favor, would be turned against them. Lootevek realized he had to form a plan and act quickly.

An idea to resolve the situation came to him. He would marry Sara. That would appease her and her father, and it would put him beyond the power of the other two females. The minister would be pleased and complimented. Itooi, seeing him the center of attention and treated with respect, would leave him alone long enough for his anger to cool. And he had plans for me, also. He would raise me to the dignity of a high official, and thus cement my friendship. He would make me his best man.

"Reverend! Reverend!" he cried. "It happens that one wants to marry! One wishes to continue life as a married man!"

The minister looked at him and frowned slightly. He was really on his way farther north, and had planned to stop here at the post on his return, six days later. And although he was a devout man of God and lived on a highly spiritual plane, he had just noticed that the barometer was falling.

"Why didn't you tell me that as soon as I arrived?" he asked, with some irritation. "If I delay now I will be caught in a storm."

"One would have spoken sooner, Reverend," Lootevek said modestly and without guile, "but it had not been decided at that time."

"You did not know two hours ago that you wished to marry?" the minister said.

"True love grows quickly," Lootevek said, bowing his head.

"True love is also everlasting," the minister said, "and therefore it will live six days. I will return at that time and then the ceremony will be performed."

As anxious as Lootevek was for an immediate solution to his problem, he did not feel he could oppose the wishes of God's ambassador. So he said no more as the gaily dressed crew and the minister climbed into the boat and put off. But he had gained his point. The people standing around had heard his declaration, and realized that he was going to be a bridegroom. As such it was necessary that there be peace and good will around him. There was, and again he was accepted as the sensation of a day which had, truly, been crowded with sensations. He was given coffee at the house of Ganella, and seal meat at the house of Gaba. That night became another whirlpool of gaiety in which—as Lootevek had figured—even Itooi smothered the fire of his anger and was not unfriendly. Lootevek again danced and danced and talked big talk about a wedding in the huge workshop, and of a mammoth coffee party.

But the next day he awoke sober. In spite of the wild promises he had made the night before, he was now forced to realize that they were beyond his financial resources— which were nonexistent. The people had forgiven him in the light of his new role—but what was to be done to maintain their present attitude? The answer might be found in Mr. Nielsen. Full of hope he went to the store.

"It happens that one desires to open a little credit account," he said.

"Does it?" Mr. Nielsen said. His pipe remained in his mouth. "Who?"

"As a man who will be a bridegroom in six days," Lootevek said, "I am the one who wishes it."

"When you are married and respectable," Mr. Nielsen said, "and when you have started to earn an honest living, come back and maybe I will talk about it."

"The Reverend has promised to marry me on his return," Lootevek pleaded. "All the people have heard him. Sara and I will live the rest of our lives as man and wife."

"Poor Sara," Mr. Nielsen said. "I will tell you what I will do, Lootevek, because I am a soft man and can refuse a bridegroom nothing. I will open an account for you of one-half a krone."

Lootevek's eyes opened wide and for a moment stared straight into those of Mr. Nielsen. Then he shut them tight, and in a furious attempt to figure, he ducked his head completely under his hood. When his round face again came into view, it showed a realization that half a krone was not enough to buy a new anorak for his bride. This alone would cost four and a half kroner, and he would need silk ribbons for Sara, shirts and underwear for himself. And the party!

Lootevek, flatteringly enough, thought of his best man and brought his problem to me. He had been through more emotional crises in the last twenty-four hours than he had encountered before in his whole worthless life, and his talk was impassioned and persuasive. He went further and so persuaded me of the white man's traditional cruelty toward the native that I was carried away, and went to see Nielsen myself.

When I had finished, Nielsen looked at me but said nothing. With a quizzical expression he reached up on the shelf and brought down the files. He showed me Lootevek's account, which, if not profitable, was interesting. In the last year he had earned exactly thirteen and a quarter kroner. His bill with Nielsen, however, was now twenty-two and a half kroner. It was evident that Lootevek was something less than a good risk, and Nielsen's position was well taken.

Having at that time a bachelor's sympathy for the establishment of marriage, and filled with the spirit of charity, I went into conference with my fellow traveler. He promised to donate all the coffee and sugar which could possibly be consumed by the wedding party, and I decided to pay Lootevek's debt at the store and open an account of twenty kroner in his name. We sent for him and informed him of all this.

Again his face disappeared as he put all his mental effort into wrestling with the figures. When he popped out of his sea of arithmetic he pulled me to one side, with the expression of a man who was about to do me a favor.

"Peter," he said, "I can see you are my friend, and from now on I will devote my whole life to you. I have just figured that these expenses to you will be forty-two and a half kroner, and all because of the intention of two small and worthless people to marry. That is far too much, and I feel that I do not deserve it. So I tell you: if you want to make the amount smaller, please give me forty kroner in cash, instead of the other plan. This will save you two and a half kroner and I will be that much less humiliated by your charity. I am going on a big hunting trip pretty soon, and when I return it will be easy to pay my debt to Mr. Nielsen."

I tried to convince Lootevek that it was better to start married life with no debts, and in spite of the passion of his arguments, I won. I paid his debt at the store and gave him twenty kroner in cash, instead of establishing credit. Even so, Lootevek left me feeling, I think, that I had deprived him of twenty kroner.

I had to leave that same day to look at some asbestos deposits in the vicinity, and was gone until the actual day of the wedding. These days were fine days for Lootevek: his sins were forgiven, he had a position in the community and money in his pocket.

When I was ready to return to the post, it was the minister's ship which stopped by for me and picked me up to save me the overland trek back. And when we drew up to the landing place there was Lootevek, on a little cliff, directing our course with loud—and happy—shouts; warning us against rocks and showing us where to land.

"Well, my dear Lootevek!" the minister said. "I am truly delighted that I shall now join you and Sara together for life."

"Oh, Reverend," Lootevek said, stretching out his hand to a plump and beaming girl next to him, "this is Anina. And

if joy and happiness shall have anything to do with it—
Anina must be my wife."

"Yes?" said the minister. "I did not remember." He took
out his diary, looked in it and gave a slight start. "I do not
understand this."

"Well," Lootevek said, "you see—the case is this. Peter
is my friend. He has promised to give a great and expensive
party for me. He promised to be present at the church and
take part in the dance. So will Mr. Nielsen, and so will the
many visitors who will be present. Before, when you were
here, Peter and all these people were angry at me. So what
did I do? I promised to marry Sara. But now they all love
me and are my friends—so must I still marry Sara? Oh no,
Reverend! Oh no! Now I can be married to Anina, who I
choose out of love!"

The minister was speechless with rage and I understood
easily enough what Lootevek had done to him. It is the
custom, here in the North, for couples who have announced
their intention to marry, to live together openly from that
time on. The minister realized, of course, that he had given
his official sanction to what had become, in his eyes, a scan-
dalous *amour*. As soon as he could have his crew turn his
boat around, he left the settlement, refusing pointblank to
marry Lootevek to Anina or anyone but Sara.

The news of this new disaster spread rapidly through the
settlement and finally reached Sara, whom Lootevek had
carelessly neglected to inform of his changed plans. Now it
was her turn to come to me and complain of the injustice
which was being done her—but not, as you might expect,
with respect to her having been jilted, but because she had
been promised a new anorak as Lootevek's wedding gift, and
now she would not receive it. There was only one thing for
me to do, as a white man and a gentleman. She got her new
anorak.

And then Lootevek appeared again, with sorrow and pain
and fear on his face.

"Peter," he said, "we are in trouble."

I did not interrupt him to find out by what process of
reasoning he had arrived at the particular pronoun he used.

"We were going to give a party, Peter, and now that I am
not to be married and there is not to be a party, people
have become indignant, and are using harsh words. Particularly unfriendly are the visitors—for while you were
away I went for many miles in all directions, and invited

more than twelve skin boats to come to your dance. Now that they feel deprived, isn't it likely that they will feel unfriendly toward you, also? And, Peter—of all the things which makes me feel bad, the biggest is that you cannot have the party which you looked forward to with so much pleasure!"

I began to feel that the responsibility was really as much mine as his. And, as a matter of fact, I had looked forward to that party.

"Listen," I told him. "No minister in the world can deprive us of a party and plenty of coffee. You may tell the people that the dance will go on!"

And we had some party. We danced, with the midnight sun shining through the front windows of the carpenter's shop; we danced on and on. The sun walked around and peeped into the windows at the side of the house, and still we did not stop. It even came all the way around to the back of the house, and then we quit and walked home. But by that time everybody's belly was as hard as stone, filled with coffee, biscuits and figs. We all had holes in our sealskin boots, we had danced so long, and when I finally rolled up in my blankets to sleep, I thought, "Now, thank God, the affair is ended."

But I had reckoned without the father of Anina, the girl Lootevek represented as his great love. Her father's complaints were definite and violent, tinged with sadness, but purposeful. Anina had been betrothed to another man before I—so her father said—had made it possible for Lootevek to come into the picture. And while this other man was not a "first-class man," still he would have made a satisfactory husband. Now he had canceled his proposal, and Lootevek himself seemed to have cooled off. He had told her father, "After all, old man, I have had my party and I am very happy. The minister will not marry me to anyone but Sara—so why should I bother to marry anyone at all? A wife is, no matter how one regards it, a nuisance and an expense!"

Furthermore, Anina's father went on, it was all my fault that Anina was now humiliated, and did not even have a new anorak to show for her shame. She deserved at least as good a one as that which Sara was showing off, and it was up to me to see that she did not go without it.

Another four and a half kroner, I thought, can make little difference. So Anina got her new anorak and I hastened to throw my belongings together and leave the community the same day, before my present expenses of fifty-odd kroner would be increased.

A year later, on my return, I heard the final and most significant chapter in the amorous adventures of my friend Lootevek. He had braved the attitude toward him of the people in the settlement and stayed on. He was still there when Sara's baby—in spite of her aunt's mysterious knowledge —was born. He saw Orfik pay the attending midwife eight kroner for her services, and his business sense once more took hold of him. His mind began to work.

"Why," he figured, "should I ever marry a woman whose every child will cost me eight kroner? It is much better— is it not?—to marry a woman who *receives* eight kroner any time a baby is born?"

So Lootevek, without any wild talk and without any coffee party, quietly married the midwife.

2 Arctic Nightmare

CAN AN INNOCENT MAN become the object of intense hatred through no fault of his own? Like most people I always thought this could not happen, until an experience in my own life proved me wrong.

The time was the first world war and I was living in Thule, utterly isolated from the civilized world. No ships came that far north in wartime, there was no radio to bring news from the outside world. There was nothing but serene peace— peace to work and to think.

I decided to go with some of my Eskimo friends still further north, to the most remote place I could find, to study the conditions of the Eskimos when they are completely cut off from all outside supplies and must depend on their own resources alone. I was the only white man among them, but no matter how long I lived among my Eskimo friends, though I learned their way of life, their habits, and their hunting methods, my mind still needed the stimulation and the support which only books can give.

Consequently, I got together a whole crate full of books —heavy volumes, hard books. I chose works which could beat some knowledge into me when my isolation and my desire for some mental activity would at last force me into reading what I would otherwise hardly dream of looking at. I found quite a few books of that kind and stuffed them into a crate which I placed carefully on my sled.

There was quite a group of Eskimos with me when I left, our equipment was first rate and we were all in high spirits when we set off to the north. We had to pass Cape Parry on our way. Outside the cape the ice is very unreliable and the greater part of the year one has to go across the large glacier, travel behind the cape, and then come down the coast from north of Cape Parry. This is a long way to go and a pretty hard one, so we decided to risk crossing the treacherous ice, it being so much shorter and easier. We could still see the tracks from some sled which had gone there a few days before us, and we thought it was going to be quite safe.

We soon learned otherwise, and realized we would have been much better off the long way round. The ice got thinner and thinner. Several times the old tracks had been broken by open water, which had frozen to a thin sheet of ice again. We did not worry, since it only takes a night's frost to make the ice solid and safe to travel over. But the going was still very rough. The sleds cut through the ice again, and we all had to pull and lift for all we were worth to save them. Like all Eskimos, my friends kept their good spirits, but we all cursed ourselves for not taking the long way round.

We were still at it when it got dark, and we fortunately found a cave in the cliff close by the ice where we could spend the night. There was no chance of getting all our stuff up in the cave, we had to be satisfied once we got our sleeping bags and the dogs up from the ice. We took along the food we needed that night and left all the rest with the sleds on the ice. After the strenuous trip we soon settled down for the night, and we did not let the ominous thundering of the ice disturb us. It was too dark to see anything outside, and we decided to let the next day tell us what had happened, without bothering to check anything during the night.

What the morning told us was that my sled and one other had been covered by solid ice. The ocean currents had lifted up large sheets of ice and thrown them on top of the small sleds. It was a thorough job. The sleds themselves were intact but the ice had cleared away everything that had been on them. It took us several hours to cut them out of the ice and repair them, but the whole load was a total loss. Boxes and equipment had been completely carried away by the ice. My Eskimo friends mourned the loss of my harpoon and knives and other gear, but I was mainly annoyed to see my book crate gone. I ought to have carried it up to the cave and saved it.

We had no further mishaps on the trip and were given a great reception when we arrived at our destination. The hunting was fine there, the fishing likewise, and we decided that we could not care less about the outside world. We knew people were fighting there, but it did not concern us. We had "sensible work" to do, as the Eskimos said. We settled down to hunting and fishing when the weather was fine, held great parties when it was not, and lived as only happy people know how to live.

But after a while something strange happened to me. Inside of me a great hunger began growing, more noticeable every day. My book crate was gone and I missed my books. There were nights when I could not sleep. There were days when I could not say another word about the hunting or the dogs, nor listen to what my friends had to say on the subject. It was like a famine in my mind. I was starved for books. It was a terrible thing to feel.

The Eskimos could not understand it. They knew something was wrong, they recognized the fact but were powerless to do anything about it. The ice had taken my treasure and the ice never returns what it takes.

But that was just what the ice did in my case. One day an old Eskimo called Urvulac came to our camp, and the moment he was in sight he managed, by waving his arms and legs a great deal, to make us understand that he brought startling news. I thought at once that the mail had arrived with news of the war, perhaps the end of the fighting, peace at last. For the first few seconds I forgot myself and my trouble in my eagerness to hear about the outside world.

But it was something else Urvulac brought me—a real book! With great difficulty he had fished it out of the ice when he passed Cape Parry. He told me that my book crate apparently had fallen between two heavy sheets of ice, it had been rolling back and forth and finally broken to pieces. The contents had all been lost except this one book.

I grabbed it eagerly, with trembling fingers. In my excitement I hardly had time to be polite and thank him. But at least I asked him to come and stay with us. I brought him into the tent and then settled down on my cot to open at once the treasure which he had carefully wrapped in sealskin.

The book had been in salt water for quite a while. It was yellow and swollen and greasy from having been dried over Urvulac's oil lamp—and handled by his curious family. But still it was a book. Hungrily I studied the title. "The Relationship Between Denmark and the Popes at Avignon"! It was a doctor's thesis presented to the University of Copenhagen. It did not matter to me, the content was of secondary importance. It was a real book, the print was very small and it would last me quite a while. Besides, I told myself, I know nothing about those Popes, it will certainly be great to learn something about the relationships and thoughts of those fellows. I was deeply grateful and I settled down to my reading at once.

It was a good book. The author, Dr. L. Moltesen, was clearly an able, learned man, and there was nothing wrong with his style. The subject was not my particular field and I felt very ignorant reading about all the epistles of the Popes and the contents of all the archives studied by Dr. Moltesen. But I read it all carefully and began understanding a great many things I had never thought of before. I finished the book and felt I knew a great deal about the Popes and Avignon.

The days went by, bad weather set in, and as we could not always give parties, I had time to read. I felt sorry for all my companions, since none of them could read. I was the only one with such superior knowledge. Unfortunately I had only the one book, but I read through Avignon once more. And when I had finished, I read it a third time and a fourth.

After the fourth time I began thinking on my own, and I argued with the author. I began doubting, I suspected Dr. Moltesen of making misleading statements. I felt he might have misquoted, falsified the record, but I had no proof. You need a whole library if you want to take a doctor's thesis to pieces. And I had only this one book with all its statements and claims and quotations. I realized that I was in no position to argue with the good Dr. Moltesen, and decided again to trust him blindly. So I read through his thesis again. I soon knew it by heart, but as the days passed I simply had to have the printed letters enter my head through my eyes. Just to see them was a relief. I could not leave the book alone, no matter how much it annoyed me. The relationship between Denmark and the Popes became the source from which I took the strength to maintain my culture and my civilization.

After a while it got to be a game. I wanted to see how fast I could possibly read the book without skipping a word. The record was four and a half days. I had other things to do, but most of my time was spent with the Popes.

Soon I hated the Popes like the addict hates the morphine he cannot do without. A bitter, intense hatred developed in me, but soon my feelings shifted from the Popes and concentrated on the author. I knew that the first job for me once I returned from Greenland would be to trace this diabolical man, this evil Dr. Moltesen, and exterminate him. I thought of the professors at the University. Were they corrupt or only feeble-minded to accept such a hoax and make the author a doctor? It made me laugh to think that they had been unable to see through him. Just one look at the book would suffice to know the author for what he was. But I read the book again.

Again and again! Over and over I read the book. It was a fever, it was a nightmare. I knew when I got to a certain page with a large cod-liver-oil spot that I would find a number of highly complicated names. But I knew them without looking at them. I knew the whole book forwards and backwards, by heart.

But, fortunately, the Lord is merciful! He does not let time stop. I felt He could if He wanted to, but I didn't know it. All I knew concerned the Popes at Avignon, nothing else. Time did pass, however, and suddenly summer was there with plenty to do out of doors and no time left for reading. I did not even have time to miss my book, should I have felt like it.

I was spared another winter with the Popes, which would surely have been too much for my sanity. When the summer was over we went back to my quarters in Thule, where I had all my books. I was grateful for the relief they gave me and I had peace in my mind once more. But if I ever came across anything concerning the Popes, Dr. Moltesen, or Avignon—or even southern France—I was apt to get a nervous relapse.

Two years went by, peace came to the world once more

and it was time for me to go back to civilization. Knud Rasmussen came to Greenland and we returned together.

We were greeted as arctic explorers when we got back to Copenhagen. We had returned from a Polar expedition and that seemed sufficient excuse for a celebration. There had been no official banquet in town for several months, apparently, and our return offered a good opportunity for banquet-starved officials. We were both surprised and we were humble in the knowledge that there is little reason to celebrate people just for following their hearts' desire and living a simpler, freer life than most, but we did turn up at the official dinner.

Knud as head of the expedition was given the place of honor at the banquet, next to the Premier. I was second in command and was seated next to the foreign minister.

And his name was Dr. L. Moltesen!

I was dumbfounded, paralyzed. I stood in front of him utterly spellbound. I sat next to him unable to utter a word. When I heard his polite, friendly voice, I saw in a haze the ice and the little tent, my cot and his terrible, dirty, greasy book. All my thirst for revenge was awakened. There was a deafening roar in my ears, and my plans to exterminate this man took hold of me once more.

After a while I came to my senses. I was dressed in my tails, after all, there was wine on the table in front of me, there were toasts and speeches. A killing seemed inappropriate in such a setting. I could not disrupt the whole banquet. In the end I postponed my revenge and concentrated all my attention on the food. That was probably his salvation.

Food is not a thing to be treated lightly by returning arctic explorers, and what we were served at the banquet was worthy of my full attention. Slowly and carefully I devoured every crumb that was placed before me, and I had time to listen to the soft and friendly voice of my neighbor, even though I was in no position to understand his words clearly. For dessert we had ice cream with a center of frozen macaroons. There were candied raspberries and chocolate sauce and small polar bears made of sugar. Under such conditions one does not slay foreign ministers. A different setting is needed.

At last I had recovered sufficiently to speak clearly once more. And I had full control when I turned to my neighbor.

"Do you know, Dr. Moltesen," I told him in a calm voice, "on this expedition I brought along only one single book, my only reading material. And the book was your thesis 'The Relationship Between Denmark and the Popes at Avignon.' "

The man was genuinely pleased. He seemed quite excited and made many polite exclamations.

"Your book had quite an extraordinary fascination for me," I told him, quite truthfully. "It really made me think. I have even kept the book. It is very dirty and worn by now, of course, but I would be happy to send you my copy as a sign of my appreciation."

He told me he would be delighted to have it for his library, and the next day I went through the stuff I had brought back with me. When I found the filthy thing, I took it along to the bookbinder, who gave it a scornful look.

"I don't care what the price is," I told him. "And it is not going to be cleaned, only bound—in the finest binding you can give me for this treasure!"

He did the job and I am sure the book is still in the Moltesen library.

But here is the strange thing. I later went to a party where religious history happened to become the topic of conversation. There were some very learned men there, they knew all there was to know on the subject, and the rest of us fell silent. Most people don't know much of such things, but for once I felt that I had an opportunity to shine. I wanted to surprise them all with my superb knowledge of the Popes at Avignon, and I interrupted the learned men with some very clever remarks.

They hesitated a moment only. Then I was curtly brushed off: "My good man," they said, "your ideas are completely obsolete. They have been proved wrong by all the latest documents found in the archives of——" And they were off again.

I did not listen any more. In a reasonably polite way, they had told me to stick to my own field and not speak of things I knew nothing about. But I really thought. . . . Surely I had read that. . . .

Suddenly I discovered that I had forgotten every word of Dr. Moltesen and his Popes. And I began to wonder whether I should not buy another copy of the book. After all, it was a wonderful time—and a wonderful book. Or so it seemed.

3 An Eskimo Takes a Bride

Two LITTLE GIRLS brought the exciting news from tent to tent: "Imenak has arrived! He has left his sled down by the ice and he doesn't unload it!"

Nobody could fail to understand the meaning of this. Imenak wanted to get away in a hurry. He had already given himself away by paying too much attention to Arnaluk, the beautiful daughter of Otonia. And there was no doubt of her feelings. It was common knowledge that she had several times lately eaten the lice which she removed from his hair when he put his head in her lap to be relieved of the annoying little animals. What then could be more obvious than that she loved him.

Imenak was a very good hunter, he was young and he was good looking. His father was highly regarded and lived with his brothers at a settlement farther north. He had given his son a number of good dogs and the young man already had several bears and walrus to his credit. No wonder that Imenak was now looking around for a wife to take care of all his skins and to make clothes for him. As long as he remained single his mother did it for him which meant that Imenak always had to wait until his father had been taken care of. His young sister and old grandmother made him his mittens and sometimes a pair of kamiks, but a young man who is a great hunter needs a great deal of clothes. A wife is a necessity.

Arnaluk was free and unattached. She might not yet know all there is to know about sewing and she was far from being an expert in preparing the skins. She was still failing in many of the duties of a woman. But she was strong, hard working and good looking. Her teeth were pure white, her full cheeks were always smudged from the skins she was chewing in order to make them soft enough for kamik soles. The brown and black smears looked rather cute. And Arnaluk had the flattest little nose—and thus the most beautiful—of all the girls in the village.

Many young men had tried in vain to become a son-in-law in Otonia's house, since Arnaluk's father would only accept a man whose fame and family were equal to his own. A few quiet words had been enough to turn down the suitors. No scenes were permitted and an outright quarrel was out of the question.

The suitor would pay a visit and stay as a guest in Otonia's house. Sometimes the men spent the night in the Young People's House where Arnaluk slept, but the girl took no interest beyond the friendly smiles she gave everybody. The boys would never pay any attention to her. They would not make themselves the laughingstock of all the listeners by talking to a girl or even looking at her except to let her dry their boots or mittens and once in a while to let her pick the lice out of their hair when the animals were getting too vicious. Arnaluk was very good at catching the little gray bugs, but she always threw them in the fire and laughed when they exploded with a tiny "crack."

The eager young men would always sit quietly on the side bench over their meal. It was not seemly for them to speak first when there were older people present. But if a man was very set on his errand, he might finally speak up.

"One should have mended a pair of kamiks," he might say. "Unfortunately one has nobody to do the sewing."

There would be a few minutes of silence. The meaning of the words was obvious.

"There might perhaps be a woman further north," Otonia would finally answer. "Somebody might be found there to take care of a pair of kamiks."

Thus it was said, the refusal was public and the suitor had been told off. He would never show a thing, only continue his meal and maybe say a few words about his useless dogs which would make them all exaggerate their praise of his animals. The man would prolong his meal as much as possible since his departure had now been made quite difficult. He knew that roars of laughter would follow him out. The best was to wait until somebody else had an errand outside and then try to sneak out unnoticed. The suitor would never say goodbye, just drive off with his dogs as quietly as possible. A young man did not carry much luggage and nobody could tell whether he was going hunting or was a rejected suitor going home empty-handed.

Gossip travels fast, however, and the moment a suitor had left Otonia's tent the news made the rounds: "Otonia has turned down another man again!" The names were mentioned, each new and unsuccessful proposal was whispered about up and down the coast. The Arctic Eskimos are not numerous, it is far between their villages and they thrive on gossip.

But everything was different the day Imenak arrived. It was well known that last spring Otonia had spent quite some time with Imenak's father. They had stayed together in an igloo while they were waiting for walrus. The evening had been very long with nothing to do but talk.

Imerasuk was proud of his son Imenak who had just caught a walrus that same day. It was the first one they had caught and it was a fat and glistening animal.

"This poor boy of mine," Imerasuk had said. "By the merest chance he has happened to catch this walrus today. It's a great pity for him since he'll now be expected to have the same luck all the time. And it is well known to us all that he is totally lacking in any kind of skill."

The other men praised Imenak and said that the young man would surely become a great hunter like his father.

"Nothing of the kind," Imerasuk went on. "What a misery! Now in my old days it seems that I shall have to move to another settlement since my fellow settlers are given to lies. My son is not the only member of my family who would surely starve if the neighbors did not help. The boy is utterly dependent on his luck. I fear for the fate of my son when he grows old. No father can possibly trust him with his daughter since she would be bound to starve."

There was a breathless pause since they all knew the importance of Otonia's answer. At last the old man spoke up:

"If the girls in my village were only not so miserably useless and at the same time so ugly that they have to hide their faces! Otherwise they would have had a chance of being fed in their old age."

The question was settled. The faces in the igloo were set in masks of frozen calm. No hint of expression revealed the faintest interest in a conversation which merely dealt with women and thus could be of no importance. But two of the men went outside, saying that they had to look after their dogs. Once outside, they took a careful look at the sky and decided it would be too windy for the ice to settle tomorrow. There would be no good hunting and they might just as well go home right away. As they drove off, the other men knew that this latest news was going out in the world with them. Soon it would be known all along the coast that Otonia had promised his daughter to Imenak, the great son of Imerasuk. All the other young men would know that there was no hope for them any more since Imenak was stronger than them all and came from a great and powerful family.

Imenak had been lying on the floor in the igloo while his father talked with Otonia. He soon began snoring to show that he had not heard a word they had said and that in any case the whole subject did not concern him in the least.

The next few days he could not help noticing, however, that the girls began eying him curiously and small hints popped up in everything that was said to him. Imenak felt quite shy and wanted to get away from it all. At last he got one of his friends to go bear hunting with him in the region of the Humboldt Glacier far to the north. Thus he would be left in peace and at the same time show that he did not depend on any woman.

They did not return until the ice was breaking up. Imenak brought back with him a number of good bearskins, but it was noticed right away that he had cut off the long mane hair which the Eskimo women use for the tops of their stockings. His sisters felt quite hurt and told their girl friends about it:

"A bear hunter returns but, of course, he must throw away the mane hair of the bear which we could use for stockings!"

It was easy enough to figure out. People giggled and talked and Imenak felt their eyes constantly on him—which is the worst kind of torture for an Eskimo. And so at last he went down to Cape York where Otonia and his daughter Arnaluk lived.

The girl had had her troubles too. She had felt the curiosity all around her and had taken to sleeping more often in the Young People's House instead of with her parents in order to show her independence. Her mother laughed at her but was proud of her modesty.

From the moment Imenak arrived, Arnaluk did not show herself outside. She stayed in her tent all the time. Outwardly she was calm but she felt as if she was going to burst. Soon she would be the wife of a great hunter, she would be able to invite all her new neighbors, urging them to eat while she complained bitterly that nothing in her house was worth eating since her husband did not know the first thing about hunting. Alone in her tent she was dreaming about all the things that make life wonderful for a young Eskimo girl.

Imenak had to call on all the people in Cape York. He did not go first to Otonia's house, nor did he make it his last visit. Either way he would have revealed his eagerness and showed that his visit had a special purpose.

When he finally called on his future father-in-law, Otonia received him in a friendly way without giving him any special attention. Otonia's wife served auks in rich oil and when they had all eaten a while, their tongues loosened. Most of the people at the settlement were present since they did not want to miss anything.

"Well, well," sighed Imenak at last. "One certainly would like to settle down close to a bird cliff this summer and fill up the bags with such good auks."

Nothing was said since they all knew that one cannot decide whether to settle down until one has a woman. Imenak had had his say.

That night Imenak slept in the Young People's House, but Arnaluk remained in her parents' tent. The next night the same, and the following one. Imenak did not seem to be in a hurry. He went seal hunting during the day, caught a great many and drove by Otonia's house with a sled loaded with seals. But Arnaluk did not appear, nor did she turn up at the communal meals. She ate by herself in her tent.

One day an old woman finally commented to Otonia's wife on the long absence of her daughter.

"She is such a shy girl!" said the mother proudly and everybody heard her. A few of them laughed, but hurried to explain that it was only because some of the puppies playing by the fire seemed so funny.

Finally it was discovered that Arnaluk had to leave her tent for a few minutes in the evening to follow the call of nature. She always looked around very carefully first. Imenak was waiting for her and pounced on her the moment she appeared. But he was not fast enough. Arnaluk jumped back in the tent and the young man could hear her say in a loud voice that she had just taken a look at the weather but it did not seem very inviting.

Imenak waited a moment before he went back to his sled where he now decided to spend the night. It was quite warm, the Arctic sun was in the sky all night long and Imenak could stay outside and keep an eye on the entrance to Otonia's tent. But Arnaluk did not come out any more. She only lifted up the bottom flap of her tent now and then and did not have to let him see her at all.

The excitement was growing in Cape York since they all knew it would be too bitter a defeat for Imenak if he had to return home without his girl. But they never discussed it with him, they only talked about hunting and the weather. Imenak made only very short hunting trips now and spent most of the time in the settlement playing with the other young men. Arnaluk paid no attention to their games, she remained stubbornly out of sight and was highly praised for her maidenly modesty. She could be heard singing to her young sisters, telling them that she would play in the snow with them next winter. This was an open challenge and at last Imenak was forced to take the offensive.

In the winter it is impossible to get a woman out of a stone house and, consequently, a marriage can take place only in summer. There is only a small hole in the floor of the winterhouses and if a woman just spreads out her arms and legs, nobody can force her out. In the summer it is different since a tent is no great obstacle.

Finally Imenak went into action. With a great jump he was in the middle of Arnaluk's tent. The children screamed and their mother told them to be quiet. Otonia sat on his bed and greeted his future son-in-law with a smile.

"We seem to have visitors today," he remarked but he quickly left the tent while his wife remained quietly in her corner.

Imenak jumped on the bed where Arnaluk had withdrawn as far as possible, clutching the tent pole with all her might. Two old women sitting next to her were screaming with laughter.

Imenak grabbed the girl who screamed and kicked in vain. He got hold of one knee and one arm and pulled her to him. She held on to the tent pole and the whole tent was trembling as he pulled her. The mother called out that Arnaluk was not playing fair and that the whole tent would fall down.

"I don't care! Nobody can get me out of here!" Arnaluk screamed in a wild fury, and bit him in the hand. Imenak pulled and she kicked until finally the pole gave way and tore a gaping hole in the wall of the tent.

"An opening should be used!" cried Imenak jubilantly and with one kick he split open the entire wall of the tent. He rolled her through and now they were both on the outside where they were met by shrieks of laughter. The whole settlement knew what was happening and they were waiting to see the couple come out the regular exit. This way it was even more exciting.

Outside there was more room for fighting. Arnaluk still held on to the tent pole, but he got one of her hands loose by beating her over the knuckles. He tried the same thing with the other hand which flew suddenly from the pole straight into his face. The sharp nails tore five long gashes from his eye down the whole cheek and the blood was streaming down his face. The Eskimos cheered for this honorable feat.

At last Imenak got the wild woman up on his shoulders while she still beat him over the head and tore out fistfuls of hair. She was kicking wildly but he had her in such a grip that she could not stop him from walking.

The audience knew that the end of the show was approaching. Down by the meat rack two young men were looking casually at the sky apparently without having seen or heard a thing. Judging from their faces they did not even notice the kicking, screaming girl on Imenak's shoulder. The proud bridegroom stopped for a moment to show that nothing unusual had happened although he carried a shrieking bride on his shoulders.

"It is not unlikely," he said casually, "that one might go away for a while."

"Oh? Somebody is leaving?" they answered with a disinterested air. Imenak's face remained calm although he had to use all his strength to keep her in place.

He got her down to the place he had prepared and threw her down on the sled. But still the crazy girl did not give up. She jumped up and tried to run away from him. Imenak had to run after her and grabbed her in such a way that they both fell down. She kicked him in the face and soon blood from his nose mixed with the blood running down from the gashes in his cheeks. He got her on the sled once more and this time he gave her a real beating, but as soon as he stopped she got up again, spit in his face and took up a defensive position once more.

At last Arnaluk's mother had had enough. She had enjoyed the fight immensely, she was very proud of her daughter's modesty and defiance which she knew would be praised up and down the coast to the honor of her family. But enough is enough.

She called down from her tent: "It's time to give in! A young woman has given sufficient proof of her fear of mar-

riage which is the terrible fate of all women. Alas, resistance
is of no avail. All men are pitiless brutes and the masters of
our weaker sex! It has been seen once more that there is no
escape!"

The words had been said. The mother had given the signal
and Arnaluk subsided at once. She settled down on the sled,
still gasping from the struggle. People returned to their
tents and Imenak made the dogs ready for the trip. When
one of them tried to get away and return to the tents,
Arnaluk grabbed the whip and lashed out viciously like a
man.

"Miserable dogs!" she called out. "Don't you know we are
going home!" She was a wife already and as such had the
right and duty to berate her husband's property to win the
praise of others.

They made the return trip in a leisurely pace to have a
few days to repair their clothes and let their faces heal.
Imenak had some sewing things along, since the young wife
had nothing. She had been robbed and carried off by force
and her husband had to look after her.

When they arrived at the first settlement no questions were
asked. They were received as if Imenak had always had
Arnaluk with him wherever he went, but as soon as they left,
the talk began. The obvious signs of damage to Imenak's
face and clothes were all to the honor of the bride.

Imerasuk met them as soon as they arrived at the settlement. He had been out hunting and brought home a great
many delicious seals.

"There is reasonable hope that my skins will be cleaned
faster now that my son has someone to help with the work,"
was all he said. But this was the welcome greeting and the
recognition of the marriage.

Arnaluk entered the tent of her parents-in-law and sat
down. Nobody greeted her and she said nothing. Imenak had
caught a few seals on his way home. Now he cut open one of
them and brought the liver into the tent. He put it on a
flat stone and cut it in beautiful, pink slices.

"Perhaps one would condescend to taste the liver of this
measly little seal I had the undeserved luck to catch," he
said.

"What a misery! It's a true shame to offer such poor food
which is not fit for dogs but it seems to be all a useless husband is able to bring home," said Arnaluk as she offered the
liver to her new family. She was blushing deeply since it

was her first experience as a married woman and hostess. Nobody gave any sign that the situation was at all unusual and they all ate with great appetite. Afterward the young girls were told about Arnaluk who had won great honor by resisting her husband so heroically and showing such stubborn reluctance to get married.

4 Dead Man's Cache

ELMER IS DEAD. Old Tulimak brought me the news and we sat for a long time without talking, reaching out once in a while for the coffee pot on the stove, mourning a man who was a good friend to me and a good friend to all the Eskimos. It is hard to think of him as dead and even harder to think what an ordeal he survived, only to lose out to common influenza. After a while Tulimak and I talked, and it was decided that now I am released from my old promise. Now at last I am free to tell the strange story of Elmer Boyle and Gotthart Snider, though I've not used their right names for fear of hurting someone even yet.

It began a long way from the Arctic, in a little town in New England where both boys were born and grew up. They were about the same age but different in every way. Elmer never had the breaks. His trouble started before he was born, when his mother was a pretty nurse in the local hospital and got too interested in a sailor patient with good looks and a smooth line.

When the sailor got well he took the nurse out a few times and the sailor did what a lot of sailors do and then went away to sea and probably never gave her another thought. Pretty soon she had to give up nursing and go away somewhere for a year. When she came back she had Elmer and, of course, no reputation left at all. A thing like that will set tongues to wagging anywhere, but they wag worst in a New England town.

Naturally nobody would hire a nurse who got into that kind of trouble, so Elmer's mother took up dressmaking. She did pretty well, because she had to work cheap. Nobody would think of paying her the same price a decent woman would charge, any more than they would think of saying "Good morning" to her on the street or of asking her into their homes.

Elmer grew up under that cloud, without any friends or any other clothes except mostly cast-offs, and no spending money. The kids made life hell for him all the time, so he took to hiding out in the woods. He built himself a secret hut and spent most of his time there, filling up the emptiness inside him by getting acquainted with the birds and animals and all outdoor life. It was the one place he felt happy and like a whole person.

Then times got tougher and he had to quit school and take a job in a local factory, and that was pure misery. He didn't dare complain, though, because everybody said what a fine Christian man the owner was to give a good job to someone like Elmer. The real reason was he could make Elmer work longer and for less money than boys who just wanted spending money.

There was only one good part about that job: the night watchman was an old Hudson Bay man, and sometimes Elmer would sit around half the night listening to stories of bear hunts and dog sledge runs under the Northern Lights. Elmer made up his mind that some day he was going to do those things himself. His mother had been withering away for a long time, like a flower cut off from water. When she died, mostly of pure loneliness, Elmer just boarded up the house and disappeared. Nobody knew where he went and nobody much cared, least of all Gotthart Snider.

Gotthart was a big, mean, overgrown bully, the son of a German butcher and always a troublemaker in school and out. His favorite sport was picking on smaller kids and beating them up, and of course picking on Elmer was the most fun of all, because Elmer had nobody to stand up for him. Gotthart knew the old Hudson Bay man, too, and in a way that's how this story all came to happen.

Somehow the stories he heard gave Gotthart the idea that the Arctic was a great place for excitement and adventure and easy money without much effort, which suited him just fine. Still, until he got into the Big Trouble, he never really figured on going north.

He was running around with Mabel Greencut, the daughter of the factory owner, and in no time his money was used up, but not his passion. He needed more money, so he just helped himself to some that belonged to, of all people, Mabel's own father. He got caught, because along with everything else, Gotthart wasn't very bright. He got a good, stiff prison term, and when he got out he had a sneaking hunch he wouldn't be welcome in his home town.

Some of the crowd he met in jail were going north to work in a mine up around the Coppermine River, where they looked more at a man's muscles than they did at his past. Gotthart remembered how the old Hudson Bay stories used to fire him up, so he decided to go along.

In no time he found out that toiling in a mine with clouds of mosquitoes so thick he couldn't breathe wasn't his idea of adventure. By that time the mine bosses had found out that having muscles didn't make Gotthart any bargain, either. He complained so much and so loud about everything that he was getting the rest of the men dissatisfied and cutting down on work, and he was always whining about having a stomach-ache or a lame back so he couldn't work. They were trying to figure out how to get rid of Gotthart, short of kicking him out into the wilderness with winter coming on, when he settled it for himself.

Six men came along in a big canoe, heading north for a winter of hunting and trapping in the real Arctic. Seven men had started, but one took sick and had to be left behind with some holy brothers in a cloister hospital. Now they were short-handed and willing to offer a share in the expedition to another man.

"I'll go," Gotthart said. He figured anything was better than mining.

They looked at his muscles and accepted. The mine crowd was too glad to be rid of him to disillusion them, so off they went.

At first it was easy, just Gotthart's style, sitting in the canoe while wind and current did all the work. Then they came to a wild rapids where all their heavy stuff had to be portaged while the steersman ran the canoe through almost empty. "I should have a man in the bow," the steersman told them, "to fend us off the big rocks. Somebody with experience."

The other men looked at the white, thundering rapids and shook their heads. Gotthart looked at the heavy packs that had to be lugged a mile or more and spoke up fast. "I'll handle the bow pole. I'm an old man at it."

When the rapids caught hold and they began racing and

whirling and bouncing, with jagged black teeth of rocks reaching out on all sides, he almost wished he had taken the portage. He was half blind and dizzy from the speed and the spume, but for once he was too scared to fold up. He yelled his panic into the roar of the rapids and jabbed crazily at the hurtling rocks, but by a miracle they got through without a scrape. Gotthart was shaking all over and sick with his fright until the steersman said, "You did a mighty fine job there, fellow. You're a real boatman."

Gotthart stopped shaking and started bragging. After that he rode every rapids and missed all the carry work, but before long the others began to see what kind of companion they had picked up and they weren't too happy. An arctic winter is bad enough to take without being cooped up with somebody like Gotthart. But they had him, and they couldn't get rid of him now.

The expedition was to split up, part of them staying in the lower Arctic and the rest going on far up into the real barren tundra beyond the tree line. When they reached the first company post it didn't look too bad. The company hut was sound and comfortable, there were plenty of provisions and at least a scattering of stunted trees. Gotthart looked it over and wanted to know which bunk was his.

"Huh-uh," the boss said. "We stay here. You go on north with Ralph and Billy to the other post."

Gotthart wasn't happy, but he couldn't do anything about it. He got more unhappy when he saw his winter home up in the bleakest tundra, without trees or grass.

The hut was there, but some Eskimos had helped themselves to a couple of siding boards to fix a sledge runner or something, and there was no wood to patch it with. All they could do was tear the whole hut down and rebuild it smaller to eliminate the hole, and that was mighty hard work. Ralph and Billy were hard workers themselves, and they expected as much or more out of Gotthart. He whined and complained and that didn't help relations, either.

With that job done, they set him to mending nets while they began storing up whitefish for winter food. The nets were always getting ripped on rocks, so his job was never finished. With winter coming on, the other two couldn't wait around for Gotthart to take his time. They gave him a couple of warnings and then they took him out and gave him the beating of his life.

"We took you on because you said you'd work," Ralph

told him grimly. "Now you're going to work and do your share, or you don't eat or sleep inside. There's no time to coddle slackers in the Arctic."

Gotthart sobbed and whined, but after he missed a meal and found himself locked outside with a cold night wind coming up, he howled his surrender. For a while he really did work, because he was afraid not to. As long as he did his job, they were easy and friendly. When he shirked, like the day he failed to bring in a full supply of firewood, he got the same treatment, only worse.

He thought he would die then, but that was only the beginning. When they started setting traplines for muskrats and martens and foxes, they made him go along to learn the job because he was expected to run his share of line and produce his share of pelts.

By noon of his first day with Ralph, Gotthart was so tired he lay down and cried, but there was no rest for him. "Get going or stay here and die," Ralph told him bluntly. "We're stuck with you, so we mean to make a man of you or kill you trying. This is nothing. Wait until snow comes and you have to stay out alone from Monday to Friday running your set."

Somehow Gotthart made it back. Then he had to chop ice and get water as well as work on frames for stretching skins before they let him fall into his bunk. His last thought was a fierce determination to kill his tormentors. He would shoot them the moment the first snowstorm came and then report that they were lost in the storm.

With every day of added hell, Gotthart's lust for murder grew in him. They drove him unmercifully, day after day, and while Gotthart was still convinced he was being worked to death, he was actually getting hardened so the work was not nearly as strenuous as he still imagined. For a while he nourished himself on his dream of freedom.

Then the wolves began to come down with winter. He heard them howling outside at night and the bloodthirsty sound filled him with trembling terror. Billy and Ralph talked of experienced arctic trappers killed and mangled by the brutes. Gotthart suddenly realized how helpless he would be alone. To paddle back up that wild river unaided was impossible, and he knew no trail and had no dog sledge to carry provisions. With that realization, his dream of murder evaporated, and he began to feel like a rat caught in one of his own traps. When he wasn't too weary to think at all, he lay in his bunk and wept tears of self-pity each night.

Day by day the work speeded up and the men drove him more mercilessly. Then came the snow, endless and terrible and frightening, and the fresh agony of learning to use snowshoes. It was like running upstairs all day, until his legs wanted to break off at the knees and the agony of cramped muscles made him howl. "You'll get the knack," they told him without sympathy. "In a month you'll walk as naturally as you did without them." Gotthart began to yearn for the comparative ease of life in prison.

He proved such a poor trapper that in disgust they left him at home to prepare skins, cut firewood, and do other menial jobs to pay for his grub. When he tried to shirk even those duties, he was beaten harder and warned with frightening grimness of even worse penalties. The Arctic lays its terrible weight on all and there is no place for weaklings or non-producers. Gotthart looked ahead at five more months of agony and burst into tears.

Then one day he peered across the snow and saw a dog team approaching with two muffled figures trotting easily behind the sledge. They swung up and halted. The taller man threw back his parka.

"Well, I'll be damned! Gotthart Snider."

It was Elmer Boyle, of all the people on earth. Elmer had followed his dreams to the Arctic long before and found his world in the frozen wastes. Tall and husky and bronzed, he was working for the Canadian government, delivering mail and messages to remote Eskimo tribes and isolated trappers. With him was a young man named Ryan, a *chechako*, a newcomer in his first year north but already making a place for himself with his enthusiasm and his eagerness to learn.

After that first startled greeting, Elmer was no more than cool to his old schoolmate. He knew Gotthart too well from personal experience and knew of his prison record. Gotthart, on his part, was cautious. This rugged, confident giant bore little resemblance to the helpless boy he had picked on remorselessly at home. He measured the muscular frame, gauged the steady gray eyes, and shivered.

Ralph and Billy returned to give the newcomers a boisterous welcome. They knew Elmer well and liked Ryan on sight as much as they despised Gotthart. After the first shock of amazement at finding that two such opposites had been boyhood neighbors, they excluded him from the conversation for a long time. It was not until the next day that he learned what was on their minds.

"Ryan wants to join our crew and we want him, Elmer," Ralph said. "You can probably guess what a worthless burden Gotthart has been to us. If you'll take him off our hands, back to the nearest post, and leave Ryan, we'll be everlastingly grateful. If he stays here any longer, we won't be responsible for what might happen to him. You look like a person who could handle him for a short trip."

Elmer turned those cold gray eyes on Gotthart for a penetrating moment. "I can handle him."

"Now, wait," Gotthart yelled, frightened at the look and at his own memories. "I'm not going off into the wilderness with him. I can't stand such a journey in this cold. I won't go."

"Gotthart," Billy said softly, caressing his rifle. "Maybe you don't know that a trapper always checks his supply of sugar and tobacco. Ours has been disappearing too fast. Robbing supplies in the Arctic is a major crime. You could be shot for it, and nobody in the Arctic would blame the man who did it."

Gotthart subsided, blubbering and shaking. Elmer faced him grimly. "I'll take you, on one condition. You do your full share of the labor and you'll get your full share of food. Do less and you'll get less. Lag behind and you'll be left behind." Gotthart could only remain silent, but in his heart raged a new tempest of murderous hatred and all of it was suddenly directed at Elmer Boyle.

From the start, the journey into the sub-zero cold of full Arctic winter was ten times worse than Gotthart's imaginings. It was bad enough to learn that he must run on snowshoes instead of riding the sledge runners. Luckily, he was hardened enough by then to keep up, but he wailed steadily. Elmer ignored him. By night they pitched a thin tent and, if they found a few sticks, had a brief fire for warmth. Otherwise they cooked on a kerosene primus stove and had no heat.

The gale hit them without warning, coming in the night. Gotthart awoke as the tent whipped away, and with it his boots and mittens. Dogs and sledge were lost somewhere behind a white wall of screaming torment that engulfed them.

Somehow Elmer got his own spare boots and mittens, got his companion dressed and dragged him to the poor shelter of the river bank. Gotthart howled and cursed all the way. "You're dragging me somewhere to die."

"Don't be a fool," Elmer shouted above the wind. "Why should I do that? I promised to get you out and I will."

The gale howled on without letup while they huddled and felt the numbness creep over them. By the next day they were half frozen. Elmer stood up with a struggle. "Come on. We can't keep this up much longer. Follow me and don't get lost."

"I can't," Gotthart wailed. "I won't. You can't make me."

He tried to fight back, and suddenly he was being jerked up with amazing strength, then hurled to the snow with stunning force. Again and again Elmer lifted him and threw him down, smiling as Gotthart cursed and cried and pawed at him.

Suddenly Gotthart realized that he was getting warm, that blood was once more coursing through his body. Elmer grinned at him then and stopped. "It was the best way to get us warm. Now we can huddle down again with our sleeping bags and last out the day."

That night the wind died. Elmer dragged the cursing Gotthart up and forced him to stumble around until they found the half-buried sledge, its cargo intact, the dogs snugly curled nearby. Their tent was gone, with the caribou skins they put under sleeping bags for warmth, but Elmer was optimistic. "The snow is packed now so we can make ourselves an igloo each night. It's warmer, anyhow, and there's no frozen canvas to struggle with."

The big snow knife carved out heavy blocks. These were set in a circle and gradually built into a solid dome. Gotthart momentarily forgot his hate in admiration as Elmer cut his way out after placing the last block. When he would have dived inside, Elmer caught him back. "Not yet. Take a knife and help bevel the cracks between all the blocks. They have to be packed with snow like mortar to keep out the wind."

Finally the job was done, the corn meal and seal oil cooked for the seven dogs, and then their own slim supper. "The dogs are fed first," Elmer explained, not unkindly, "because they haven't the resistance we have and our lives depend upon them. We'll all be on short rations until we reach my big cache on the coast, unless by luck we sight a bear or caribou. I only hope the dogs' strength holds out until we make it."

Gotthart was silent, hating Elmer for his logic and his knowledge, hating him for feeding dogs ahead of men. Still he was forced to admit that their snug night in the igloo was the pleasantest so far, although much too short. Elmer rousted him out long before light to take full advantage of the packed snow. With luck, they could make the cache in five days, eat their fill and rest a day or two before pushing on to civilization. But in the Arctic man could rarely trust in his luck to hold. Theirs ran out in a day and a half.

The second gale hit them a little past noon, more savage than the first had been. The howling wind buffeted them and slashed their faces with a million knives. A white wall hid the dogs. In that screaming, agonizing tumult there was no sense of direction.

Gotthart stumbled and fell and huddled there, sobbing wild curses, his face whitening with frostbite. Elmer caught hold of his arm and struggled to drag him to his feet. "We've got to go on as long as we can. Every inch we make it toward the cache is another chance to survive. Get up."

"I won't!" the other screamed. "I won't move. I can't."

Elmer stepped back, his face grim, and swung the long dog-whip. Gotthart screamed again as the lashes stung him mercilessly, over and over, until the pain was greater than the agony of exhaustion. Somehow he got to his feet and they stumbled on.

They endured that nightmare journey almost two hours before Elmer was willing to give in. The moment they stopped, the dogs simply curled up in their tracks and vanished under a blanket of sheltering snow. For the two men there was no such easy rest. Gotthart stumbled in a daze of exhaustion while Elmer found packed snow, cut the blocks and began their igloo. In the teeth of the terrible wind, Gotthart had to brace the walls with his body to keep the blocks from being hurled down before the lower rounds were finished.

When Gotthart howled and protested that he could not breathe in the storm, Elmer, too tired to argue, did the job himself. He came back to find Gotthart dozing on the floor. Nothing had been done. No hard-packed snow was melting for water. The snow had not been brushed from their sleeping bags nor the ice beaten out of the mattress skins.

"You damned, worthless, no-good whelp," Elmer roared,

and his fist lashed out. Gotthart fell back, blood streaming from his nose. He struggled to get up and Elmer knocked him down again and again until exhaustion had replaced rage. "Get the hell out and cut blocks for drinking water, damn you. And none of this loose snow, either. Find packed stuff so we'll be sure of plenty."

Gotthart stumbled out into the terrible storm with a new and deeper rage festering in his mind. He had wanted to destroy his tormentors before, but those feelings had been mild compared to this new fierce longing to kill Elmer Boyle. Suddenly it came to him that soon he could enjoy that pleasure without any fear. This storm was really his ally. When it ended and they were close to the previous cache, so close that not even a dub could miss, the deed could be done. A shot in the back, a body left for the wolves, and Gotthart would have everything to himself. He could invent any of a dozen fatal accidents blamed on the storm and no one could doubt or disprove him. When he returned to the igloo he was almost happy in his new-found hope.

All that night the storm blew in savage gusts and by morning there was no sign of letup. Gotthart was hungry and said so. Elmer shook his head. "Sorry, but I'm afraid you'll get a lot hungrier. This storm might last for days, but our food supply won't. One of the first rules in the Arctic is to fast the first three days of storm. That still leaves you enough food and strength to go on again. Otherwise we might eat everything and die of starvation waiting for it to clear, or be too weak to travel when we could."

Gotthart made so little protest that Elmer gave him a look of sharp surprise. They settled down with their pipes and their thoughts. The storm raged unabated through the day, and eventually the weight of solitude and the pangs of hunger drove them to talking. They avoided childhood and the immediate past and for a time were almost friendly.

Elmer estimated, he told his companion, that two to three days of clear travel would see them at the cache, where a generous supply of food for men and dogs had been stored for just such emergencies. They were following the river which emptied into the sea. A scant twenty miles west of its mouth was a tiny promontory with a slight rise at its tip, too small to be called a hill but easy to identify. Here was his cache, raised on a high pole out of reach of marauding bears and clearly visible. Gotthart listened and suppressed a smile of triumph. Elmer, the fool, was making his plan childishly simple.

At last the storm began to wane. They set out before it was over, because now every minute was precious. Gotthart did his full share of packing for once, telling himself that he was preparing his own survival after Elmer's death.

They made the coast at last, only to find the shore piled high with ice. They had to stay inland over rough ground and inch their way, but at last there came the moment when Elmer saw a landmark. "We're ten miles from the cache, Gotthart. Ten miles west along the shore and we're saved. We'll camp now and finish in the morning when we're fresher."

That night the third gale hit them and pinned them down for a day of torture. Gotthart was sure he was dying of hunger, but Elmer laughed at him. "You'd be surprised how much you can take. A fast like this is good for you. Stop whining and think of the feast we'll have at the cache."

The next day the wind was down enough to travel and they set out in new high spirits. Presently Elmer went on ahead to get his bearings from a high ice peak. Gotthart and the dogs dropped in their tracks. He was too tired even to unlash the rifle on the sled. That could come later. The moment Elmer reported the cache in sight, he would find the strength to complete his plan of murder.

Gotthart awoke to see Elmer stumbling toward him, his whole figure glistening with ice. "Hurry!" Elmer yelled. "I'm drenched and freezing. I fell into a crack where two floes had parted and had to swim to solid ice. Get an igloo built quick and get my sleeping bag beaten out. If I don't get a change fast, I'm done for. Get moving, man."

Gotthart gaped at him stupidly. "Igloo? But . . . but you never taught me how to build one."

"Then I'll build it," Elmer panted, "but get my sleeping bag beaten out and my change of clothes. Hurry, you fool."

He worked furiously, cutting and setting the blocks. Gotthart did as he was told, but his mind was whirling with this unexpected good fortune. Now there was no risk at all, no rifle slug to be found, no possible question of accidental death.

With the house done, Elmer swiftly undressed and crawled into the sleeping bag. "Take my clothes outside. As soon as the water freezes you can beat it out of them as ice. It won't be warm but at least it will be dry and we can make the cache before dark."

Gotthart took the clothes and vanished outside. Elmer fell into a stupor of exhaustion, cold and shock. At last, after an endless time, he roused himself and yelled for Gotthart. There was no answer. He called again and again and at last forced himself to brave the savage cold long enough to peer outside.

A deep, terrible curse burst from his lips. There was no one outside, no frozen clothing, nothing but a fresh trail and at the end of it, far to the west, the tiny figure of Gotthart clumsily driving the dogs toward the cache.

For a time Elmer's rage bordered close to madness. He was left without food or clothing, to die here so near his cache. At last, back in his sleeping bag for protection, the rage wore itself out and with the creeping cold came a dreamy sense of well-being.

The day dragged on and the cold bit deeper and in time Elmer knew that Gotthart was not coming back. By then he was too far gone to care. . . .

On the ice, Gotthart was alternately jubilant and frightened. His hated enemy was dead or dying, and no one on earth could blame Gotthart. They might even hail him as a hero and reward him for his courage in trying to get help in time.

When he finally saw the little unmistakable promontory with the hillock at its tip it took him moments to realize he had found his goal. Then the knowledge struck him and he forgot the dogs, forgot everything, to stumble crazily out over the ice toward the haven of promised food and fuel.

He reached the hummock and climbed and stared wildly, incredulously around. Here was the exact spot Elmer had described. Every landmark was clear and unmistakable. Everything was in its place . . . except the pole that held the cache.

He ran wildly, he cried and sobbed and blubbered, he cursed and called and even prayed, but nowhere was there a sign of a pole above the broken expanse of snow and ice. He climbed onto the highest jumble of rocks and ice chunks to see if perhaps another point might be the right one. He could see nothing and he was too utterly weary to hunt further.

He must have sleep first. He thought of the sleeping bag back on the sled and cursed his foolishness in abandoning it. Now he lacked the strength to go back and get it. He had to sleep a little first. Then he would be stronger.

Three Eskimos, Tulimak, Papeek, and a friend came to their cache of caribou and stared with rage. A bear had been at it, only hours before to judge by the tracks. The meat was devoured, the cache stones scattered. This was serious and infuriating. In the code of the Arctic, the robber of a cache deserves to die. Besides, this particular robber could supply his own flesh in place of what he had stolen.

They set out grimly to track down the bear, and that is how they came upon a hastily made igloo and a man without clothing or food and almost dead from the cold. But the Eskimos are wise in the ways of the north. They cared for Elmer and brought the blood back to his veins. Then, warmly wrapped in skins, they took him to their village and nursed him back to strength.

In the spring, when the ice broke, Elmer and his saviors set out by kayak for the post. On the way they passed the little point where the cache was stored, and Elmer asked that they go ashore to see if, by chance, Gotthart had reached the cache and revived himself enough to escape.

With the snow gone, the cache was plain to see, the stout boxes of food for man and dogs, the spare skins and clothing, the fuel for the stove. They were there, scratched and marked by a prowling bear, but safely closed. On top of the little mound they made on the hummock, the highest point anywhere near, the place a dying man would climb for his last despairing search of the horizon, they found a hideous thing.

It lay sprawled across the little artificial hill. Foxes and ravens and gulls had been at it, but there was enough of the clothing left to identify the body.

Gotthart had lain down for his last sleep on top of the very snow-buried cache that could have saved his life.

They found the pole down by the shore. Some bad-tempered bear, irritated at this man-thing poking up above his familiar world of snow and ice, had batted it down and eaten the fresh meat tied to its top. The snow had quickly hidden the pole.

But any man who knows the Arctic knows a thing like that happens all the time in the North.

5 The Partner

~~~~~~~~~~~~~~~

IT'S OFTEN HARD TO TELL what makes a man go up to the Arctic year after year, until he has spent maybe half a lifetime in the Polar regions. Sometimes it is a tradition in a family. Boys follow in the footsteps of their fathers and become experienced trappers before they are out of their teens. Their lot is nothing to envy. The profit is small and most of these sturdy men could make a better living at home or as sailors going south to a comfortable life instead of north to the arctic darkness. But there is something which pulls these men northward, something which never lets go of a man once he has been up there a year or two.

There are those, of course, who are not suited for the loneliness in the Arctic. They have to get out at once. And there are some who are disappointed when they find arctic life is not an uninterrupted series of adventures. There is, naturally, much in the life of an arctic trapper which is different from anything at home, but his Polar existence is essentially monotonous. The Arctic is always the same: cold, dark and indifferent.

Most of the trappers and sailors I have known in the Arctic are no different from other people; they are solid and normal men. They can take the loneliness, but the darkness is sometimes too much of a strain on the nerves. When a man is left utterly alone for four months of darkness, an event that interrupts his known routine often presents a situation he cannot master.

I remember a man like that, whose nerves snapped under the strain. He was a good trapper and a fine fellow who had spent winter after winter in Greenland. His name was Olav, and since he is still alive, I shall not mention his last name. He was an old-timer in Greenland. A simple man, perhaps, without much learning or imagination, but as good as they come and a first-rate trapper. I had known him for many years, and he had always spent the winter in Greenland with the same partner, Thomas Vold. The two of them went up and

251

stayed alone together, miles and miles from the nearest man, until they were picked up in spring to go south with their catch. But one year Olav quarreled with Thomas about his share in the catch, with the inevitable result that the partnership split up. The next year Olav got himself a new partner.

I was serving then as first mate on the *Blue Whale,* the ship which brought the trappers up to Greenland. As soon as Olav came aboard with all his supplies, he introduced me to the new man. His name was Gustav Krakau, and I knew right away that he was a stranger to Greenland. Gustav Krakau, Olav told me later, had never before been out of Denmark. He had some money, apparently, and he had paid more than his share of the supplies. That may have been part of the reason why Olav let himself be talked into taking along such an inexperienced man, but I think it was just as much due to Gustav Krakau's manner and the way he talked. Even the old-timers seemed to like him and trust him.

They had quite a lot of supplies along, more than we were used to, and we teased Olav about it. The old man is a millionaire now, the boys said, look at all the stuff he has along: crates and crates of dried fruits and cans and cans of fancy stuff. We got it all on board and left the next morning, but the first day out Gustav Krakau got sick as a dog. Nobody made anything of it at first, but Olav did not like it. He felt it was a reflection on his own reputation to have his partner behave as a landlubber, and that made it all the worse. The crew began pulling his leg, joking day and night about "the tough new partner." Krakau stayed in his bunk and didn't touch any food, but as soon as we were in the ice and the sea got calm, he was all right again. Once he came on deck and we got to talk to him, he turned out to be a man who knew a little bit about everything. He didn't talk much about himself, but he seemed to come from a good family. He had brought along a lot of books to read during the winter, something unusual for a trapper.

Olav was in for teasing again, about the Greenland library. He wasn't very proud of all the books, but he stood up for his partner, declaring that there was no law against a trapper reading if he felt like it.

After a few days, we came to the fjord where Olav had had his blockhouse for many years. The two men left us with all their boxes and crates and stood waving goodbye to us as we sailed out the fjord and turned north again.

When the *Blue Whale* came back for them next summer,

Olav was alone. As soon as we approached the bottom of
the fjord, we could see that something was wrong. When
Thomas Vold was Olav's partner, the two of them always
came out in the rowboat to meet the *Blue Whale*, as all the
trappers do unless they have lost the boat during the winter.

No boat came out to meet us. We could see the dogs running
around on shore, but at first there was not a soul to be
seen. At last Olav came out of the blockhouse, alone. He
was a ghastly sight. He looked like a broken man.

He just stood there waiting for us and as soon as I came
on shore, I noticed in a little patch of clear ground behind
the blockhouse a simple wooden cross. A name had been
carefully carved in the wood—Gustav Krakau—with the date
of death.

We could hardly get a word of explanation from Olav. He
had the looks of a haunted man; his eyes were shifty, and
he looked away when we talked to him.

Finally, the skipper decided to open the grave. Olav refused to go with us. He did not want to come near that little
wooden cross. We got out some spades and soon the body
was uncovered. Gustav Krakau had a large hole in his head.
It didn't take much knowledge to see that he had been shot;
a great part of his head had been blown off. And still we
didn't know just what had happened. It might have been an
accident, but Olav would not explain. We would have to report the death as soon as we got back, of course, and we had
to bring Olav with us to the proper authorities. The skipper
told me to put together some kind of coffin for the body of
Gustav Krakau and we set off again.

The return trip was a miserable affair for Olav and the
rest of us. He walked around by himself, never talking to us,
just looking at us with his scared, restless eyes. Most of the
time he spent alone in his cabin, muttering to himself, never
turning up for any meals.

As soon as we reached port, the passengers went on shore
and nobody stopped Olav from leaving with them. But the
skipper went straight to the authorities to give his report, and
the following day Olav was arrested.

I think it was only after they put him in prison that Olav
finally went out of his mind. I think I can swear to it that he
was still normal on the trip home, but he had felt all our
eyes on him—questioning, curious, accusing.

I was present in the sheriff's office when Olav made his

statement the following day and told the whole weird tale
of that winter. He was hesitant at first, incoherent and confused, but once he really got going, nobody could stop him.
His worn hands were twisting nervously and his eyes looking
off in the distance as he began:

"I should never have taken him along, of course. I can see
it now, but that's only because one knows so much after-
wards. I can see it as I sit here and I'll try to tell you all
about it because I want you, I want somebody to understand what really happened. You may still not understand it,
Sheriff, but perhaps it doesn't matter too much."

And without holding anything back, hesitating only now
and then to fumble for the right word, this shadow of the
Olav we had known gave his account of Gustav Krakau's first
and last winter in Greenland. He began right at the beginning, the moment when the *Blue Whale* left them in the
little fjord.

Gustav had been very eager and excited, but that first moment when they were left alone, he had suddenly grown
solemn. He grabbed Olav's hand and promised to show himself
worthy of all the confidence and friendship the older man had
shown him. Olav didn't care for such talk. He told Gustav
gruffly that it was all nonsense, turned his back on him, and
told him to carry up their gear to the blockhouse as fast as
he could.

After the first few days with Gustav Krakau, Olav knew
he had never met a better man for a companion. Gustav was
clever and he learned fast. He had never seen a walrus before, but as soon as he was shown how to hit the animal
right behind the ear, he got the knack of it in no time.
He had no idea about skinning and flensing animals, but he
stood watching Olav like a little boy. Then he asked for permission to do the next walrus himself, in order to learn it.
And he worked all night long before he was satisfied.

He was a wizard in the kitchen. Olav had never seen cooking like it. Besides the usual supplies, Gustav had brought
along all sorts of things: curry and spice sauces and stuff
Olav had never heard about. The way he made the food made
Olav feel like staying on at table long after the meal was
finished, just to keep the good taste in his mouth.

From the time he was a small boy, Gustav had done a good
deal of hunting in the woods at home. He had dreamed of
being a trapper one day, but his mother had kept him from
it. She wanted him to study, that was why he had plowed

through so many books. It got to be a habit with him, and
he kept on reading.

He was a good man with a gun, and he and Olav had
plenty of meat during the late summer. When fall came
with the first frost, they saw their first bear. Gustav got all
excited and asked if he might have the first shot. Olav told
Gustav to go ahead. Gustav was like a child when he felled
the bear, and he made a real good job of it. Later on, they
saw bears every day, several big ones in one day sometimes.
Gustav skinned them all and he studied their insides to see
what they had been eating. He did the same with all the
animals, and he wrote down in his books what he saw.

After a while, it was getting noticeably darker every day,
and soon the sun would be gone for a good many months. It
was time to set the traps, and that was something new to
Gustav. He worked at it at home by the blockhouse first,
and he got to be pretty good at it. In no time he caught on
to the trick of setting the traps and covering them with a
thin layer of snow to hide them from the fox. In a couple of
days he was as good as Olav, and they set out together. At
first Olav went with him, showing him where to put the traps
and how to find them again when he came back

After that, the two men split up the territory between them.
Everything to the north was Gustav's, while Olav kept to the
south. They made a regular routine out of it. Every Monday morning they set out with two dogs each. The dogs pulled
the little sleighs with the sleeping bags and food, and they
could move faster that way. Olav had had the same four
dogs for years, and it was funny the way they took to Gustav
right away. The old partner, Thomas Vold, had always had
a hard time getting along with them, but Gustav had a wonderful way with the animals and they were friends from the
first day.

Gustav went north and Olav south and they kept walking
away from each other all day Monday and Tuesday. At
night, they slept in some small huts which Olav had built
years before. Half of Wednesday they kept on walking, check-
ing the traps, but in the afternoon they turned around. Wednesday they slept in the Tuesday huts and Thursday night they
spent in the Monday huts. Friday they were back at the
blockhouse again. If they met a snowstorm, they had to stay
over in one of the small huts, of course, and they wouldn't
get back until Saturday. Sometimes they did not meet again
until Sunday, and once in a long while they did not see

each other until the end of the next week again. But Olav had stored plenty of food in all the huts, they were both careful, and he knew he did not have to worry about Gustav.

Soon he noticed that he was really looking forward to Friday. He began missing Gustav when he was all alone with the dogs, and he was eager to sit listening to his strange partner again. Life with Gustav was quite different from all the winters he had spent with Thomas Vold. They hardly spoke a word to each other, Olav and Thomas. What did they have to talk about? They knew the work and did it well enough, both of them. That was all. Gustav was the opposite. He always had lots to tell when they met again. During the week he had seen so many things he had to talk about —things Olav and Thomas always had known but never talked about, because they did not seem worth wasting a word on.

What a talker Gustav was! When Olav was alone again during the week, he couldn't help thinking of all the things Gustav had said. In the end he got so used to all this talk that he began saying things on his own.

After a while, it got to be with Gustav just like with the heat in a house: you can do without it, but you get mighty cold. Olav missed him more and more during the week; Gustav made the winter quite different for him.

Christmas came and they even had something extra to eat, they even washed and shaved themselves and lit candles. Olav put on a clean white shirt. After all, he thought, it's Christmas only once a year. But Gustav did not seem to be moved by the Holy Day. He went out to check his traps just like any other day. Olav didn't like it, but there was nothing he could do, since they were partners and Gustav was just as good a trapper by then as he was himself.

It was shortly after New Year's Day when Gustav complained that he didn't feel so well. His arms and legs were like lead if he walked any distance. Olav could see that he moved very slowly and went early to bed, but he always took a book along with him and told Olav about some of the things he read. Olav never understood much of what was read to him, but he listened carefully and thought about it afterward.

The next Monday they got ready as usual. Gustav still moved slowly, but he seemed all right as they parted. They said goodbye to each other and trotted off again, one to the north and the other to the south. The week went by like any other, Olav looked after his traps and had a pretty good load with him when he returned on Friday. Gustav's dogs were by the blockhouse already, and Olav could see the lights in the house. It was the first time Gustav had returned before him, but when Olav entered, he found the other man in bed, looking very sick. Gustav told him he had had some fever and had returned the day after they parted. He had felt pretty bad for a while, but he was all right again, he said. He had only wanted to wait for Olav before he set out to make up for the time he had lost. Now he wanted to leave right away to get the animals in his traps before the wolves got them.

He was right, of course. They had to think of the catch before anything else; that was what they were there for. Olav didn't say anything, although he had been looking forward to spending the weekend with Gustav. He felt very lonely as his partner left. He had never thought of it before, but now he knew that Gustav had spoiled him with all his talk.

Monday he set out again and he had extra good luck that week. The load was heavy, and it was late in the evening before he came back to the blockhouse on Friday. There was no light in the house. Gustav should have been there, since he had started out a day before Olav.

But something was wrong. Olav could hear the dogs inside the blockhouse howling and barking as he came closer. His own dogs began barking too, but there was still no light inside the house. It was very strange, and Olav felt scared. He took his time with the dogs to give Gustav time to wake up and come outside to meet him. But then he noticed that there was no smoke coming up the chimney and quite a lot of snow had settled in front of the door.

At last he went in. It was pretty dark and he got out his matches. It was just as cold in the house as outside. The dogs jumped on him, howling. Olav took off his heavy clothes and lit a candle. Gustav was in bed with his back to Olav.

"Gustav!" he called. No movement! It didn't take him long to understand that Gustav was dead.

At first he would not let it be true. He made a fire in the stove and cut some ice for the pot. The whole water barrel outside was a solid block of ice, and it had always been the duty of the first man home to thaw some ice. Olav even began scolding Gustav for neglecting his duties.

He didn't want to look at Gustav. As long as he didn't he could pretend that the man was asleep, that he would soon wake up. He fed the hungry dogs, told them that Gustav was drunk, that that was the reason why they never got their food. He knew it was a lie, but he felt he had to say something.

He kept up the pretense that Gustav was asleep. He knew how miserable he would be once he admitted that his partner was dead. Suddenly he felt utterly exhausted, tumbled into his own bed, and fell asleep.

I remember Olav made a pause in his story at that point, staring at us with those faraway eyes without recognizing us, turning at last to the sheriff again with pleading in his voice as he went on: "You don't know such loneliness, Sheriff. You don't know that darkness. You don't understand how a man can make himself believe something he knows is not true, something which is obviously a lie." With a deep sigh, Olav went on with his story.

When he got up the following morning, Olav made hot cereal for both of them.

"Do you want some?" he called out to Gustav. There was no answer, since the other man was dead, but Olav didn't want to let Gustav see that he knew it.

That was Saturday morning, and Olav decided to keep Gustav in the house until Sunday night. He wanted some company over the weekend at least, then he could bury him Monday morning and set out on his usual round, so he wouldn't have to sit alone at home feeling miserable. He decided to check Gustav's traps, too. There must be plenty of foxes in them, and he would bring them back to Gustav.

Nonsense! He told himself. Gustav was dead, what would he do with the foxes?

Suddenly he decided to have a look at the dead man. Gustav was lying hunched up in bed with his legs pulled up. He looked just as if he were sitting in a chair. He was frozen stiff, of course, but the face looked as if Gustav were laughing. Olav lifted him up and put him down on a chair by the table, then he sat down to his lonely breakfast.

Olav talked to the dead man as he ate his food. He felt that he had to give Gustav the answer to all the things they had been talking about the weekend before, about the soul, about religion and immortality. Gustav had said he did not believe he would go to heaven, he didn't know where it was or what it looked like. It was hard to answer a man like that, but Olav went on talking.

Gustav just sat there laughing. That was the way he looked anyway. And Olav talked to him, otherwise it would have been too lonely. He supplied the answers himself, told himself all the things he thought Gustav would have answered. That way he could talk back again and forget that his friend was dead. It was hard to keep up, of course. There wasn't really much to talk about, and Olav didn't feel like saying the same things over and over again.

In the evening he took Gustav outside. He put him on a sleigh and pulled him over to a small cliff behind the house. First he put the body down in the snow and then covered it with stones, lots of stones piled neatly on top of the body. He didn't want wolves and bears to eat his friend Gustav.

It was a strange week. Olav looked after his own traps first, then Gustav's. And he took all four dogs along. He didn't want any of them to stay at home and howl as soon as he approached the house again, coming back for a lonely weekend.

When he got back the following Sunday, Olav was very tired and decided to stay in the house for a whole week. He had to soften up all the skins and put them up for drying. There was a lot to do, and he was alone with the job.

As he sat by himself in the blockhouse, Olav began thinking that it had been better, after all, when he had Gustav at the table with him, even though he was dead. Now Gustav was outside, freezing in the terrible cold, poor man. That was all nonsense, of course, he thought. But still, he was so utterly alone and—well, Gustav wasn't really buried, after all, just covered with stones. And Olav had to sit there and eat all alone. He had to go out by himself, look after the dogs by himself, and now one of them was having puppies on top of it all. Gustav had been looking forward to that.

It was nobody's business, Olav thought. Since he was all alone, it didn't really concern anybody, and it was his intention all the time to put Gustav out again, to bury him decently. But just while it was so terribly dark, for a little while only.

In short, he took Gustav in again. He regretted it once he had him inside, but then it was done and he had to stick to it. When he had him sitting there on the other side of the table, things seemed a little brighter. Olav talked to him and went on answering for him. He knew Gustav pretty well, by then, so it was just like playing with dolls. And he was sure Gustav would never have objected to it.

They had quite a good time together, he felt. Olav prepared food for both of them and set a place for Gustav. He even served him, and he got angry when Gustav didn't eat and he had to give the food to the puppies. He pretended to be angry because Gustav was so finicky about his food—that was part of the game.

When he went to bed that night, he left Gustav sitting by the table. That was a great mistake, because he woke up in the middle of the night and Gustav was moving! He could have sworn to it that the body was moving. He was wide awake in a second—and here is the strange part: he really wanted to be afraid that Gustav was moving. He knew all the time that the body was only thawing, but he did not want to admit it. If he did, he would have to give up the game of make-believe, of pretending that Gustav was still alive.

When Gustav died, he had been all hunched up with one arm bent forward a little so Olav could put it on the table edge for support. Gustav had looked quite natural that way. It was this arm which began thawing, that was the whole explanation. Olav had to have some heat in the house to thaw the stiffly frozen foxes, but he should not have let Gustav thaw with them. That night he was so scared he could hardly move. He even said the Lord's Prayer, although he really knew all the time that the thing was quite natural, that the body was only softening. And toward morning he calmed down again.

"Come along, my fine friend," he said to Gustav as he got up. "You are going out in the snow again. You are all through scaring decent people."

And once more he covered Gustav with stones before he set out on his rounds. He worked out a new system with the rounds. First he looked after half of his own traps to the south and half of Gustav's to the north. That way he came back to the blockhouse twice a week. And not for a second did he dream of doing Gustav out of his share of the catch.

Every time he got back to the lonely house, he felt drawn to that stone grave again. The urge got too strong and after a couple of weeks he gave in again. He brought Gustav into the house and put him down at the table once more. He served him his food as before, and the puppies got what was left on the plate. If anybody sees me, they'll think I'm crazy, Olav thought. But he didn't care. He just kept talking all the time, for Gustav and himself. If he stopped for a moment, the cold silence would come between them again and he would have to admit that his friend was dead, and he didn't want to do that.

When the light began coming back to Greenland, a little more of it every day, Olav thought he would get over it. Once he could really get a good look at Gustav, it would be too crazy to carry a dead man back and forth. He had seen too many friends and fellow trappers die to be impressed by death, but everything was different with Gustav. Every time he returned to the house, he was determined not to take him back again, but he always found some excuse. Actually, even in death, Gustav had such an influence on Olav in life that Olav couldn't ignore him. It began to irritate him a little.

There was hardly a weekend when he did not have Gustav in the house with him. The body got a little worn from all the handling, of course. The sun was getting warmer every day and sometimes it would shine right in his face. He noticed for the first time that Gustav's skin was a dark yellow. He was furious with him, telling him that he was dead and should stay dead. He didn't want to see him again, he shouted to the body. This is the last time you'll be in a room with me, he yelled at Gustav.

Gustav just sat there grinning at him. He had been a little too close to the fire and his mouth had sunk a little, making his grin even more gruesome. Olav knew that he was sure to go out of his head altogether if he kept this routine until the warmer weather set in. Gustav would thaw completely and his body would have an unbearable stench. But how could he stop it?

One day he noticed a snow sparrow outside and he knew he had to do something. The bird was a sure sign of spring, the fox trapping was over for the winter, the ice would soon break up, and the *Blue Whale* would return to take them back to Denmark.

He was afraid, he was really scared when he returned to the house with the last traps. Scared of Gustav, scared of his ghost—for he was really a ghost, the only difference being that Gustav didn't walk around by himself, because Olav carried him. It was just like when he was alive, he could make Olav do things he would never have done voluntarily by himself.

The idea came to him all of a sudden. He knew what he had to do—and he knew that it was the only right thing to

do. He took Gustav in and went on talking to him as if he
had nothing up his sleeve. He smiled to himself when he
told Gustav about all the things they would do the next day,
just to reassure his friend. After a while, he told Gustav
that he had to go outside for some more coal for the fire.
He had his gun outside, of course. He didn't close the door
all the way, left it open just a little crack. Gustav couldn't
call out and complain of the cold, poor man. But Olav knew
he was going to fool him this time.

He sneaked back to the house with the gun in his hand,
ready loaded. It took him at least an hour to get the barrel of the gun through the crack and get it in the right
position. Gustav sat there just where Olav had put him. He
had his back to Olav, but he was turned a little sideways,
just enough to let Olav see his smile—a disgusting grin
which wasn't really like him at all.

This time he was alive, Olav felt, but he had had enough
of him now. And he cocked the gun. Taking good aim was a
slow business. Even if he was a dead man, it was, after all,
a friend that Olav was going to shoot. Just as he was going
to pull the trigger, Gustav moved. The arm was getting soft
again. It was hard to shoot him while he was still moving.

But Olav had to rid himself of Gustav. Suddenly he got
furious with Gustav for trying to scare him even at the
very last moment. And then he shot.

A deafening roar shook the small blockhouse. The whole
back of the head was blown to pieces. At last he was really
dead and would never again visit Olav. After all, Olav would
never carry a man with half a head into the house.

He buried his friend the real way this time and made a
wooden cross for the grave. It felt good to be alone. Nobody to pay any attention to. He didn't miss Gustav. His
friend was dead now, true enough, and it was a great pity,
but there was nothing he could do about it. Quietly and
peacefully, Olav prepared for the trip home. The *Blue Whale*
would come any day now, he knew.

During the voyage home, Olav wanted to throw himself
overboard, he said. The only thing which kept him from it
was the thought that people would only think the worst of
him. Nobody spoke to him on that trip back home. He had
a cabin alone by himself, nobody would eat with him or have
anything to do with him.

"I knew what they thought of me and I knew what would
happen," Olav finished. "And I was right. This morning the

whole police force came to get me. We only came home yesterday and I walked alone to my house then, but today you needed four policemen to bring me down here.

"I am no murderer, Sheriff! I only used my gun to make Gustav leave me in peace once he was dead. I only killed a dead man. There is no law against that! Or is there? You tell me."

Olav was taken back to his cell that night and in prison they must have called him a murderer, told him that he had killed his best friend. That proved too much for him. Olav had always been a strong man, a good and honest one, but this was more than he could take. All that winter he must have been on the borderline, and that night he finally lost his mind.

An autopsy quickly confirmed his story. The medical examination showed that the body had been dead for some time and frozen stiff when it was shot in the head. Olav's name was cleared, there could be no question of murder, and the sheriff announced that no charge would be raised.

But it was much too late. Olav was incurably insane by then. He didn't understand what the sheriff told him and kept up a constant, incoherent muttering to himself. He was brought to an asylum and he is still there.

He was one of the strong and good men in the Arctic who couldn't take the unusual, the event outside his routine. He didn't have much to fall back on, he didn't read much, perhaps he didn't think much, and he couldn't stand being alone.

But who knows, maybe the same thing would have happened to him if he had lived down here in more civilized regions.

6 *The Day I Harpooned Myself*

YOU CAN SPEND a long lifetime harpooning whales and walrus and seals, but you never quite realize how they feel about it unless you harpoon yourself. That is exactly what I did to myself one day, but I don't recommend it to anybody.

Unpleasant experiences aren't rare when you've spent much of three-quarters of a century in the Far North. I've had to amputate my own frozen foot. I've set my broken arm in a "cast" of wet sealskin. I've been attacked by many animals, including a rogue whale, and I've been captured by the Germans, who confiscated my peg leg to keep me from escaping —although I escaped anyhow, hidden away in a crate. Still I don't think I ever spent a more agonizing interval than when I was impaled by a harpoon, nor have I ever suffered more than on the trip during which this occurred.

It all started in February of 1912 when the mail arrived at the trading post in Thule. The mail, which had left Denmark the previous September, informed us that Ejnar Mikkelsen, a noted explorer, had set out to cross Greenland from the north and had expected to be at our place by February.

Came March, and I said to Knud: "We better go look for this fellow." He agreed, and we enlisted the services of my father-in-law, Uvluriaq, and an able young hunter, Inukitsork. After a conference, we decided to head for Danmarks Fjord, some 700 miles northeast of Thule.

However, when Knud and I and the two Eskimos started for Danmarks Fjord in 1912, it meant sledding across Greenland's icecap, a great flat dome, crevassed on the edges, covering 700,000 square miles and in some places 8,000 feet thick. As far as I know, no one had ever attempted the crossing before.

We took 53 dogs, pulling four sleds packed with all the provisions they would hold. Following the sleds on skis, we made excellent time. There were times when we traveled as much as 30 hours without stopping. After 19 days, we reached the northern edge of the icecap and found that it dropped off perpendicularly, leaving ice cliffs about 100 feet high.

This sort of traveling can be done by compass, but not very successfully. We wouldn't have attempted it unless we knew that I, a somewhat experienced navigator, was able to use a sextant and tell, quite accurately, where we were at any given time. One thing went wrong. I am blond and therefore susceptible to snow-blindness. By the third or fourth day, my eyes were killing me.

When I kept them closed, it felt as though they were filled with sand. That was bad, but when I pulled them open, literally, once a day to take observations, I had the feeling that someone was sticking hot knives into them.

Nevertheless, we had reached the area for which we were aiming, and now we seemed to be stymied. "Here's a crevasse that seems to go down to the bottom," Knud said. "Somebody's got to be lowered down there somehow and then get out in front, where he can probably pick out the best place for us to try to come down with the sleds and dogs."

"I'm the strongest," I said, which was the truth. "I'll go."

We tied our harpoon lines together, and figured they would reach pretty close to the depth of the crevasse. Then we chopped at the ice until we had a sort of post around which to twist the line, and I started down between the walls of glistening ice.

I looped the line around one thigh so that I could pay it out gradually. Even so, I was going down faster than I expected. Then it happened.

The type of harpoons the Eskimos use come in two parts. The tip, which isn't too different from the barb on a fishhook, is attached to the line. It has a socket in one end into which the harpoon handle is set when the harpoon is ready for business. One tip had been left on the spliced line.

"I'd better take this off," Knud had said when he was tying the knot.

"Don't bother," I said. "I can get around it when I reach it."

But the snow-blindness and the effort to grasp the line with my mittened hands had taken all my effort and thought. I remembered only when I felt a deep jab in my thigh.

So there I was, hoist on my own harpoon, unable to go up or down. I shouted, but it was no use. There was a stiff wind up above and the men who were holding the line, fearful themselves of being pulled over the brink if they slipped on the glassy surface, couldn't hear a sound.

"So," I thought, "this is the way those animals felt while I held the other end of the line, so proud of my strength and my marksmanship."

At least I had sense enough not to struggle violently and waste my strength. Ignoring the pain, I sat there for a long minute, thinking out a plan. I tried, slowly and cautiously, to pull myself up the line. The wet leather of my mittens against the wet sealskin line gave me no traction. The mittens must come off, but would my bare hands do any better? If they didn't, they would soon be numb—and then what?

I dropped the mittens. Reaching high, I found I could gain a few inches, but the moment I let go with one hand I slid down again, impaled more firmly than ever. I tried again, and this time when I pulled myself up, I gripped the rope with my teeth. Then, using one hand to help steady myself, I reached behind me with the other to see what I could do with the harpoon tip. My heavy bearskin pants impeded my investigation, but finally I got a firm grip on the dart.

At this point another thought struck me. Sealskin is tough, but how long would a thin line hold under the pressure of teeth clenched in desperation? Could I free myself before I chewed myself into an icy grave?

The vision of dropping 50 feet onto rock-hard ice gave me the added strength and courage to yank out the harpoon tip, regardless of the flesh that held it firm. Somehow I got safely around it and continued on down the line. It ended 10 or 15 feet before the bottom of the cleft, but I was in no position to worry about that.

I just let go. I fell into a bank of relatively soft snow and lay there, staining the snow red. I knew that my companions would haul up the slack line and hurry to the edge of the cliff to watch me emerge onto the low land. Perhaps when they saw the blood on the harpoon tip, and waited in vain for me to show, they would figure I had dropped to my death, but for the present I couldn't relieve their fears. I was just too weak to move.

After ten minutes or so, I was able to stagger out into the open where I could be seen. I waved to those on the cliff and then started to look around. Off to the east there seemed to be a spot where, for a short distance, the ice sloped toward the shore. I pointed to it and collapsed again.

By skillful manipulation of the teams and sleds, my companions got down the choppy ramp with the loss of only three dogs. We retrieved the bodies and ate them, because we were completely out of food. I lay back in the snow in a sort of coma while the others set out on a hunting expedition. They were gone, it seemed to me, forever. All I had strength enough to do was to keep winding the two watches I always carried as chronometers.

When the rest of the party returned, I chided them for taking four days, but they silenced me quickly by showing me the carcass of a musk ox they had killed. Slowly, with the help of food, my strength returned. We started to look for any trace of Mikkelsen but found nothing. (Much later we learned that Mikkelsen had returned safely to Denmark.) However, there was much new land to be explored and mapped, and we kept busy until September.

We were down to three sleds by then, but we loaded them with fresh musk-ox meat and climbed back onto the icecap. This time it took us 25 days to cross. Rasmussen became seriously ill, which added to our woes, but finally, shooting the sun each day, I was able to guide our party to the spot where we should descend.

Down we came, happy to have seven dogs left—we had had to kill the others and divide them between ourselves and the survivors. We came to the spot where Thule should be, only to find we were on the wrong side of a wide, deep bay. Nothing to do but climb back onto the icecap and come down on the opposite shore. We were so weak that it took us ten days and cost us four more dogs.

I felt worse than anybody because I realized that, lying in the snow after my harpooning, I had thought four days had passed when there had been only three. That one day, with the speedy declination of the sun in September, had thrown me far off my calculations of where we were.

But all pain and hardships were forgotten when we finally caught sight of Thule far below us. We stopped to congratulate ourselves and I sprang my big surprise—a tiny supply of tobacco I had saved. With true heroism Knud and the Eskimos decided to save it until our arrival in Thule. When the first Eskimo came running out to meet us, Inukitsork said proudly, but very, very casually: "Have a smoke?"

7   Marriage, the Harbor of Safety

IS IT OF ANY ADVANTAGE to be beautiful? Yes and no.

Nauja was said to be a beauty, and her beauty was discussed in many Eskimo settlements. Men came to take a look at her, and some of them, I might say, were not contented just with looking. Nauja could not therefore be said to be without some experience of life. Young people moreover like fun, and when Nauja decided to go somewhere away from the village to catch salmon by herself, she could not be alone. Several of the young men always went along, and after some argument between them just one stayed, the others returned to the tents.

Nauja had a lot of fun watching these arguments. Often there were real wrestling matches, and stones were thrown in the air and even harpoons were lifted. It was all very thrilling, but she sometimes became scared, it even gave her that cold touch down the spine, that all women feel at least once in their lifetime.

Nauja had been through this time after time. After what happened up there in the mountains, she could never leave the boy at once. She might stay away from the rest of the tribe for ten sleeps or more.

But after that time the boy always began to bore her, and Nauja went home. The mother, old Aneenak, was wise. She knew that it was good for a girl to collect memories, and she liked to have something to tell the other women at the place for visitors, who could only look backward but not forward for the thrills of life.

Aya-ya-ya-ya-ay
The virtue is only to be found in old women,
And I am so sorry, I am so sorry, that I am old!
Aya-ya-ya-ya.

That was the song of old Aneenak, the last chant of a full life, the feeling that made her a poet.

"Fight and trouble and worry! Mad men and angry words!" the song continued. "One trembled with the yelling and roaring of the men. I am sorry that I am old, so sorry that I am old."

Nauja soon felt all those things of which old Aneenak sang. A man grabbed her by the waist and threw her up on his shoulder, carried her down toward his sledge and at the same time looked around to protect himself against attackers from behind. Nauja screamed and spanked the air with arms and legs.

She did not know what was going on at all, but she had to show her female embarrassment by this. At the same time, this man was evidently strong and mighty to walk right in between the igloos, kick down the wall in the house, and haul away this one girl, whose broad cheeks and flat nose made her talked about even a long way off. This man must be without fear of men and a good judge of women. Therefore she did not bite his ears, or press her fingers in his eyes, or otherwise demonstrate, but only swung her arms wildly over her head.

And when Nauja caught a glimpse of the other women standing defeated and depressed in their awareness of her triumph, she screamed all the louder to celebrate the triumph before them. Nothing was at all unpleasant; it was in fact charming to be resting on a man's shoulder and feel his arms and hands on her body.

"Away-ay, away-ay"—the dogs got a terrible smash of the whip, the sledge was kicked at the same time, so it started rolling, and the party was off.

With the sled were some men from way up north. They had been far south, trading with the white people; and on their way home, they felt lonesome and woman-hungry, so they stopped. This was only natural for them, since they had to show these people from the middle of the land that they were to be feared, and that payment was to be given for the honor of having such good hunters pass by. It was only to be expected that a girl or two or three would be taken along. Nothing particularly wrong would be done to the women—nothing at least that they might not expect in their own tribe. Besides, up north the meat was always plentiful and the men were able to support an additional wife without too much difficulty. Nauja's own father could do nothing to hinder her leaving, neither could any of her boy friends dare to use their bows and arrows, or lift a spear. Their courage reached only as far as their own kinfolk, from whom nothing was to be feared.

In addition to Nauja, two other girls were taken. This was quite a blow for her little village, but at least Nauja had company. Her abductor looked big and strong and between fingers and tears she counted his dogs. There were plenty of them. She saw a big load on the sled. She made in fact quite a few observations, none of which were unsatisfactory.

Nauja of course had to keep on crying. She did not want her abductor to think that her change was for the better. So she sat in bad temper of mind on the sled. And every time Awala, the mighty man, talked to her, she just mooed a little to show her disgust and discontent. But he seemed not to mind this, for he kept smiling and he sometimes yelled to his dogs to make haste: "Here we are with a new girl, let us show her it is dogs, not lice, that are dragging the sled."

They went up overland, cutting out the northern peninsula. Now and then stones peeked through the snow. Here it was necessary for the driver to jump from side to side of the long sled and push it to keep the runners from being worn by the hard rocks. The runners were made of frozen mud and covered with a fine layer of ice, just as thin as possible but smooth, and, once started, the sled moved over the ground without much friction.

Nauja stayed on the sled. Awala would not ask her to walk even when it went upward; he was not the type of man who wanted to hear critical remarks about the strength of his dogs. But after a while there came a stretch with lots of stones, and Nauja jumped down, took a hold in the sledge on her side, and pulled toward her; he pushed on his side, and they managed to keep out of the dangerous protruding sharp stones. She hopped up again, laughed a little to let him know her contempt for the whole affair, for his lousy dogs, for his inability to drive them, and to show her surprise that a man was unable to handle this alone.

But soon after, when they went downhill, she helped him, braking the sled that might run faster than the dogs could gallop along. This of course was done only for her own safety, but as they went over the ice footing at the bottom, she again left her seat and helped him get clear of the packed-up ice hummocks and out on the smooth pan.

Here they saw some of the other sleds ahead of them. These had stopped to repair their runners, since they had suffered heavily from the stones. Some had big pieces of the mud torn off, and the drivers had to smooth the cracks down with their knives. Other sleds were in worse condition, and the hunters had to chop pieces of frozen meat, plaster them on the runners, and then plane them down.

Awala's sled was unharmed, but he took a look at the runners. Nauja helped him tip the sled over. During the day the thin ice layer under the runners now and then wears out, and lukewarm water must be put on again. Of course you can't stop and make up a fire and take the time for this, so everybody has to add what he or she can deliver from the human body. And why should Nauja deny this, or the two other kidnapped girls? Everybody who had urine to spare did, and such help always makes for good mutual understanding.

After this, Nauja and Awala did not see the rest of the party that day. Awala built a little snowhouse, when he thought the day had been long enough. Nauja did not speak, but she was cold, so she helped fill out the cracks between the snowblocks in the house. Thereby the whole work was completed much faster. The meal at night was fine: frozen caribou meat followed by the real food, boiled ribs with plenty of tallow.

Soup and small pieces of tallow floating on top of it no woman can resist, and Nauja realized that it would be of no use to do so in any case. So the next morning found them in peace when the other sleds came up and they were urged to go on.

Together the whole party drove over a long stretch that day. Nauja had never been so far before. Every time they stopped during the day, she talked to the two other girls. None of them had anything special to complain about, but their honor compelled them to cry a little and to assure each other that they were going to run away and go home at the first opportunity. And they all said that somebody would soon come and fight for them and take them back, just as surely as the snow was on the ground.

The whole party camped together. The men had some meat caches at the place, and while they worked at the meat, Nauja told the other two girls that she was going to run home. On their part, they had to follow her, and that was what they did; though Nauja had hoped they would persuade her to stay.

Girls are girls, thought Awala as he watched them running away. He laughed.

A young man who had had his first woman on this occasion got worried, but Awala was wise. He told him: "Just let them run. They will come back, I know women. After a little walk anger cools down, and girls return. And should they keep on, we can catch them easily tomorrow by sled, and when they are hungry and cold, oh how happy they will be seeing us after them."

That same evening, as Awala had said, the three girls came back by themselves, almost before the igloos were made for the night. They did not try to explain, they just went in, each of them going to the man to whom she now belonged.

"Somebody has been out for a walk," said Awala. "It is time to cook." And he chopped the meat into pieces suitable to put in the pot.

"A mitten was lost," said Nauja, "but it was found again."

Ever since that time Nauja was a wife in the big man's house.

When the party arrived home, Nauja was afraid, for she had already heard of Seewagak, Awala's other wife. Some of the party had told her, but not Awala himself, for he was a hunter and his talk was not about women.

Seewagak had the gifts of women—gifts which surpass those of men, though men never realize it. Seewagak came out and saw the newcomer.

"One has come home from trading," she thought, "and one can never know what one will bring."

She greeted her new partner like a sister. But Nauja made no remarks: she just unloaded Awala's sledge, and Seewagak helped. This was the easiest way of getting over the embarrassment she felt as the object of attention from everybody in the village. She could see them looking at her. They made remarks and laughed. They ran for the other sleds and asked questions. But Nauja just unloaded.

Later they went into the igloo, and Seewagak showed Nauja her side of the house and told her which one of the lamps was to be taken care of by her. Seewagak helped her, she took the boots from her feet, she helped her husband and did all the work. Nauja saw right away that Seewagak was a hard worker and able to do much. The husband made no remarks. As the time came to sleep, he turned over to Nauja's side, and there he slept for the night. And the next night and the next night too.

Every day the men went out hunting. Usually they came home at night, but often they stayed out for several days, and this was when the women at home had their fun. They visited every house in the village and talked and talked as women do. The three newcomers were accepted, and after they had no more to tell about their homes and their village, they just became part of the tribe and were no longer considered strangers.

Awala kept on liking Nauja. He took her along sometimes to places a few days away, but as it became spring, and it was good to get rabbits for stockings in traps, Seewagak had to go along too, since she did better work with the skins.

Time went on. Nauja made a pair of boots for Awala, but they did not fit too well. He said that his feet hurt him walking after caribous, the mountains acted funny under his soles. Nauja blushed and was ashamed. After a while, she saw that Seewagak went out visiting some houses to talk. Her tongue was with her, Nauja knew that.

Nauja then made a pair of mittens for her husband, but Awala neglected to take them when he went out in the morning. Seewagak was still sweet to her. She did the cooking, she did the work of the house, she fixed the blubber and the skins to be scraped.

But that night when Awala came home, he seemed different. Nauja jumped from the bedplace to help him get his boots off, but he just pushed her aside and asked Seewagak to take over. He sat close to the old wife and talked to her about the dog that had pups that morning. The world had changed for Awala and for Seewagak too.

"Somebody wants food," she said. "Let untired ones cook." She threw the meat over to Nauja. "Make the fire big on your lamp," she commanded. "The terrible man ought to eat, and lots of it, for his hard trouble today."

She said "the terrible man" to please Awala, and she talked loud without any smile on her face.

Somebody came in to visit. "A pleasure to see somebody," yelled Seewagak, the first time she greeted a stranger this way. "Sit down and have a bite between the teeth." Nauja had to serve, and after this she was told to go after ice for water for the next day.

She didn't even know where to get the ice. Seewagak used to do this. But now she had to go out into the darkness to look for it.

"And look after the coat of the strong-minded man," urged Seewagak. "After it is dried outside, turn it inside out and have it done by tomorrow."

Nauja slept alone that night, and she did so for many nights from then on. She decided to return home. Her mother was crying, she knew, and her little sister wanted her help. She felt unhappy, and Seewagak, who used to help, was now full of talk and only commanded in the house, so that Nauja's ears were hurting. Awala did not mind: all he did was come home and go out. He slept close to Seewagak, and Nauja had to keep awake most of the night to dry his clothes.

And she was told to sew and make boots and mittens and coats for the different young boys in the house—the men who helped Awala and who were, therefore, to be taken care of.

But as the sun went high without sending pleasure to Nauja, one day Awala remembered her again. A trip to an egg island was planned, and Awala's outfit was arranged.

"It will be better to take your blanket along." That was all he said to Nauja, but it was enough, and everybody understood. Nauja was to go with him, and why should she keep it secret?

"Oh, let one's pots be cleaned," she yelled to Seewagak, and it was as eating tallow from a young caribou to see her hurry up and take her orders. "Let me not be missing anything, see that there is enough sinew in a bundle to sew holes in the boots, if the big hunter wears them out. And have at least a pair ready when we arrive home." Nauja said it loud, and Seewagak had no answer. How could she talk, she who was just a woman in a house which is supposed to help the provider?

Nauja saw the sun and was happy. She collected eggs and she made dried yolk for the winter. This was done by cracking the eggs and carefully drinking the white away. This was then spit out and the young people sat together and had quite a contest seeing who could spit the whole white farthest in one part. Lots of fun!

The yolk was then taken into the mouth and spit out into the long dried intestine of a seal. It looked like a big worm. The filled intestines were to be hung up where the sun could not strike them, because they had to dry slowly if they were going to be any good. In the wintertime, nothing could be nicer than to sit around eating dried eggs, because they stick to your teeth, making it difficult to open the mouth. Nauja prepared many of them. There were eggs in any amount, they did not have to go far to collect what they wanted.

Inuitek was with Nauja. He was young and clever. The older men went out on the ice and hunted seals that slept on the floe in the sunshine. But Inuitek stayed with her. He liked eggs very much; he said that they gave a man strength to talk smoothly. So they stayed and played day after day. Nauja became quite dull in her mouth, for she had swallowed too many eggs in the beginning. Now she detested them and wanted to eat meat. The men coming back from the ice boiled eggs every night, but she was on the edge of vomiting, and her stomach refused them.

Inuitek laughed and told her that she looked nice. Her face was painted with yolk—how could she help that, when she was working every day with the stuff? He also told her that her nose was almost invisible, when he looked at her from the side to examine.

"No nose, just cheeks to be seen," he yelled. Nauja had never been so flattered. The young men in her tribe at home did not tell her such things. They did not even know that women like to listen to these words. He also told her that he thought of going musk-ox hunting far, far away. He wanted to be a man, he said, the kind of man people talked about. Next winter he would catch many foxes so that he could go and trade with the white men. He said he was going to have a sled; he already had four dogs for it. "Maybe somebody arrives home from the south with a wife from the south," he said. But after a while he told her that he might not. "One likes to have a wife looking nice. Not a woman with a nose protruding like a narwhale's horn in the face. But where can I get such a woman? When I grow up, there will be fights every day to defend one's wife, but where to get one worth such a danger all my days?" Inuitek and Nauja lay in the sun and looked up into the air.

No more making dried eggs this season. The eggs now had the chickens inside, and Nauja could eat them again. When she boiled them and swallowed the entire egg, it amused her to feel the young bird that would never see the light sliding down her throat, falling down into the stomach.

Such a summer she had never had before. One night she stayed awake and listened to Inuitek's breath three men away from her. She thought of the wife he was looking for. He had told her his future. He was to have a wooden sled, knives, several pots, and tools from white men. He needed a wife who would be envied because of her fine husband. He might even procure the worst of all things: a gun that could kill animals at any distance, a gun that would make him feared. Yes, if he only had a gun, he could get anything. He had once told her that a man with a gun could buy the wife he wanted from anybody; he had then stopped talking and looked out over the ice, but Nauja had wished he would keep on talking.

Nauja could not sleep. She saw that Inuitek lifted his head. So did she, but her husband, the mighty Awala, was sleeping peacefully beside her. And his one arm, which seemed to be heavier than anything on earth, rested across her. So Nauja only looked and Inuitek looked; the night was long because it was in the light summer, when the tent never became dark, but it was longer than Nauja could ever have imagined.

Nauja thought of the song the girls used to sing at home:

> A-ya-ya-ha.
> When the world is warm,
> It is fun to go up on the hill.
> The sun keeps watch and shows it to all.
> Aya-ya-hay.
> When the dark winter hides the wanderer,
> It is cold and I am sorry that
> It is impossible to play in the hills.
> A-ya-ya-ha.

Next day Inuitek went out and got a seal. He treated everybody to a meal in the evening, and the men sang his praises and ate his food with delight.

Inuitek said he intended to go after geese in the interior of the land.

"A woman must go along, somebody who can mend one's boots. Can I take your wife along, or whoever else is able to walk as fast as necessary to keep up with me?"

He said it with his best strength, but it did not sound too well. A laugh was his answer.

"Oh, everybody hurry, come close! A big hunter is amongst us! Someone never found out before! A man wants to trade a wife, he will leave his own behind and take somebody else's. Where is his beautiful wife? Could it be a dog or a stone? Oh, finally one got an offer that flattered one's ears."

They all understood and they all laughed up in the air. Inuitek blushed and Nauja blushed. She was the one requested, she was the woman who was wanted to go with a man that had no wife of his own to offer for a change. Awala grabbed her and beat her badly.

"Oh, it is like a woman to try to belong to somebody else. Let me try to see if I can make her feel who is the master. Her cheeks are handy to hit, in order to feel if she is present." He gave her one blow after another. He kicked her, and when she fell down, he threw her far away from where he stood. But he only was warming up. So he was the man whose wife was wanted by a young boy who was lucky enough to catch a seal and liked to brag! Was Awala a man regarded as weak—one who could be talked to by children? He hit the innocent Nauja. He beat her like a dog. And when he finally got tired, she was full of blood and half unconscious from the blows. But she was also aware that she had been fought for. She saw that the other women in the party were scared, for a woman is after all born to be the victim of men. The two girls from her home village were never wanted by somebody else; one of them had even been given away voluntarily. So this beating would be related far south to her mother, and would fill her with pride. "Nauja the kidnapped girl, she is the object of desire from many, many men."

And life went on. Nauja and Seewagak. Sometimes the one was in favor and ruled the house, sometimes the other, and the other had to obey.

Awala had his fun from it. Whenever he came home, both of the wives ran out to greet him. Both of them brought him mittens and dry clothes. He accepted from one and let the other's stuff drop to the ground. Then they knew. But he sometimes liked to fool them; he took the service from one of his wives, and let her start commanding and acting like mistress of the house. She might even be the hostess of a party at night, when the neighbors came in to eat. "Sit down and have something to eat," she might say. "Let the other one take your things. Hurry up and cook more food for our great guests, bring water to please them, hand them a skin to wipe their big and industrious hands!"

Awala could often not help laughing, because he might then go to sleep at the lamp where the servant wife sat, thus confusing both of them. Sometimes he even slept in the middle part of the house. Awala was full of humor, but what woman likes to be laughed at?

Then came the big blow.

A long, long way from where they lived, on the other side of the inlet, so far away that everybody thought it was there that the wide sea reached up to touch the sky, there were fierce people living. They were fearful and strong. They never raised girls themselves, because conditions of life were too hard; they killed almost every little baby girl at birth. Their young men had to be strong enough and clever enough to steal women from other tribes.

On a certain day, a group of these people came visiting on their fast sleds. Some of them went to Nauja's place, which they must have been watching for some time, because they planned their visit for a day when most of the men were hunting. No resistance was offered. The men at home even welcomed the visitors and smiled when these started talking aloud.

"Oh, since we are men here, we care for our dogs and our game. We procure meat and eat it, gather for the winter so we can have something to eat when we sit together and tell about the great visitors we have been honored with."

At night the strangers selected women, and Nauja was taken. A nose so flat and a pair of cheeks so big, small eyes that disappeared when she smiled. No man could pass her by without forgetting the rest of the world.

"If it comes to the women, nobody here cares! We are men, and we just have them to please visitors." But the visitors selected four women and took them along; they also stole provisions enough to get home. There was not even a fight, and Inuitek did not resist.

Nauja did not cry, she felt disgust for such men who would not protect her. She had been through the same thing before. Life needs experience, she thought—anything but monotony until one feels old and tired.

Across the sea, over heavy ice hard to travel on and only passed after terrible ordeals, they took Nauja and the girls. These men talked differently and their clothes looked foolish. But she soon learned their ways.

Nauja became the wife of two men, for women were scarce in their country, and friends could share the happiness of life. No woman, thought Nauja, could have it better. She slept in the middle of the house. It was winter when she arrived, and the igloos were chilly. But in the middle of the igloo she kept warm and was comfortable. The two men lay along the sides and felt the coldness of the snow walls. Just as she had done for many winters.

There was no work that caused any real trouble for Nauja. The men kept their own clothes dry and mended. When she made them a pair of boots, she was thanked and praised. Could she help smiling, thinking of being thanked for doing her sewing as a wife had to? If they had only heard of that at Awala's place! She thought of Awala. A man who did not stay home to defend his home. Now he could turn to Seewagak. Let them be, for a marriage with two husbands was the life!

The men did the cooking, and she did the talking. She was not a kid any more, and she knew her limits. Men like women and they are right to take a little trouble for them. When Nauja asked for water, the men always raced to be the first out after ice to melt. They brought in the blubber for the lamps, they asked her what part of the seal she preferred to eat.

Life went on once more, happiness can be found all over the world. One of her husbands was a medicine man and full of wisdom. His ways were not like those of the hunters. He went up into the mountains alone and stayed isolated for days, until he could feel the spirits calling him. After this he was weak and required much food and fat meat to eat. Sometimes he arranged for meetings in a big igloo built for feasts and dancing. There he sang tunes and helped the tribe by telling the will of the spirits. In the beginning Nauja was scared of him, but she gradually understood that he was the easiest of the two, after all. But sometimes he became angry and furious like a madman. There were no beatings, however; when a woman has two husbands, one can't be allowed to hurt her and spoil her for the other.

Natark, the other man, was strong and a good hunter. He brought in the animals, but Sagdlok added to the house by the gifts given by the people he helped. And he understood Nauja's desires.

Once she said she would like to eat tongues of caribou. That is rare food for women, for the hunters eat it on the hunt, and a man would be laughed at if he kept it for the women.

"Oh, look at him," they would tease him. "Here is a good provider who thinks a lot of his wife. Why does he go out at all? Let him rather stay home and take care of her, she may want something else too. Let us hunt for him and bring the best things home to his wife."

To prevent such talk, Sagdlok told the hunters in his songs —when his mind was absent and his soul visited the moon— that tongues of caribou were to be brought to his house, for the Great Spirit demanded it.

Summer followed spring, and the caribou began to migrate north. The people met them in herds and killed them, until their arms could not lift a spear from the ground. There was a feast and a dance so great that the like had never been seen before. Sagdlok, who by his songs had caused the caribou' coming, was naturally the hero of the feast. But he had no leisure, for he had to keep on singing and was called to cure those who had eaten too much. His pay was tongues of caribous, for his spirit knew no other recompense.

So Nauja had her caribou tongues. She had too many of them, in fact, but they kept on coming in (Sagdlok had forbidden tongues to be eaten by anybody in the tribe except in his house, in order not to offend the caribous.)

Soon Nauja felt sorry she had asked for such tiresome food, and she invited everybody to partake in her meals. But they had all heard the medicine man's order, and nobody dared. They even gave her more tongues, even after Sagdlok went away to another village to cure and to call the spirits and help his people.

Natark stayed home. He loved his friend, but he had no talent for medicine. He hunted and believed in travel from place to place; he wanted to look at the land and to learn from the animals.

He was her husband, but he was just one of two in the house, and he was scared of the other.

"If we run away, could he follow us?" asked Nauja, when they found out that they did not want to have somebody else in their house.

"He can find a man even on the other side of the earth. He traced you and told us where to find you, when we brought you here." Nauja and Natark were afraid, but they looked at each other and wanted to run away.

Nauja remembered Inuitek, and she told Natark about his bragging. Natark remembered him well but had never thought of a fight with him. Men over there did not dare, he observed; they are only there to bring up wives for us. She did not like this talk, she said, but told him of her mother and her father. He liked to listen to tales and sayings about foreign people.

Natark did not like it when Sagdlok came home and required to be nursed like a baby. He had tired himself by singing and did not regret that his meat was captured on another man's hunt. Natark had been lucky in the last days, for he had seal meat and liver to offer. But Sagdlok brought tongues and more tongues with him, as he came in and threw himself down on the skins. Nauja could hardly bear the sight, and told him so. He looked bewildered and was unable to talk. Hadn't she herself asked for tongues, hadn't he promised her all she wanted, and hadn't she been thankful toward him when she found out that she alone could eat tongues in any quantity?

Natark laughed, and Nauja, too. Then she ate the liver from a still warm seal, but Sagdlok only glanced at her.

He had come here after a tiresome trip and had even hurried home, carrying these tongues to please her. He expected charm and love, and now she cared for liver and nothing else. He was tired, and he felt terrible at seeing her eat. The blood from the warm liver ran down her cheeks, her little nose was all painted with blood, and her fingers grabbed at the food in a way that could stir up every man in the whole world.

Nauja smiled at Natark. Since he had been at home so long a time with her, it seemed only just that she should take care of Sagdlok now, at least for a turn.

Disappointed husbands always have some way of making their regrets known. Awala would have beaten everyone in the house to show that he was the master. But Sagdlok had his co-husband to consider. So he chose another way. He began to talk about his successful trip and about what he had heard from people way down to the east.

Nauja listened: the news might be about her own people and about her folks, whom she now heard about only occasionally. She wiped her fingers and her face in a foxskin, sat down beside Sagdlok, and asked him to continue. Natark offered her more liver, but she was not hungry. He cut out the eyes of the seal and pressed the slimy mass out in his hand and held it toward her. But she merely sucked the delicious stuff up with a gulp and did not even take her eyes off Sagdlok. She expressed no thanks, no surprised exclamation. Nauja was absorbed by the news about white men living close enough to be reached in one winter's travel. They were even medicine men themselves and seemed to have a very strong medicine, for a man called *Gésé*, or something like that, was hanged on a pole and nailed to it with arms extended, but afterward he was brought down again and came to life by himself. Sagdlok had not found out if this performance went on very often, but he understood there were many things for him to learn.

Sagdlok was a wise man: he did not tell all his stories at once. He only said he was sleepy and wanted to lie down to get a nap.

Natark stood there with his seal, trying to tempt Nauja with the smell of a steaming pot of ribs, but she did not notice him. She was deeply touched by what she had heard from Sagdlok. She remembered that when she was at home, and when somebody had been down and seen the white men, there was always something to talk about for years, and the whole village would sit and listen, spellbound. Nauja realized that if she could manage to go over to the east and see the white men, she would have her fill of adventure. There would be nothing in the world left for her to see. Whatever would happen to her in the unknown future, she would have the reputation of having seen everything and done everything in the world.

What power she would have in the years to come!

Sagdlok was awakened from his sleep by Nauja's diving down under his bedskins. Natark heard them whisper, and he sat up waiting for them to be hungry, when *he* could be the man again.

Days came and went. Natark hunted. Sagdlok stayed at home and speculated, thinking that renewal of his repertoire as the medicine man of the tribe would do him some good. If those white men, people who were his colleagues even if they knew more than he, could teach him some of their medicine, he could even do more than Suna—the upstart who was trying to make himself believed. He would like to go, and he intended to induce Natark to go, because Natark was the man who owned the dogs and the sled which, as a holy man, Sagdlok himself did not possess. As soon as Nauja and he were alone, Sagdlok told her about how he wanted to find the truth from the white men, and a trip there would give him power beyond anybody's. Nauja listened intently, because she too wanted with all her heart to make the fantastic trip—a journey never even hoped for by any of the other women.

Natark was the hunter, the provider of blubber and skins, whereas Sagdlok got only fancy things as gifts. If, then, Natark felt his minority when it was a matter of talking, his love for Nauja led him to figure out a tremendous plan. Natark planned to propose a trip to visit the white men. Nauja was to go, too, but she must understand that he, Natark, the great hunter, was responsible for the trip. That would put him in her favor, and he would buy her so much woman's stuff there that she would have things to marvel at for winters to come, and never forget to love him.

"It may be handy to dry some meat if a long trip is to take place next spring," he remarked. "White men live many sleeps from here. A journey must be figured in moons and not in sleeps, but it can be done."

There was no answer. Answers were not necessary, as everybody knew. Nauja had only to let the news spread out. Sewing was done and provisions made. Their neighbors gave them skins to trade for needles and knives. Commissions were arranged, and there was great excitement. Natark and Sagdlok became more and more taken up with their work, and little time was left for interest in Nauja, but she didn't miss them because there were fur coats and boots to be made, and the fanciest clothes ever seen to be prepared for herself.

Finally, the party set out on the long trip. On their way they wore their old traveling clothes. The distance turned out to be much longer than expected, so Natark had to hunt during the trip, and Sagdlok was busy night and day persuading the gales and taming the snowdrifts. Both succeeded in their tasks and finally they arrived.

What a sight! What emotion! Four houses made with lumber, and white men in long black robes! People came out and welcomed them. They spoke Eskimo language to some extent, and they brought them inside and gave them things to eat.

Sagdlok told them he came to get information about their medicine, and Natark said he came to trade and bring fine things back to his hunting grounds. Nauja said nothing, she only looked around. She saw people from all over the world, even some from her own place, including her cousin, who told her about her folks and said it was now common to go to visit the white men and trade foxskins for their tools and needles.

Nauja also met Inuitek, her boy friend from up north at Awala's place.

She spent hours talking with him and listening to him, and her two husbands were so friendly to him that Inuitek had her all for himself.

How nice it was to have white men in the country who could gather people from all over!

Sagdlok became friends with the men in the long black coats. He soon found out, however, that there was a misunderstanding about the man who was nailed to a pole with arms stretched out. This had happened as Sagdlok first heard, and the man was still alive; but the man was not present. He could nevertheless hear people when they spoke to him. Every day they yelled at him all together, and somebody pressed small pieces of white-painted wood on a big box. This made the box scream in a funny way. There was a competition between the man who managed the box and the people who yelled which ones could do it loudest, and white men said all this was done in honor of the man hung on the pole.

But one night Sagdlok came home and looked sad. He ordered everybody to get out but Nauja and Natark, and then he told them that there was to be a divorce, since the white men had refused to teach him anything as long as Nauja had two husbands. Natark, Sagdlok suggested, had better go home right away and leave him with Nauja. But Natark refused to do so. "Of course," he said, "I am a man and do not give attention to a woman, but you can't look out for her clothes and her food. She needs a hunter, that is, she needs me."

For the first time a quarrel about the wife. Both wanted to keep her. Finally they decided to let her make her choice herself. This was very foolish for Eskimos; had anyone ever heard of such a thing before?

Natark took all his skins and bought pearls and needles, chisels and a mirror in which Nauja's cheeks looked bigger and nicer than before.

Natark was highly regarded by the white men, as he brought more skins than the rest of the hunters. They therefore gave him many gifts and he always brought them to Nauja. She smiled and showed a pleasant face, but he walked away quickly because he did not want to give her the impression of meaning anything by this: he just wanted to give her a few things.

Inuitek had not very much to give Nauja, but he had his gun paid for. Before she had arrived, he had brought in his catch for three years. He could now kill anything alive from a great distance, and had only one wish in his soul: to possess Nauja.

"You did not put up a fight for anybody, when some were taken away from our old place!" said Nauja.

"If I had, who would have gotten you?" was the answer, and she was stuck with its truth. Women all over the world run up against the truth now and then, and such truth makes them silent.

Next morning, the argument between Sagdlok and Natark was of no use. Neither of them had a wife any more. She was gone. A little young man had taken her—just an unknown boy. He had made quite a sensation some time before when he wanted a gun and got it. Evidently he was a boy with ambition. Where he belonged nobody knew, and who could go after a man with a gun? He might go to any place

and hide, he had no reason to follow the coast and take to
the water. His dogs could be fed by caribous inland.

Nauja had all the beautiful things Natark had given her:
she had taken them with her, just to show that she appreciated them. At least this consoled Natark very much. The two
men went home alone. Natark had forgotten his commissions and felt people laughing behind his back. Sagdlok had
forgotten his keen interest in learning the medicine of the
white men, but a little piece of wood was given to him—it
looked like the man up on the pole with arms spread out.
This, it was said, could give peace and cure everything.

What more did he need? He intended to use this hereafter
to restore those who had eaten too much. Put it on their
stomachs, it would be medicine enough to pay for the whole
trip.

Natark and Sagdlok were friends from childhood, and
Sagdlok still had brains and plans. He told Natark that they
must say that this little piece of wood with the man nailed
on had been terribly expensive to procure: they had been
forced to give all of the foxes and their very wife to get it.

But it was worth even more than that. Sagdlok knew that
people believe better in things that are hard to acquire than
in gifts. So they went home and became famous for their
trip and the results of it, while Nauja, the beautiful Eskimo
girl, continued her adventurous life.

Is it of any advantage to be beautiful? Yes and no.

8 Hunger

ONE DAY, SOMEWHERE IN Hudson Bay, I lay freezing in an
igloo. There was neither food to eat nor blubber to burn,
and such a storm raging outside that any immediate hunting
was impossible. I lay there dreaming of food—all the delicious things that can be set forth upon a dining table appeared tantalizingly to my mind's eye, and nothing much
else seemed worth thinking about. I began to tell my companions about omelets as we make them at Cape York—so

daintily delicious one could swallow them in large pieces without even chewing—and many other tasty dishes.

Old Ututiak and his wife, Manik, were with me. We were on a hunt which up to now had been none too successful. We weren't too bad off, however, as we still had dogs we could eat, but it was mostly the miserable weather that bothered us.

"Tell us something, Ututiak," I said, "something about the worst hunger you have ever suffered, so I can think about something else than Cape York and the abundance of food there."

"Ah, you talk of hunger," said the old man. "You are a white man and will never know the Great Want, for since you whites have come up here, life is not nearly as hard for the Eskimos as before. Yes, I can tell about Want, for I learned to know hunger in my childhood days. My wife, too, knew hunger early in life. See how calmly my old woman sits over there, hardly thinking about the two days that have gone by since we last ate. Ah, you must learn to know this land. It can be barren of everything, and yet so full of life that all the people in the world could eat their fill.

"I recall my worst experience. It is such a long, long time ago that I don't like to think of it very often, but I will tell you of the worst hunger I have ever felt.

"It was a long time before you white men lived in this land. Once in a while the whalers came and we traded with them, but they always sailed quickly away after the catch. So we people were all alone here in the Great Winter that lasted two years. All summer the ice never broke up, and snow still covered the land. That has happened only twice in my long life, and now I am a very old man.

"All summer we had gone hungry, and lived in poverty and need, and now came the darkest month—that month which is the worst for us people up here. At that time we lived at Ussugarssuk, and most of the men wanted to chance going farther north, but my father and his partner stayed on to catch seals in the open water and through the breathing holes in the ice.

"There was nothing but hunger and want. My own mother was dead, and my father was married again—to a sister of the other man's wife. Each of these women had a child, and their old mother lived with them—now in the one house, now in the other. At that time I was just beginning to be a hunter. I had a gun—a muzzle-loader, the kind we don't use any more. Mostly, we used bows and arrows on our caribou hunts.

"Then the other man died, and his wife moved in with us, and my father and I struggled to provide for all. Besides those whom I have mentioned, my foster sister lived in our house. I mean Manik, here, whom my mother had once bought and raised to be a wife to me. She was a little younger than I was, but strong, and had begun to sew.

"Our dogs were very poor, because they didn't get any food. One day my father said he would take all the dogs and go out to the edge of the ice to look for bears, and he would remain away for several days. But he left a couple of the dogs at home, because if a bear should prowl around at night, the dogs would wake us, and then I could get out and shoot the bear.

"But my father stayed away a long time. We suffered terrible hunger. The two small children were dead, and I often saw the women, with their curved knives called *uloes*, go up toward the hill where the graves were. What they did there I will not say. For the most part, our food was a little skin, or small thongs.

"But one night as I lay pretending to be asleep, I heard the women whispering together; they pointed at my foster sister, and said that she was strong and fat. I knew that the next night they would kill her with an axe, so they could eat her. I still lay as though asleep, but I thought a lot about what we should do and I decided to save her by running away. It seemed to me that if we *must* die, we might just as well die alone out there in the snow and ice, as to be murdered and eaten by these women.

"It's queer about women. Sometimes they are so good and kind, but in times of terrible want and need, they are always more ferocious than men. Next day I told Manik that her life was in danger, and that we must run away.

"It was impossible for her to leave at once, for her clothes weren't good enough. We had eaten the soles of her kamiks, and she would have to sew in others. So the next night I left the axe and the knives, and any other things that could kill, outside—and when we went to bed I said that unfortunately I had forgotten them, left them out where I was working, and now I didn't feel like getting up to go after them. The old woman said they must be brought in, but I pretended that I didn't understand what she meant and said: 'But what do we want with hunting knives at night?'

"Next day I told them I was going up the fjord to try to catch seals through the breathing holes. I wanted my foster sister to go along, but they didn't want to let her go. So then I said that she would have to go around on the ice to chase the seals away from the other breathing holes and drive them over to the one where I would stand. For when the seals hear anyone walk on the ice, you see, they always swim away.

"I told Manik to take a couple of sewing needles along, and her woman's knife. I took my weapons and a little axe, and out in the storeroom I took all my lead and powder, which luckily the women had not seen. Also, I took my sleeping skin, and a deer skin to lie upon. The women told us that if I didn't catch anything that day, then Manik should come home and tell them about it. I promised she would, but I knew they intended to kill her when she was alone and didn't have me to help her.

"We took the biggest dog with us, to smell out the seals' blowholes, and we loaded our few possessions onto a small draw-sled. When the women weren't looking, I also took a small pot, and then we left.

"It was hard walking. When one is very hungry, one tires easily, and it seemed to us such a long, long way to the head of the fjord where we couldn't be seen from the hut. But as soon as we were out of sight, we turned inland. If we continued inland, we would reach other people, and our one thought was to get away from the women.

"But we didn't make much progress, and that night I built a tiny igloo. It was small because I didn't have enough strength to build a bigger one, and we crawled into it and lay down to sleep. We had nothing to eat. And next day, when we should have been on our way again, we could hardly walk. But I was lucky enough to see a fox quite close by. I shot it, and we ate it at once. We gave the dog the bones, entrails and skin—all except the tail, which Manik kept to hold over her nose, against the cold. Manik and I ate the rest of the fox, and it was wonderful to eat fresh meat again. We felt new strength and set out again quickly, for it doesn't take very long to eat a fox, especially one so little and thin.

"Next day we had nothing. Then I shot a pair of ptarmigan. We divided everything between us, and made our slow way onward. We were so afraid that we hardly thought of weariness, but we became hungrier and hungrier.

"At last we walked the way we had seen white people

walk when they had drunk too much rum. We staggered so that we had to support each other. I talked of eating the dog, but Manik said: 'Oh, no, wait a little and let it live as long as possible, because I'm afraid to stay alone when you go hunting. I think of the eyes of those women, when they looked at me back home in the hut.'

"But suddenly, as we walked along, we saw the dog raise his head and prick up his ears as though he had seen something or other. I could see he had the scent of something, and luckily I grabbed him by the neck, put a line around him and let him lead me in the direction where there must be *something*. Soon he lost the trail. But he found it again, and in a short while we came to a place where a bear was hibernating.

"Oh, but I was glad! Now we would eat and live. I went quietly back to where Manik was, and took all our things on the draw-sled up to the place where the bear lay. Then we began to dig away the snow around it. It lay in a hole which it had dug in the snow, and it soon began to growl at being disturbed in its sleep. I struck at it with my harpoon, and it grew angry and came rushing halfway out of the hole. But a bear that has slept a whole winter is blinded by the sun and can't see anything clearly. So I took my gun, held it up close to the bear's head, and fired; and then it was dead.

"We were so happy we couldn't say a word, but sat down, just as if we were used to having bearmeat every day. I then had strength enough to build a small igloo, for we intended to stay there a long time. We helped each other skin the bear. It was fat, since it was a female, and as we skinned it, we ate the fat that lay between the intestines. We gave the dog the entrails, and meat, too—all it wanted to eat. Manik smeared blood on her face, as a sign of thanksgiving to the bear.

"When we were through skinning the bear, I went off a little way, without saying why I went, and looked around until I found a flat stone with a hollow place in it, which we could use to make a lamp. Now we were really comfortable. We set about making a fire at once. I had my tinder box with me, and I lit the lamp and melted some ice, so we could have water to drink. All this time we had been eating snow and ice, until our lips were full of cracks—this is very painful. But now we ate meat, and things were just wonderful!

"The next day I built a new igloo right behind the first one, which then served as a sort of entryway. And we found a couple more stones which could be used as lamps, so we warmed ourselves thoroughly and also dried out our clothes. Manik was now a regular little housewife, and she looked after my clothes and mended them, using bear sinews for thread, as we had nothing else for sewing.

"While we stayed there, a terrible blizzard blew up. We told each other that had we been out in it, and had we *not* found the bear, we would surely have died. But now we had eaten and were warm enough; our dog was with us, and we had all one could wish for. We ate all the time. The dog looked like a different creature, with a big, fat belly. We were so comfortable—in fact, I don't think I have ever been as comfortable since.

"When we had no more meat left than we could carry with us, I made coats for ourselves and a harness for the dog out of the bearskin. We also made new kamiks of bearskin, and then we continued on our way, going in the same direction—away from the women.

"We had talked about taking meat back to the women, but we couldn't carry any more than we ourselves would need to eat on the return journey. In that case we would have arrived there with only very little meat. Anyway, if my father had not returned, they must be dead by now, and so we went forward. We would never see them again.

"We traveled toward the unknown. We talked about the people we would meet—perhaps they would be enemies, but they couldn't be worse than the women in our own home, from whom we had fled.

"Our legs seemed stiff when we began to walk, for we had lain still so long, and eaten so much. But we were so much stronger that we walked faster than before. And each night we made fire and heated water and cooked meat, which was a wonderful help.

"The last couple of days I had noticed deer tracks in the snow, all headed north. So it must be the time of year when the caribou began their northward trek. I knew that soon we would reach the places where one could always find caribou. So I began to make myself a bow from a deer horn which I had found, and a bowstring from bear sinew. But before the bow was finished, we came on the caribou.

"One morning as we lay in our igloo, just as I was awakening, I heard the dog barking outside our hut. So I listened and heard a noise outside. At first I thought it might be the rushing of a river, but that couldn't be possible at this time of the year. Then I thought it sounded like a bad storm, and then I thought it might be people. But when I went outside, I saw that there were caribou all around us—every way I looked. It was the clattering of their hooves on the ground that had wakened me.

"Oh, but there were many of them! They came and kept on coming, and there seemed no end to caribou, looking both toward the way they were going, and the way from which they came. It was well for us they weren't headed right toward our hut, for it would have been trampled down, and we ourselves crushed to death. Now I knew that we had finally reached the place where there never was hunger or need, which I had so often heard about.

"I shot only a couple of them. We ate the marrow bones and the tongues, and now we had sinew thread enough to complete my bow, for I wanted to save my ammunition. In those days one never knew when one could get more of *that*.

"Now we were saved. We thought no more of the people we had wanted to reach. We thought only of the caribou. My, but they tasted delicious! It was just like the pictures we see from your land, where you guard the herds. We traveled with them by day, and halted at night. Sometimes they gained a little on us, but we caught up to them again, and there was quite a feeling a familiarity between the deer and ourselves. We killed what we needed, and could pick and choose. We had new fur coats, and new sleeping skins, and everything we needed.

"It was a pretty hard time for Manik, though," added Ututiak. "Do you remember how we spoke of its being difficult to make all kinds of clothes—and that I, of course, should do the man's work and scrape the skins to make them soft? It wasn't so easy for me, either. Now we are old and can laugh at it, but at that time it was a serious matter.

"Sometimes we felt so alone and afraid, for of course we couldn't continue living like that. Our greatest fear was that the sewing needles should wear out. They broke often, and each time I ground them on a stone they became shorter, and we could hardly sew with them any longer.

"But finally we reached other people. They were an entirely different tribe from any we had known before, but they were friendly to us. We met up with them at a place where they lay in wait for the caribou on trek, and we told them our story and stayed with them for a long time.

"Now we were no longer children, but grown folk facing

life, and you may be sure that I have never regretted that I saved my little foster sister, because, you see in saving her, I saved a good wife for myself."

The old man smiled at his wife, who smiled back at him, and a feeling of harmony filled our little igloo, as we lay there.

Two old people, who had held fast to each other through a long life. Now he took a piece of tobacco, scraped the ashes out of his pipe and filled it anew, and his wife turned over to settle down to sleep.

"Tomorrow," said Ututiak, "we'll surely find a deer or something—and then you shall eat your fill, because you white people don't really know how to do without things and still be happy."

I lay on a long time thinking of these two old people's adventure. And I felt poor, compared to them. They had lived a life of continual struggle, and although aged, still stood firmly on their own feet.

"But tell me, Ututiak," I said, "what happened to the women you left behind?"

"I don't care much to speak of it," he answered, "but I heard later that they had been found dead. My father never returned, and they couldn't provide food for themselves. But it was gruesome, the way they were found. The two skulls were crushed, and all the meat eaten off the bones. Only the third was whole, but she was terribly emaciated. She was the oldest of the three women; she had murdered and devoured her own daughters.

"Yes, it's just as I told you," he continued. "Women can be horrible and inhuman. I have heard of men who died together of hunger, but one always found them whole. Human nature is strange and difficult to understand."

9 The Polar Bear

A MOTHER POLAR BEAR lay in a cave on a huge iceberg in Greenland. The iceberg was frozen solidly into the ice, for this was winter. And the bear lay quietly and seemed to have much leisure time. Once in a while a whimper sounded from under her. It was her little cub, lying there, snug and warm.

A polar bear cub is so little and weak when it is born. And for the first nine days of its life, it's blind, and has no hair on its body. So the mother tucks the cub close under her body, where it can be warm and safe. You see, there's no grass, no leaves to lie on in an ice cave, so the mother bear must stay with her baby all the time, or it would freeze to death.

An iceberg is big—it's nothing at all but ice. Here the little family lay, all snug and peaceful.

But the mother bear had heard disturbing crashes around them, and one day a strange rumbling sound was heard over and under their cave. Suddenly there was a crack which frightened the huge animal out of all sense and feeling. But the little one lay quiet, conscious only of the milk it was sucking into its mouth, and it felt that the treatment it now received was most uncomfortable.

The mother sprang up, so that the cub rolled out on the cold ice. Then she took the cub right into her mouth, so that only its head hung out, and rushed away. And just in time, too, for the iceberg, which had seemed so big and solid, soon began slowly to tip over. Then with a crash it broke into pieces and lumps, and was now only a lot of huge ice floes lying here and there.

But now the mother bear was far away. She had rushed off at top speed and kept going for a long time before she stopped to find a spot where she could rest and hide herself and the little one. Here she carefully laid the cub down in the snow. It hurt the little warm, naked body to be dropped out of its mother's warm mouth into the cold. And bitter cold, too, for this was the month of February, when it is so cold that the quicksilver in the thermometers freezes.

Soon the mother bear found a place inland, where she could dig herself a hole in a huge snowdrift. And there she lay, hibernating, until it was time for her to come forth.

Little by little the eyes of the cub opened, and hair grew on its body—fine white fur. Soon the cub dared venture away from the mother, and crawled up on her body. And one fine day he even poked his head out of the cave and peeked out at the world.

The cub hadn't known that while it lay there, sucking milk from the mother bear, the mother was getting thinner and thinner, because she wasn't getting a thing to eat. Soon the mother bear could no longer endure this hunger, and she had to go out for something to eat; but just at the same time, her cub was big enough to take out for a walk.

The wind blew pretty cold on the cub, and he shivered, but the mother bear pushed him forward when he wanted to go into the cave again. And soon they had gone so far that the cub couldn't find his way back to the cave. So he *had* to follow his mother.

When the cub was tired, he sat down and whined, but the mother acted as if she didn't hear him, and kept on walking, so the little fellow had to run and catch up with her before she was out of sight. He ran to his mother, as if begging to be allowed to rest. But his mother kept on walking, and the little one became so tired that he ached all over his body. He had but one wish—to be allowed to lie down.

Finally the mother bear stopped. She made a hollow in the snow in the lee of an ice clump, and lay down. The cub crept close to her warm body and soon fell asleep. He didn't know, you see, that this was all a cunning plan of his mother's. She *had* to go out for food for herself and her cub, and she'd discovered a breathing hole where a seal came up for air. But so the little one might not disturb her on the hunt, she had walked and walked around the place some distance away, until she saw that her cub was all tired out.

As soon as the little one had fallen asleep, the mother rose. The cub felt cold when the mother's warm coat wasn't close by him, but he was *so* tired, poor little thing, and *so* sleepy, that he just slept and slept, whimpering once in a while— and didn't even know his mother had left him.

The mother bear crept quietly up to the breathing hole in the ice. With her sharp claws she scraped the ice away so the hole was larger, then she sat very quietly, waiting. She was absolutely still, completely motionless—for should the seal hear the slightest creaking in the snow, it would swim away.

The bear could hear the seal blowing until bubbles came to the top of the water, and the minute the seal stuck his head above the water to get a good breath of air, the bear lifted her huge paw and struck it on the head, crushing it with one blow.

The seal never felt a thing. Exerting her great strength, the mother bear pulled the seal up onto the ice, and began to eat. It was her first meal in a long, long time, and it tasted so good, so good. But she saved a little piece of blubber in her mouth for her cub, and hurried back to the place where she had left him. He was still asleep, but shivering from the cold, and whimpering in his sleep. The mother curled down beside him, to warm his little body, and now both slept soundly.

At daylight the little one woke, and his mother gave him the piece of blubber to sniff at. It smelled so good that he began to lick it, and soon swallowed it. It had a most excellent taste, and the cub was happy again, but, being a little stiff in the legs, he wanted to go to sleep again.

But there was no thought of that. They must go farther, and the mother pushed him out of their little hollow in the snow, and again they began to walk. Every bone and muscle in the little body ached. He was still so tired from the day before that he could hardly drag himself along. He whimpered and complained, but his mother paid no attention. She kept right on walking. She knew, you see, that the cub must learn to overcome the hardships of life, and that to be strong when he was grown, he must begin while he was little. That, of course, is true of people as well as bears.

This night passed like the one before. When the cub was worn out, he was put to bed—his mother caught a seal, and next morning he had a nice piece of blubber to eat. So the days went by.

But things weren't always so easy. Often there were no seals, and then both mother and cub went hungry. But as time went on, the cub was less and less tired at night. . . . Sometimes when he'd been put to bed, and his mother sat by a breathing hole in the ice, the cub woke and felt so alone that he set off to follow his mother's footsteps. But when he came loitering over the ice, the seal under the water heard him and swam away to another breathing hole. Then his mother gave him a thorough drubbing—cuffed and kicked him—and heartlessly chased him back to his bed. The unhappy cub didn't understand what it was all about. At first he thought it was all in fun, but he soon found it wasn't.

Now he learned that his mother could be severe as well as kind, but still it took a long time before he really understood that he must obey, and stay where she had left him. Many cuffs and kicks were necessary before the little bear's brain understood it.

Then he was unhappy—and sat there crying mournfully to himself. He didn't know of another thing in the world but his mother, and there was no one else to turn to. He longed for her warm pelt to curl up under, but *now* when he came close to her, wanting to play, and to seek shelter from the cold, his mother kicked him and snarled at him, so he was beside himself with despair. He didn't know, you see, that this was a school all bear cubs must attend, so they'd learn to stay away from the mother during the hunt —the hunt which was so necessary that they both might live.

But when he felt most sorrowful, his mother usually came back to him with a piece of blubber, and then she was kind, and licked the cub, and let him eat and drink, so he soon forgot all his unhappiness and slept again—all snug and comfortable.

And so the little one grew fat and as large as a half-grown dog. The sun was higher in the heavens—the days were warmer, and the cub was full of frolicsome tricks. He loved to play with everything he found. If they moved onto an island, he rolled stones off the cliffs and crawled up the icebergs so he could slide back down on his smooth, gleaming white fur. This gave his mother time to hunt. And as time went by, the hunting became better and better. The seals wanted to lie out in the sun. They clawed at the ice around the breathing holes until they'd made the holes big enough to crawl out of, and then it was easy for the mother bear to get plenty of meat for both.

For all the cub knew, he and his mother were alone in the world. His mother provided the seals they ate, and since the weather was fine, there were lots of seals around, so they had nothing to worry about.

But one day something happened.

An old he-bear came toward them, from the open sea. He had been out on the drift ice, and for a long time he had had nothing to eat. He was an old brown bear, not much good for hunting any more. His teeth were worn down, his claws dull, and he didn't have the strength he had had when he was young. And his fur was worn thin, so that he was cold and ugly as well as hungry.

His nose was up, sniffing the air. Far off he could smell that there were other bears around, and although bears always keep away from each other so they can hunt undisturbed, the old he-bear wanted to find other bears, that he might live on the left-overs from their hunts.

The cub was happy and frolicsome. He had just crawled up on a piece of ice to slide down, and was enjoying himself hugely. He'd crawled up and slid down a few times. But suddenly he spied the old he-bear. Having never seen anyone but his own mother, he was of course surprised at the sight. He stood still and stared in astonishment, but finally decided to go closer and greet the newcomer.

Oh, that old scoundrel, who stood there while the cub came closer! An old he-bear considers his own young a great delicacy, and here was a dainty meal running happily toward him. But he knew, too, that the mother bear must be around, so he'd have to be quick.

The cub was fat and had short legs, so he had no chance to escape, even if he had tried. But being accustomed only to friendliness, he thought the worst that could happen to him would be a cuffing if he disturbed the old one on the hunt. And it didn't look as if the old one was hunting, anyway, so there couldn't be any danger.

But suddenly a shadow appeared before him. It was his mother, who, although on the hunt, had spied her unexpected enemy, and had seen her precious cub in this great danger. For an instant she stood as if paralyzed, staring at the old he-bear, who seemed to be grinning in anticipation of a nice, tender bear steak.

However, the mother soon overcame her fright and sprang forward. She rushed at the old bear, and before he knew what had happened, a rain of bites and blows fell on him. He sat down to gather strength to defend himself, but the mother bear kept at him. Raging, she fought for her cub's life, and not for an instant did she stop her terrible attack. The old he-bear soon bled from many sores, and tried to save himself by flight. Then he thought that he certainly must be stronger than the young mother, and now began a fierce fight between male and female bear, a fight in which none could say who would be the victor.

The young mother was quick, with sharp teeth and ready claws, but the old male had many years' experience in this sort of fight, and he still had enough strength to strike the mother down with one blow.

He struck terrible blows with his paws—blows that made huge furrows in the snow as the mother bear sprang nimbly aside to avoid them. And each time the he-bear had struck out with his paw, the mother-bear jumped up on his back and bit him in the sides and wherever she could get at him, until his blood poured from the wounds.

But his furrows in the snow gained him nothing in the

fight, and her bites glanced off the tough head of the old bear. The unhappy mother could feel her strength going. It wasn't so easy now to spring aside when the old bear struck at her, and finally she received a blow on her back that seemed to lame her whole body.

The old bear seized the mother in his embrace to crush her to death by the weight of his body. But at the last instant, when he thought the victory was his, the young mother, in a final effort, grabbed his throat in her teeth and hung fast. The old bear fought on, but he couldn't get air and he was getting weaker and weaker, until at last he fell over and lay still. Then the mother let go her hold and dragged herself over to her cub, who had watched this—the first fight he had ever seen.

The mother's wounds were bleeding, and for the first time in the little one's life she could not play with him. She crept weakly away from him, a pitiful sight, and lay down to sleep without giving him food. The cub felt quite misused. Several days passed before he was given food again—but the wounds of wild animals heal quickly, and soon his mother was well again.

Now they traveled toward the land, and she taught the cub to hunt small animals and rodents. She tipped over the larger stones and showed him where the small mice, called lemmings, live. The cub caught them gleefully and found they tasted delicious.

Now the cub was getting so big that his mother found it difficult to catch enough seals for both of them, so they turned toward the sea—way out to the edge of the ice, where there are many seals, and where the catch is easy. Once a storm came, and the ice floes drifted out to sea, carrying the bears with it, but they were not afraid, for wherever they went, there were plenty of seals. In this way the young one learned to hunt so he could take care of himself when he was grown.

This little bear story was told by an old Eskimo woman to my little boy, at his bedtime. All little boys in the Far North love to hear about bears, for when they grow up, they too will go with sleds and dogs to hunt bears.

My little boy didn't care much about going to sleep. He'd rather climb up to the head of his bed and play with his toys, which stood on the dresser. But this he was not allowed to do, for he'd get chilly and catch cold.

The old woman gave him many warnings, and she often told him that a big bear walked outside the windows and peeked in, ready to bite the heads off small boys who wouldn't go to sleep nicely.

One day during the Christmas holidays, we were going to visit some of our family. We traveled with dogsleds, and the boy was still so small that he was bundled in a big fur sack so he wouldn't get cold. Then we tied him tight to the sled. But at night a terrible storm arose, the wind howled and the snow whipped into our faces, and the dogs couldn't pull the sled any farther against the storm. We managed to reach a cave where there was room for all of us and for our three sleds. We pounded the snow from our clothes, tied up the dogs, and made a big fire of blubber, both for light and for cooking. The dogs had to stay outside, and they dug themselves down into the snow, where they lay warm and snug. When the rest of us had eaten, we were drowsy and lay down to sleep.

You can't carry a bed when you go traveling with a dogsled, but must sleep in a huge fur sleeping bag. My little boy now lay in such a bag, right between father and mother, but he had slept so much during the day that he was wide awake now. So he crept a little bit out of the bag to take a look around.

Suddenly he saw a big bear standing looking at him. It came closer, and he thought it must be the bear the old woman told about, so probably it would be best for him to lie down again. He crawled back into the bag, but in doing so, he woke his mother, who helped him get settled, and then *she* looked out through the top of the bag. To her fright, she saw the bear close to us.

"Quick—get up!" she screamed. "There's a bear in the cave, about to attack us!"

You may well believe there was action, and that quickly. You see, one sleeps naked in such a sleeping bag, and one's clothes are put into another bag, so they'll not be frozen stiff by morning.

When I heard that there was a bear in our cave, I was wide awake in an instant, and sprang up. But it was cold, and I wanted to draw on a pair of trousers. In my haste I put both legs into the left pants leg. I lost my balance, turned a somersault, and rolled right over in front of the bear, so I had nothing to do with shooting him. Fortunately, two Eskimos who were on the other sleds in our party shot the animal.

When I got to my feet, my little boy was laughing at me. He thought it was *so* funny. And later, when we reached the family we were to visit, he told them he wished another bear would come, for then his father turned such amusing somersaults.

One day, when spring came, I shot a mother bear with two cubs. I took the cubs home to my little boy and girl. And they played with the cubs. Every morning they came into the living room, and the bear cubs and the children and a couple of pups played together all day. But one day when I came in, I heard the children crying, and they told me that the bears had hurt them. So we dared not keep the cubs inside any longer. They had grown too big and were stronger than the children. We tied them outside the house, where the children might still play with them and feed them.

But again I noticed that the young bears struck at the children. Their claws had grown so big and sharp that they could tear the children's clothes and make pretty bad scratches on their bodies. So then we put the two bears in a cage, and let them out only when they were taken for a swim.

We rowed them out to sea in a boat and let them swim back. But they grew too big for us, and when a ship came to Thule, the captain took them along with him and eventually took them back with him to Denmark.

III

THE ESKIMOS: PAST
AND PRESENT

I TRAVELED in and out of the Arctic for almost three quarters of a century, though when I look back on it, this does not seem like a long time. Nevertheless, I can see the tremendous change that took place during these years. I experienced the advance of civilization and I saw the natives slowly accept the ideas of the outside world—for the arctic regions are by no means immune to progress and new developments.

It has been maintained over and over again by certain thoughtless people that the native man was far better and happier before he met the white man with his inventions and tools. I have seen any number of films and read countless books with the same theme, whether the native in question was a Negro or a Polynesian, an Indian or an Eskimo. The story is always the same: The native tribe was happy and carefree, innocent and well off until the evil day when the white men arrived. That day marked the beginning of their inevitable doom. They were torn from their native Eden, infested with disease and vices, and soon the tribe broke up and perished.

I have never been able to understand why the white man should insist on seeing himself in such an unfavorable light. I know from personal experience that this picture is entirely wrong in the case of the Eskimos and the Indians in the Far North. I know them both quite well, and I have a certain right to speak about them, for I am one of the last civilized men who met the Eskimos when they still lived like men in the Stone Age. In Committee Bay I have met Eskimos who had no knives. The only cutting instruments they had were made of old metal straps from barrels. For flensing they used sharp stones or knives made of bone. They were walrus hunters, and it would take them days to flense and cut up one single walrus. While they worked with their miserable tools, hundreds of walrus would pass by their camp. If they had had steel knives, as they do now, the whole job could be done in half an hour and they could get out again while the hunting was still good and maybe get a whole winter's supply in a day or two.

I have gone reindeer hunting with the natives on the tundra in the Northwest Territories. Hunting is not easy on the tundra—the endless, barren, flat land where there is no rock, no bush, nothing to hide behind. When the reindeer stay together in herds, they are safe, because they have a clear view in all directions. To get at them, one has to sneak up to them from a great distance, against the wind. After a while one has to crawl on the snow, and finally one has to lie down flat on the stomach without moving and wait until the animals come close enough for the range of the weapons at hand. The reindeer have very poor eyes, but an excellent sense of smell. They get no clear pictures of fairly close objects as long as these are stationary. As long as the Eskimos don't move, the animals may come within their range, but if they make one careless movement the reindeer are gone.

The Eskimos had a very hard job in the days when they did their hunting with bow and arrow. In winter they might wait for days and days until the animal came close enough for the very limited range of their arrows, and they often had to return empty-handed—not because they were lazy or careless but simply because their primitive weapons did not go far enough and their aim could never be sure enough. Today the Eskimos all have rifles. They can get more meat, more furs, more supplies of every kind. Their life is more secure and less frustrating than before.

Those who believe in the unfailing, original bliss of the natives might do well to remember some of the discoveries of the archaeologists. They have found remains of native villages where the whole population had perished in some sudden catastrophe. The tools and equipment were still there, and skeletons of people of all ages. One thing is certain: the people who thus give valuable material to the archaeologists met a tragic end.

I have come across such ruins in the extreme north of Canada. I have seen the pitiful remains of people who perished in some unknown disaster. From the evidence, famine seemed the only reasonable cause of the tragedy. In certain ruins, for instance, we found skeletons of dogs whose skulls had been cracked in order to remove the brains. Such a thing is obviously done only by starving people. For the last thing an Eskimo will do is to kill his dog; in ice-covered country, he is quite helpless without a dog to pull his sleigh.

Or consider the importance of the humble match. Like most people, I have read countless stories of explorers running out of matches. But that never bothered them as long as the natives were there to help them. In a short while the natives—whether Indian, Eskimo, or whatever—would provide a roaring fire by rubbing sticks of wood together. The people who write such stories have obviously never been the ones who were compelled to make fire in this primitive way.

I have tried it myself. During the first world war I was the only white man living in Thule. From Thule we made long trips across Smith Sound to Ellsmereland, where it was then still permitted to go hunting. We crossed the ice from Etah to the rich hunting grounds on the other side of the sound. Our main purpose was to get snow hares, whose soft fur is used for stockings in Thule, as there are no longer any reindeer along the coast. The hares are much more plentiful in Ellsmereland, where the vegetation is richer. The first time I went hunting there with my friends from Thule, they suggested that we should get enough fur to last through several seasons. I asked them if they really expected that many hares.

"Many!" they exclaimed with conviction. "There are so many hares that it looks as if the ground has lice!" That was their best possible way of expressing an unlimited supply.

On one such trip we ran out of matches. We all knew the old method of making fire by rubbing two sticks of wood together, but we had no idea just how slow and difficult it was. Two men sit facing each other, pulling as fast as possible the string which is attached to the vertical stick grinding back and forth in the same spot on the horizontal stick. There must be no slackening of the speed. If the arm gets tired, which it always does, and one stops for a second or two for a rest or to change position, the sticks cool off, and one has to start all over again. If there is the least breath of wind it is impossible to produce a flame, the whole struggle has been in vain, and in the end one eats frozen, raw meat for supper and breakfast. No, it's a pretty good thing to be able to pull a box of matches out of a pocket and get fire at any time.

Think of the old cooking utensils made of stone. One needed time and patience to prepare food in those old pots. Among the Eskimos, there grew up a class of people whose job it was to tell stories and make the impatiently waiting people forget the food which never boiled.

The Hudson Bay Company has done more than any other company in the world to make life simpler and easier for the people living in the Far North. True enough, I have heard stories about the Hudson Bay Company exploiting the "innocent" native population, but such tales always proved to originate with people who had no personal knowledge of the facts. Such accusations have never been made by people who have been able to observe the actual situation objectively.

The Eskimos are the people who live farther north than everything and everybody else in the world. Where they came from, why they went so far north: these are questions whose answers are lost in the dark fog of the past. The one thing which seems clear is that they did not voluntarily leave the forest land to settle down on the shores of the Arctic Ocean.

Once they were there, the struggle for survival taught them to be independent of the forests. In place of the barks which the Indians used for their canoes, the Eskimos learned how to cover their kayaks with sealskins and walrus skins. Since they had to make their homes without wood, they constructed their famous igloos. They deserve a great deal of respect, these hardy people, not only for being able to stay alive, but for developing a spiritual and economic culture where no other human beings could live. It is true, of course, that the Eskimos were compelled to develop that hardness without which they could not exist, and their present admirable characteristics are the result of a natural selection in the struggle for survival.

But the fact remains that their existence was hazardous and insecure before the arrival of the white man in the Arctic. Any unexpected event, the least change in their routine, might lead to disaster. A lack of ice at the right time meant starvation, perhaps, because fishing and hunting trips would have had to be postponed indefinitely. The Eskimos constantly set out on long and hazardous journeys, not only due to inclination or restlessness; their daily needs made it imperative for them to be at the right time just where they would find the animals necessary for their survival. They needed lard, which they could get only from certain animals, but at the same time they had to go far inland to get reindeer skin and the sinews they used for thread. They needed walrus skins and sealskins, but they also had to fish for salmon in the lakes. On the tiny islands far out at sea they found their birds and eggs. All year round the Eskimos had to be on the go. Their cooking utensils were made of stone, and to renew them the Eskimos had to travel a considerable distance before they found the right kind of soft stone. Such expeditions might take a year or two, and fashioning the stone into pots and pans was a strenuous job which demanded a great deal of time and patience with the primitive tools at their disposal.

All that is different today. The Hudson Bay Company has meant salvation for a great many villages, perhaps for the greater part of the population in the northernmost part of the world. The Hudson Bay Company moved into remote regions where nobody else could or would invest capital, and the name became synonymous with security and comfort to the natives. The establishment of regular trade routes meant a revolution in the arctic form of life. One of the results was an improvement in health which an outsider can hardly believe. Those who talk so glibly of conditions in the Arctic, after spending a month or two there, have virtually no idea how vastly the life of the Eskimos has changed since the arrival of the Hudson Bay Company.

I want to stress that it is the *regular* exchange of trade which has been so important. There have been many so-called "free traders" who had no scruples in their dealings with the natives. They grabbed what they could, not caring that the Eskimos might be much worse off than before once the trader left, once they could no longer get what they had learned to depend on for their comfort. When a native has had some tool which made life a little easier, it is much harder for him to do without it than if he had never known anything but his old primitive way of life. I have met many Eskimos who had rifles without any possibility of getting ammunition. I have known Eskimos who had paid dearly for their kerosene stoves, which they could not now use, since they were hundreds of miles away from the nearest fuel supply.

Perhaps a true-life story will show better than many words what the "native bliss" really was like.

There used to be a small settlement of Eskimos on an island called Igloolik in the eastern part of the Fury and Hecla straits. The place is a veritable wildlife paradise. There were seals and walrus and caribou. In spring there is an overabundance of eggs. There are polar bears and foxes and wolverines, and plenty of salmon in the lakes. I don't think I have seen better hunting any other place in the world. No wonder these Eskimos settled there permanently.

The following events took place there in 1921, when there was no such thing as commercial flying in the Arctic. Motorboats could not get through the heavy ice of Hudson Bay, and no regular traffic by sea was possible. Igloolik was nearly inaccessible, but a wonderful place for people who felt independent of civilization and trading posts.

Once in a long while these Eskimos made a shopping expedition to Fullerton, the nearest place to the south, or up to Ponds Inlet, where a Hudson Bay post had just been established. In previous years the natives had sometimes gone up to the eastern tip of Bylot Island to wait for the whalers, but it was a hazardous undertaking. Sometimes the whalers did not show up and sometimes they could just be seen far out at sea while ice kept them from approaching the coast. By then the Eskimos might have to wait until the next year before they could cross Baffin Island. The Eskimos said that the establishment of the new post at Ponds Inlet meant the opening of a whole new era of security, since they could go there, do their shopping, and return again, all in the span of one year.

They had more fox furs than they knew what to do with in Igloolik, but they had none of the things they could get in exchange for their furs. At last a group of the Eskimos on the island decided to make the long trip to Ponds Inlet. There was great excitement in the village, since they would be gone a whole year. Their friends and neighbors gave them commissions of every kind as they prepared for the long journey by sewing new clothes—a strenuous job, since sewing needles were among the most sorely needed objects.

As soon as daylight was beginning to return to Igloolik after the dark winter, the travelers set out on the road to Ponds Inlet. Their equipment was very primitive and they were all used to spending their days on dog sleighs and their nights in a snowhut, so they made slow progress. One of the things they had to do without was wood for making sleighs. In the village there were two wooden sleighs, but since the traveling party were going to a region where they could get more wood, they had decided to let their friends who stayed behind keep the precious sleighs.

These sleighs were made in the same ancient way it has always been done in these treeless regions. First several reindeer skins were tightly rolled together. Next the long, narrow roll was pushed through a hole in the ice of a lake and left in the water until it was thoroughly soaked. Finally the dripping roll was put on the ice, covered with heavy ice-blocks and left there to freeze in the right shape. Soon the Eskimos had two stiff, strong—even if somewhat heavy—runners which would last the whole trip. For crossbars they used large salmon which had been frozen in the same way, or walrus meat which had been cut to the right size and shape. The result was not very snappy-looking, but a useful and serviceable sleigh with the extra advantage that it contained spare supplies for an emergency. And they set off happily with these sleighs for the long run across Baffin Island.

The island is very well suited for this primitive means of transportation, except for some large stretches of deep, soft snow which slow down the sleighs. The people from Igloolik made fairly good progress, but not as rapid as expected, since the snow was exceptionally deep that year. They didn't mind, however, since they were in no great hurry. And building their snowhuts at night was an easy and quick job with all that soft snow.

One night they were all asleep in their warm huts when something which is feared above all the hard arctic winter took place outside in the darkness: the mild weather set in. Most people who have traveled in the Arctic know this phenomenon, which usually takes place twice during each winter. In the bitter cold a warm wind will suddenly send the temperature above the freezing point, and everything starts dripping. Clothes get soaking wet, and a great part of one's food may get ruined. It is most unpleasant when it occurs, but to the Eskimos from Igloolik it was much worse than unpleasant. It spelled disaster for all of them.

In their three huts they were sound asleep, oblivious of the outside world. But their dogs did not sleep, they knew what was happening. They had been let loose to keep them from eating their harness. Every evening the Eskimos put sleighs, harness and all the supplies on top of very high snowpiles, beyond the reach of the constantly hungry dogs. The people slept. They were exhausted from a long day's driving; a change of weather was not enough to wake them up. They did not know that their sleighs were thawing, getting soft, slipping off the snow. In their sleep they had no idea of the terrible thing that took place outside. In no time the hungry animals had eaten the sleighs—runners, crossbars, and all. The food supplies, harness, clothes—all went the same way. The Eskimo dog knows how to hurry when unexpected food comes within his reach.

The Eskimos did not wake up until some of them felt the roof of the igloo sinking. Then it was too late. The dogs had left nothing. There was no food, there was no means of transportation left. And as their bad luck would have it, the mild weather had met them in a district where the hunting was exceptionally poor. There was hardly a chance of catching anything to eat—and no possibility of going on without sleighs.

They were soon tortured by hunger. The dogs were rationed, eaten one by one, but they did not last long. The Eskimos ate all the clothes they could do without. Any hope they may have had of being rescued in time rapidly dwindled. Soon death claimed its first victim, then another. The living ate the flesh of their dead friends. Eskimos are not cannibals, but they may be forced to commit acts beyond human judgment.

Nobody knew of the fate which befell the lonely travelers. Nobody expected to see them again until nearly a year had passed, and there was no cause for alarm. Even if people in the outside world had known what had happened to them, there was little chance of coming to their aid in time.

Later on in spring, when the sunshine lasted all through the night, an Eskimo named Patlok crossed the island with his wife. He was a prosperous man, had his own beautiful wooden sleigh, and could visit the trading post every other year if he wanted to. It was Patlok who discovered the lost travelers. One morning his dogs behaved strangely. After a great deal of sniffing in the air, they changed their course and began speeding up. Patlok thought they would lead him to a flock of reindeer or some other game, and let them follow their own course.

At last he found a tiny, broken-down snowhut. And he found two women. At first he could hardly believe that they were human beings. They were too weak to move and they could hardly talk. They had eaten their clothes until there was hardly a thread left on them. He carried them into his sleigh and began questioning the stronger of the two, a woman called Atakutaluk.

"Where are the others?" Patlok asked.

"One does not know," was the answer.

After a long pause Patlok asked again, "Have human beings been eaten here?"

"One knows nothing," the old woman answered, but she pointed to a big snowpile behind the remnants of an igloo. When Patlok looked further, he found the bones of the other people, those who had starved to death. Some of the larger bones had been split in two to remove the marrow.

Patlok offered food to the two women, but he warned them. After a long period of starvation, the sufferer actually feels no pain any more, and it takes quite an effort to swallow food. Once the starved person begins eating again, the pains come, and then the dreadful hunger returns. The first few days are very critical, since it is easy to eat more than the starved system can take.

Atakutaluk was a wise and strong woman; she controlled her hunger, eating only a little at a time and not very often. But the other woman could not resist the temptation. She jumped on the food, and when the others warned her against overeating she cried and screamed for more food. Patlok had food enough, and he did not have the strength to keep it away from her. But she did not eat for long. After a short while she began vomiting and complained of sharp pains in the stomach. She did not gain much from her rescue for she died within a few days.

Atakutaluk, who knew the art of self-control, lived to a ripe old age. It was she who told me of the whole tragedy.

What can one say to a woman calmly describing such a disaster? I listened to her and found no words. But Atakutaluk was an Eskimo. She saw that I was deeply shocked when she told of eating her husband and her three children. It is considered very impolite for an Eskimo to "remove the smile from the face of a guest," so Atakutaluk hastened to reassure me. She had found herself a new husband, she told me. And she had had a child with him and was the step-mother of his other two children, so she no longer had any debt to the "Great Being."

Such a story was not unique in the old days. A great many similar tragedies took place among the Eskimos, but they do not happen any more. The arctic life is growing ever more secure and the population is increasing year by year. Eskimos in places like Igloolik all have wooden sleighs these days, and a pot made of stone is only a curiosity. There is hardly an Eskimo who does not have the most modern tools and weapons. They are available to him in the Hudson Bay trading posts. Everything which proved to serve a good purpose has become part of the arctic life. Other things, which failed to pass the test, have disappeared and are no longer part of that regular exchange of goods between the Hudson Bay Company and the Eskimo which has brought such great benefits to the natives.

It is one of the Hudson Bay Company's great merits that it kept many so-called free traders away. Also, with its vast resources, it could supply the Eskimos with whatever they needed. If something wasn't available, it could be made so. It was the responsibility of the station managers to find out what the Eskimos needed or could use, and then supply them with it. Thus, the company's activity had a social side to it.

A trader who was supposed to break new ground for the company would be sailed up to the desolate spot where the station was to be established. There he was thrown ashore with a pile of building materials and trading goods. He built his own house, opened shop, and started at his work. During the first difficult period he needed the assistance and the benevolence of the Eskimos, and a good part of the white superiority feeling—if any—would be killed right then and there. The procedure made for very independent people in the service of the company. Their education was perhaps a bit rigorous, but it hardened them for the life they had to lead. And the great advantage was that the Hudson Bay man became the friend of the people among whom he lived. It was not feasible for a man to serve the company and do his duties except in harmony with the customers he was dealing with. As a result, the Eskimos got a painless edu-cation in the white man's methods and habits, and the Canadian Eskimos were never hostile to the white men. It was fellow humans, not superior beings, who came to them.

Of course, these agents were rarely idealists or conscious dispersers of culture and progress—fortunately! They were simple people, chosen from among healthy and well-balanced men.

All Eskimos who came from distant places to trade were received royally and welcomed and invited to be the guests of the company for two days. During that time the trading was done, and they talked about the hunting conditions and prospects for the future. In this way, the Hudson Bay man procured an invaluable knowledge of the country and the people.

Whenever I observed the work of the Hudson Bay Company, I regarded it with amazement, for I came from Greenland, where development had taken a different course.

The present Danish possession of Greenland dates from the year 1721, when a missionary and trader, Hans Egede, managed to fit out a combined trading, whaling, and missionary expedition to Greenland, believing that the original Norsemen were still to be found there.

For in 981 A.D., Eric the Red had been exiled from Iceland for five years for a minor offense, and he went to Greenland. He was an intelligent man with a sense for propaganda; he gave the island the name of Greenland, described it in glorious terms, and induced a small party of friends to come with him. Thus the Norse colonies were established in Greenland, and from there Eric's son, Leif, later sailed to America.

The Norse colonies maintained connection with Denmark, and for centuries the Danish king benefited greatly from his exclusive rights to the land. Then a period of long wars and bad times made it impractical to continue the cost and the risk of shipping; the new markets in the Orient brought bigger profits for the large Danish fleet. At the same time, the climate grew colder, the ice around Cape Farewell was at times completely impenetrable to ships, even in summer, and little by little the colonies, and even the sea route, were entirely forgotten.

In 1310 there appeared at Bergen, Norway, a boat from Greenland. Sagas relate that this ship was held together by sealskin lines, without the use of a single nail. What later became of it is not known; it might have gone down on its homeward voyage. After its visit, nothing was heard of the Greenlanders for a long time. Sagas tell of years of terrible weather conditions, with ice drifting in much larger masses, winters that grew colder and longer, and torrential rains that made it impossible to dry hay for winter. But this was also the time of the Eskimo invasions.

They came from the North. The Norsemen called them the weaklings, and regarded them as spectral beings less than human, a contempt that might have been their undoing. For the Eskimos became more and more aggressive, unusually so for their general character, and in 1346 one of the two settlements, *Vesterbygden*, was attacked and burned down. A boat from the other settlement, coming the following summer, found no Norseman left.

There were no more reports until 1585 when John Davis went to Greenland. He found no sign whatever of Norse colonists, and the Eskimos had taken possession of the whole coast. They were never numerous, and it is difficult even to guess how many there were, for they traveled up and down the coast constantly in search of food and skins. It was imperative that they visit the vicinity of Holsteinsborg at least once during their lives, there to get the huge whales from whose bones they made hunting gear.

Later excavations in the Norse ruins show that there were two large communities with altogether 5,000 inhabitants when they were at their most prosperous. There was a bishopric and twelve churches with eight cloisters. The clothes and the way of life were among the most fashionable that characterized the Middle Ages.

But isolation and a worsening climate destroyed them. The skeletons found show signs of scurvy and tuberculosis, and in-breeding had resulted in deformities and undergrowth. It is not impossible that the Eskimos had a primitive, instinctive fear of this disease-ridden, degenerated lot, and therefore decided to destroy them all.

So Hans Egede came and found no Norsemen. Resolutely he started spreading the gospel among the Eskimos. Since he had to learn the language from the bottom up, his first instructions were done in simple language. He would show the Eskimo pagans a picture of the devil and then start to beat a couple of the nearest ones thoroughly, so as to show that the devil was to be feared.

At the same time, he founded a colony in the name of the

Danish king, who now again claimed exclusive rights to the country. But Dutch whalers often visited Greenland waters, and several islands, straits, and mountains today bear Dutch names. When it came to a matter of battle between the Danes and the Dutch, the Dutch lost out, and the Danes extended their colonies along the west coast. There were a few unsuccessful attempts to rent out trading concessions; then the Danish government declared a monopoly, and Greenland became—for the next two hundred years, right up until the second world war—one of the most closed countries on earth. The island was closed to all but members of the Royal Greenland Trading Company, so that not even Danish subjects could be admitted without special permission. The last region to be taken over by the monopoly was Thule. As mentioned previously, the Thule district became Danish in 1921, and the trading station was taken over by the state in 1935.

Over this long period of years, the population of Greenland underwent social and economic changes. The *Styrelsen* (the management of the Royal Trading Company) tried to maintain and protect the native way of life. For the first hundred and fifty years, its policy was to keep their hunters at their trade. Danish and Norwegian workmen and sailors were brought into the country to do the work at the colonies and the whaling stations, all those jobs that were not considered "native," a distinction that was continued right up until the recent reforms.

Many of these Europeans took Eskimo wives, and the mixture produced a stronger, more intelligent race.

As soon as colonies were started, strife arose between the missionaries and the traders, as their points of view concerning the natives were naturally quite opposed. The Trading Company · wanted the population scattered around at the places where the game was, while the missionaries wanted larger settlements where people could be close to church and school. Basic conditions solved the argument. If too many hunters stayed together in one spot, the game in that vicinity would soon be killed off or frightened away, and that would never do. Consequently, trading stations were scattered about, and even as late as 1948 not less than 170 of them were maintained, some at a considerable loss.

For many years, however, the stations earned a nice income for the Danish state from the skins and blubber that were brought in. Never did Denmark selfishly exploit Greenland, though; the hunter always got a fair price for his catch, and for a long time Greenland was the home of a contented and wealthy people.

But these favorable living conditions brought about an increase in the population that began to overtax the resources of the country. With the discovery of the Polar Current, competition in seal hunting came to the natives from the outside, and serious trouble developed.

The east coast of Greenland is nearly always blocked by huge masses of ice, carried by the East Greenland Current down through the Denmark Strait. From the time of the Norsemen it had been noticed that the fjords of eastern and southwestern Greenland are always full of driftwood, and the Eskimos there have wood for every purpose. The Norwegian explorer Fritjof Nansen became curious about this drift. When he heard that clothing, utensils, and a boat, belonging to the unfortunate "Jeanette" Expedition, had been found by Eskimos on an ice floe off the west coast of Greenland, and it was learned that these effects had been left behind by the Americans close to the north coast of Siberia, he realized that they must have drifted across the North Pole, south around Cape Farewell, and up along Greenland's west coast. He went out on his famous "Fram" Expedition, sailing east along the Siberian coast, then letting the ship drift with the ice toward the North Pole. As a result of this experiment, the Polar Current was discovered.

The Greenland kayak hunters got the worst end of this scientific advance. Large numbers of seals were discovered on the ice east of Greenland, where they went to give birth to their cubs. Sealing ships at once set out from Norway to catch the seals before the cubs could swim. These seals were taken by the thousands, and the western Greenlanders saw their game become rarer and rarer. They, of course, had to stay at home and wait for the seals to come around Cape Farewell in the spring and fall of the year.

By the start of our century, the supply of seals available in Greenland had become insufficient. The amount caught by the Eskimos from their kayaks had never made any appreciable difference to the seal population; but the Norwegians had taken a terrible toll. In the southern part of Greenland, the natives were entirely dependent upon the sealing, since there were few fish there, and poverty became oppressive to the point of hunger. The Danish state took care of the unfortunate ones, but it is never morally healthy for a population to live on charity.

As long as the seal hunting remained good farther north, there was no cause for alarm for the country as a whole, but now came a new disaster: the general increase in temperature all over the Arctic pushed the seals' migrations farther north, and along the coasts of Danish Greenland they became more scarce again.

To offset all this, progressive Danes employed by the Styrelsen tried introducing new industries. As these proved useful, they were taken over by the monopoly. Quite a number of the natives became able to provide an income for themselves by making rugs and blankets out of eider duck and other bird skins. The ground shark was hunted for its liver, which contained an oil rich in vitamin A. Fish were salted down or smoked and sold in Europe.

But with the alleviation of the worst hardships caused by the scarcity of seal, a change in the construction of society took place, and this at first caused a wound in the Greenlanders' self-respect. In early times, only the seal hunter was regarded as a man of true dignity. Those who for some reason or another were unable to go out in a kayak and hunt, and had to fish for a living, were looked down upon, they had no standing. As the seals disappeared and the colonies grew, there seemed to be less and less room for a man's pride. Sailors and workmen were recruited in increasing numbers from among the natives, and the church employed many also. The sons of such men did not even have the chance to learn to use a kayak, and this state of affairs caused a feeling of shame. A new emancipation had to take place, and in 1912 the Greenlanders obtained a democratic constitution with two kinds of council, a municipal council for each district, and two provincial councils, one for northern and one for southern Greenland. This helped their self-respect enormously, and the Eskimos were introduced to the parliamentary way of life.

In the meantime, the country grew poorer and poorer. The increase in temperature began to be really felt about this time, and especially so in the sea. Then the Danish scientist Adolf Jensen discovered in the southern fjords the presence of lots of fish of a kind never known to exist there before, the Atlantic codfish. Research was done, and as a result of it stations were built along the coast for the purpose of teaching the natives how to fish with long lines and nets and how to clean and salt the fish for export. And the influx of codfish became richer and richer.

So began what is now Greenland's major occupation—fishing, with the codfish, which are exported to the Catholic countries of southern Europe, as its chief source of revenue. Motorboats were carried up from Denmark with the ships and sold to the natives on credit, and the fisherman became the new pillar of society. Some hunters still exist, of course, and they are held in high esteem. But they are almost always low in cash. They furnish the fisherman with meat and skins, but it took them a long time to grasp the fact that they should demand money for meat. In the old days, meat belonged to everyone, so to speak, as it still does in the Thule district. It was hard for them to break such a tradition and realize that their country had become a money country.

In 1912, Mr. Daugaard-Jensen became director of the Styrelsen. He was a very able man, inspired by a deep love for Greenland, and he promoted the new prosperity resulting from fishing. But he suffered from an almost psychotic fear that the codfish would disappear again as suddenly as they had come. He was afraid that he would become responsible for getting the Greenlanders used to plenty of money, only to return them to the poor existence of former times.

"Greenland's greatest economic value is the frugality of the population," he said constantly. "We must not spoil it!"

The activity of the Trading Company was based on this principle. It was made difficult for the Greenlanders to get any other goods than those handed out by the colony manager, the Trading Company's representative, at the old trading station. These goods they knew to the point of boredom. The shop was only an outlet for the plainest possible kinds of provisions and dreary cotton goods. Nothing to arouse interest, nothing to make people want to buy and own more.

So while the waters around Greenland teemed with more and more fish, practically carrying gold to the doorsteps of the settlements, the Greenlanders were too disinterested to catch anything more than they needed for the necessities of life. When they had replaced their old peat houses with new red-painted wooden houses, when their motorboats and tools were paid for, what else was there? Nothing worth while.

At the same time, Danish fishing companies were clamoring to be admitted to the new rich fields. But Daugaard-Jensen was adamant. And the same monopoly—the one that had formerly been a blessing to Greenland because it protected the Eskimos against exploitation—now became oppressive and intolerable, a damper on all initiative, all enjoyment of life.

The second world war put an end to this fiasco. Denmark was occupied by the Germans, who also established some strongholds in eastern Greenland. But by one of those happy chances that occur so often in history, the right men were at the right places in a critical situation. I am thinking of Eske Brun, the sheriff of northern Greenland, and Henrik Kauffman, the Danish minister in Washington. Both of these gentlemen put all ordinary rules aside, and established themselves as free agents responsible to the government of Denmark after its liberation from the Germans. The result of their cooperation was that President Roosevelt signed an agreement according to which the United States agreed to establish defenses against the Germans on Greenland, not an unimportant matter in the conduct of the war, because of Greenland's meteorological importance. And Greenland would be supplied with food and other necessities from the United States.

With that, the old system in Greenland began to crumble. The American soldiers came as friendly visitors from an outside world. Goods of an unknown multitude and variety could be bought in the shops. It was as if money all of a sudden was worth more, although the goods were more expensive. Whole new perspectives opened up; life got a new meaning. Eske Brun, when he found that the poor settlements in the south were difficult to supply, simply moved their populace farther up north. The old settlement system had outlived itself; it did not fit the new times, with fishing and more time for education and leisure.

Incredible as it may sound, there were some Danes in power right after the war who tried to get Greenland closed up again, as if nothing had happened. Finally, in 1948, Prime Minister Hedtoft made a complete tour of Greenland with a commission of the Parliament, so as to see for himself how the country could be modernized. I was with him on that trip, as correspondent for the newspaper *Politiken*, and it was one of the happiest occasions of my life, for on that trip the new Greenland was born!

The state monopoly was abandoned, with immediate effect, and the country was opened to private enterprise. A five-year program was worked out, in order to establish new and modern fishing villages where the population had outgrown the old hunter settlements. The main requirements were, in the first place, to collect the population in small towns of three or four thousand inhabitants each, then to build quays and sheltered harbors for motorboats, provide supplies of fresh water, build power plants, construct schools and hospitals, etc. Needless to say, such a program would cost a lot of money, but the Danish people assumed the tremendous cost with little protest.

They were, of course, well rewarded for doing so. When I last visited Greenland in 1955, I seemed to sense the presence of a social miracle: shops and streets had been transformed, commerce had developed apace, families were thriving in the new economy, education and vocational opportunities had multiplied. The discovery of lead and zinc deposits and their development led to a new mining industry; fishing became of great commercial importance and canneries grew to major economic stature. As I walked about the land that was the world's most forgotten place fifty years ago, tears came to my eyes. In spite of the feeling of pride and accomplishment I felt in sharing in the resurrection of this beautiful island, I also thought of the difficulties and hardships which Knud Rasmussen and I had in our little trading post, and of the adventures that now seem so unbelievable in view of the industrialization and modernization of Greenland. But I also felt reassured in all this, thinking about what men can do when they want to build rather than destroy!

Like Hudson Bay and Greenland, Alaska too has developed remarkably in the last decade. From the time of its acquisition by the United States almost up to the second world war, the history of Alaska was mainly that of a small administrative system, like that maintained by any other colonial power, and the varying fortunes of its gold fields, fisheries, and sealing industries. But in 1939, recognizing the territory's strategic importance as the northwestern bastion for the defense of North America, the U.S. government began to build military bases. Kodiak Island became the site of the territory's principal naval base. A major air base and fort were established outside Anchorage. Another air base was built at Fairbanks on the air route to Siberia. Secondary airfields and ports were also constructed, highways began to multiply, communication networks were strengthened, measures were taken to maintain control of the sea routes to and from Alaska.

All these developments turned out, in view of the Korean conflict of 1950 and America's increased rivalry with Russia, to be but snail steps in view of the boom now underway. Military constructions have given birth to magnificent and undreamt-of retail and service industries. Even the Eskimos of the Alaskan Arctic have felt the impact of the demand for labor in naval oil exploration and in the building of the Distant Early Warning (DEW) radar chains.

I have seen many things in the Arctic and I have done many things there, and my body is tired, yearning for rest and relaxation. But my soul is still young and more adventurous than ever at the sight of the marvelous developments that are taking place in Hudson Bay, Greenland, and Alaska. The hope I have always entertained for the backward and underprivileged people of these places has been greatly satisfied in what I notice each time I visit my friends anew. Far from being discouraged at the changes I see and yearning for a return to times that are past, I look forward to the day when the Arctic will help man to realize his dreams of making the earth a better and more happy place in which to live.